John Galsworthy and disabled soldiers of the Great War

Manchester University Press

Cultural History of Modern War

Series editors

Peter Gatrell, Max Jones, Penny Summerfield and Bertrand Taithe

Centre for the
Cultural History
of War

John Galsworthy and disabled soldiers of the Great War

With an illustrated selection of his writings

~

JEFFREY S. REZNICK

Manchester University Press

Manchester and New York

distributed in the United States exclusively by Palgrave Macmillan

The right of Jeffrey S. Reznick to be identified as the author of this work has been asserted by him in accordance with the Copyright, Designs and Patents Act 1988.

Published by Manchester University Press
Oxford Road, Manchester M13 9NR, UK
and Room 400, 175 Fifth Avenue, New York, NY 10010, USA
www.manchesteruniversitypress.co.uk

Distributed in the United States exclusively by
Palgrave Macmillan, 175 Fifth Avenue, New York,
NY 10010, USA

Distributed in Canada exclusively by
UBC Press, University of British Columbia, 2029 West Mall,
Vancouver, BC, Canada V6T 1Z2

British Library Cataloguing-in-Publication Data
A catalogue record for this book is available from the British Library

Library of Congress Cataloging-in-Publication Data applied for

ISBN   978 0 7190 7792 0 *hardback*

First published 2009

18 17 16 15 14 13 12 11 10 09   10 9 8 7 6 5 4 3 2 1

The publisher has no responsibility for the persistence or accuracy of URLs for any external or third-party internet websites referred to in this book, and does not guarantee that any content on such websites is, or will remain, accurate or appropriate.

Typeset in 10/12pt Minion
by Graphicraft Limited, Hong Kong
Printed in Great Britain
by MPG Books Group, UK

Contents

Contents

Illustrations

List of illustrations

Acknowledgements

This book would not have been possible without the generous support of Steve Forbes. I thank him for granting me access to his outstanding collection of John Galsworthy papers and for his generous subvention, which enabled reproduction of key manuscripts and printed documents from the period of the Great War. Photographer Richard Holttum captured these images, and for his time and expertise I am especially grateful. My thanks are also due to Andrianna Campbell and Bonnie Kirschstein for facilitating my contact with Mr Forbes, to Simon Edsor and Patricia McCaldin for their guidance and their hospitality during my time at Old Battersea House, London, and to Elizabeth Marwell for preparing all the appropriate permissions.

Many more archivists, curators, librarians and specialists on both sides of the Atlantic provided me with valuable assistance and gave me permission to quote from documents and/or to reproduce images in their collections. I wish to thank Pauline Allwright, David Bell, Rebecca Hawley and Mary Wilkinson of the Imperial War Museum (IWM); Deirdre Clarkin of the United States National Library of Medicine; Charles Greene and Don Skemer of Princeton University Library; Mindy Hecker and Ellen Solomon of the Wilma L. West Library of the American Occupational Therapy Foundation; Gary Johnson, David Kelly and Kathy Woodrell of the Library of Congress; David Kessler and Susan Snyder of the Bancroft Library, University of California, Berkeley; Martin Killeen of Special Collections, University of Birmingham; Karen Lee of Cengage Learning; Leslie Morris of the Houghton Library, Harvard University; Judith Paige of the Library of the Armed Forces Institute of Pathology, United States Department of Defense; Janel Quirante of the Hoover

Institution Archives, Stanford University; Brian Rutherford of the Louis Stokes Health Sciences Library, Howard University; I. C. Wallace of Bamforth & Co. and the Bamforth Postcard Collection, Leeds, and Mitch Yockelson of the United States National Archives.

During the past decade, I presented early versions of my research on Galsworthy to a number of audiences in Britain and the United States. I am especially grateful for thoughts I received at meetings sponsored by the North East Conference on British Studies (NECBS) (panel on 'The First World War and the Construction of Memory', held at the NECBS meeting in Hartford, CT, October 1998); Institute of Historical Research, University of London (panel on '(Re)creating the Physical Body: The Case of Prostheses in the Modern Era', held at the Seventy-second Anglo-American Conference of Historians, July 2003); American Historical Association (AHA) (panel on 'Militarizing the Body: Prosthetics, Propaganda, and Medical Politics in Wartime Europe and the United States, 1914–1919', held at the AHA annual meeting in Washington, DC, January 2004); National Museum of American History, Smithsonian Institution (2005 research seminar series); University of Wisconsin at Madison, Ebling Health Sciences Library (2005 William Snow Miller Lecture, in conjunction with the exhibit ' "Casualties are Arriving Daily": Medical Transportation in the Great War'); the Wellcome Trust and the University of Manchester's Centre for the History of Science, Medicine and Technology and Centre for the Cultural History of War ('Enabling the Past: New Perspectives in the History of Disability', June 2005); IWM and University College London (UCL) ('Bodies in conflict: Corporeality, Materiality and Transformation in Twentieth-century War', the third IWM/UCL Conference on Materialities and Cultural Memory of Twentieth-century Conflict', September 2006); Center for the Intrepid, United States National Armed Forces Physical Rehabilitation Center ('Rehabilitation of the Combat Amputee: Consensus Conference and Creating a Roadmap for the Future', September 2007) and by the United States National Museum of Health and Medicine, Armed Forces Institute of Pathology (NMHM/AFIP) ('Limb Labs: Getting Amputee Soldiers back to Work after World War I', July 2008).

I appreciate the institutional support I received during the course of my research and writing. The Centre for First World War Studies at the University of Birmingham connected me to rich resources and to likeminded scholars who stimulated my thinking and supported my inquiries. I am indebted to the Centre's Director, John Bourne, for welcoming me into this community of scholars. The NMHM/AFIP offered wonderful opportunities to explore and refine my ideas about material culture studies, and to do so in co-operation with my colleagues there when I served the institution as its senior curator from 2005 to 2007. The American Occupational Therapy Foundation provided me with time to complete my final typescript, and to its board of directors and its executive director, Charles Christiansen, I am grateful.

Many colleagues and friends offered immeasurable support during the course of my research and writing. I am especially thankful to Stephen Badsey, Lenore Barbian, David Cantor, Thomas DiPiero, Margot Finn, Michael Flannery, Aidan Forth, Jeffrey Gambel, Peter Gatrell, Michele Garfinkel, Thomas Hahn, Michael Harris, Terri Hasseler, Alan Hawk, Walter Hickel, Amanda Laugesen, Fred Leventhal, Mark Levitch, Jonathan Lewis, Beth Linker, Elizabeth Lockett, Aran Mackinnon, Jessica Meyer, James Mokhiber, Colin Newbury, Adrianne Noe, John Parascandola, Paul Pasquina, Tim Pennycoff, Jane Potter, Heather Perry, Andrew Piper, Michael Rhode, John Roberts, Helene Ross, Paul Sledzik, Brian Spatola, Kathleen Stocker, Frank Turner, Janet Watson, Stewart Weaver and Donna White.

The staff at Manchester University Press – especially Rachel Armstrong, Emma Brennan, Reena Jugnarain, Anthony Mason and David Rodgers – offered generous assistance as I prepared my writing for publication. I am also grateful to Martin Hargreaves and Ray Offord for their time and their expertise.

According to copyright law the Galsworthy compositions reproduced here are in the public domain, either because they were published before 1923 or because they fell under government copyright in the first instance when Galsworthy created them in service to the Crown. In drawing these conclusions I am indebted to Jeremy Crow of the Society of Authors and to Christopher Sinclair-Stevenson of Sinclair-Stevenson Ltd. At the same time, I am of course solely responsible for any questions of copyright that might arise as this book circulates. Every effort has been made to trace the copyright holders of material reproduced here which does not fall into the public domain. Should holders step forward after publication, due acknowledgement will gladly be made.

My father's love of history continues to be an inspiration to me, and I remain grateful for his perspectives and his support of my research and writing.

I dedicate this book to my wife, Allison, for her own unwavering support and for helping me to balance my love of history with the love that has surrounded us since we met and especially since the arrival of our daughter, Danielle, in May 2007. While the joys of research cannot match those of new fatherhood, I am grateful that during the course of completing this book both combined in my life in ways that I could not have imagined.

Any errors that follow are mine alone, and I hope readers will forgive them as they join me in exploring Galsworthy's connection to the 'sacred work' of the Great War and in considering the relevance of his opinions to disabled soldiers of subsequent conflicts.

J.S.R.
Rockville, Maryland

John Galsworthy and the Great War: rediscovery and reappraisal

Born in Kingston Hill, Surrey, into an upper middle-class family, and educated at Harrow and at New College, Oxford, John Galsworthy (1867–1933) (Figure 1) was one of the most prolific and best-selling authors of the twentieth century. During his lifetime he produced an immense body of work, including twenty novels, over two dozen plays, three collections of poetry, more than 150 short stories and five collections of essays. He received the Nobel Prize in literature in 1932 and alongside this honour is best recognized for his epic sequence of novels and 'interludes' about the upper middle-class Forsyte family, known collectively as *The Forsyte Saga*.[1] Since its inaugural publication as a single edition in 1922 this story has become one of the most celebrated British period drama series ever made.[2] It was produced in part as a film in 1949, more fully for television in 1966–67, again in 1990 as a radio series and once more in 2002–03 in a made-for-television film adaptation.[3] Yet while Galsworthy's name has become synonymous with *The Forsyte Saga* his reputation in this context has belied another he achieved during the Great War, which was his humanitarian support for and his compositions about soldiers disabled in the conflict.

I learned about these aspects of Galsworthy's life and literature as I completed research for my first book on the Great War, which explored life behind the lines for non-officer 'other ranks' who served on the western front.[4] In that project I used a variety of literary, artistic and architectural evidence to draw connections between features of the mobilized British state – the so-called war machine – and the contemporary 'culture of caregiving' that chiefly involved disabled soldiers of non-officer 'other ranks'. I defined that culture broadly as the product of

Figure 1 John Galsworthy, ca. 1919, shortly after reaching the peak of his international reputation for supporting and writing about disabled soldiers of the Great War. (Library of Congress)

medical knowledge and procedure, social relationships, material culture and health institutions that combined to inform soldiers' experiences of rest, recovery and rehabilitation in sites administered by military and voluntary-aid authorities. In revealing previously overlooked features of wartime life in Britain, I argued that its 'generation of 1914' was a group bound together as much by a comradeship of healing as by a comradeship of the trenches.

John Galsworthy and Disabled Soldiers of the Great War extends my previous study and encourages new perspectives on the Great War by opening a wider window on to Galsworthy and his association with the contemporary culture of caregiving. It makes available for the first time in a single edition the majority and most significant of Galsworthy's writings connected to what he described as the 'the sacred work' of this culture, that is, the rehabilitation and reintegration of 'stricken heroes of the war' who, 'in every township and village of our countries . . . will dwell for the next half-century . . .'.[5] Rediscovering and reappraising Galsworthy through these texts and their sociocultural contexts, this book ultimately investigates two questions that have not received the attention they deserve from scholars. Why did the 'sacred work' emerge as a central feature of Galsworthy's life and humanitarian opinions and actions during the course of the Great War? And why – after the end of the war and despite his prophetic vision of the societal impact of a generation of war-disabled – did Galsworthy never again in any substantial way take up 'the sacred work' as a subject of his humanitarian concern? In exploring answers to these questions *John Galsworthy and Disabled Soldiers of the Great War* advances several intersecting fields of scholarship, including the biographical study of Galsworthy himself, the cultural history of the Great War in Britain and the fields of material culture studies and disability studies.

This book is timely not only from these scholarly perspectives, but also from that of renewed popular interest in Galsworthy's wartime fiction and dramatic canon. In 2007, the editors of *The Penguin Book of First World War Stories* reprinted his 1924 short story 'Told by the schoolmaster', in which an under-age volunteer is shot for desertion.[6] Here was Galsworthy's first appearance in a major modern anthology of Great War literature. Also in 2007, as part of its 'George Bernard Shaw and his Contemporaries season', the Orange Tree Theatre of Richmond, Surrey, revived Galsworthy's 1920 play *The Skin Game*, a story of hostilities and animosities between two rival families whose estates border each other in the English countryside. The Mint Theater of New York City had revived *The Skin Game* two years earlier, and it did so within months of the Orange Tree reviving Galsworthy's 1914 play *The Mob*, an anti-war story about a government Minister who resigns, refuses to back an imperialist war and joins the campaign against it in part by speaking at an anti-war rally.[7]

Reviewers on both sides of the Atlantic praised these new productions of *The Skin Game*, noting the contemporary relevance of the story and suggesting the potential of their revival to spark even broader interest in Galsworthy's drama and his work overall. The Mint '[offers an] arresting and admirable revival of "The Skin Game,"' wrote Lawrence Van Gelder in the *New York Times*.[8] 'It's good news for this . . . production though bad for Western civilization that . . . *The Skin Game* . . . still feels relevant,' observed Catherine Rampell in the *Village Voice*.[9] 'This . . . could easily bring about a renewal of interest in the entire Galsworthy dramatic canon,' concluded another New York critic.[10] In London, a reviewer for the *Times Online* argued that '[even] while you might suspect that [the story] is out of date and that the dramatic works of the writer better known for his *Forsyte Saga* are rarely revived for good reason', this 'engrossing, intelligent' production 'demonstrates that there's not only moral ferocity but [also] theatrical fire in Galsworthy yet'.[11] A reviewer for *The Stage* offered a similar opinion as he called the Orange Tree production 'sumptuous . . . [a] quite rattling-good melodrama [and] well-made play with the potential for tragedy, unfairly neglected for more than 70 years'.[12] Yet another reviewer praised the Orange Tree for 'continuing to throw up forgotten gems, such as this 1920 piece [The Skin Game] by . . . Galsworthy'.[13]

Following these critically acclaimed revivals, and in tune with key scholarship, this book 'throws up' a different set of 'forgotten gems' by Galsworthy. Its centrepiece is his essay 'The sacred work', which Galsworthy composed during the spring of 1918 upon request of the Ministry of Pensions for the official proceedings of the second annual inter-allied conference and exhibition on the after-care of disabled men. Held in London, that event was one of the largest and most comprehensive initiatives of the day that sought to address key issues related to the human wreckage of the war. During the course of its sessions leading allied medical authorities, voluntary-aid representatives, labour leaders, politicians and government administrators exchanged views on vital questions with which Galsworthy had become intimately familiar and which – down to that final year of the war – helped to mark the pinnacle of his international reputation for supporting disabled soldiers. As the agenda of the conference and exhibition suggested, methods of surgical treatment and standardization of artificial limbs received substantial attention, as did debate about compulsory versus voluntary retraining and provision of pensions and related allowances (Figure 2). At the same time, one of the most prominent subjects under discussion during the conference sessions and on display at the exhibition were the so-called curative workshops and objects produced therein by soldiers. Here were the very sites and *matériel* – indeed, the very tangible expressions – of Galsworthy's 'sacred work'. Thus in name, in content and in historical context, his associated essay is a touchstone for this book.

After this historical analysis readers will find sixteen of Galsworthy's compositions related to disabled soldiers and to his support of their rehabilitation and reintegration into post-war society. These texts are reproduced in two parts. Part I includes a chronological arrangement of ten non-fiction essays which originally appeared from March 1916 to February 1919. In these essays readers will find the complete body of work that Galsworthy contributed to *Reveille*, the landmark journal he edited during the final year of the war, as well as his most significant

Official Programme for the Allied Conference and Exhibition on the After-Care of Discharged Men.

CENTRAL HALL, WESTMINSTER, MAY 20th to 25th, INCLUSIVE.

Monday, 20th May.
Delegates and guests are requested to be in their places not later than 11.15 a.m. at the Central Hall, Westminster.
11.30 a.m.—Opening ceremony by H.R.H. the Duke of Connaught.
12 (noon).—Opening of the Exhibition. Presentation of Delegates from Allied Foreign Nations.
12.30 p.m.—Visit by their Majesties the King and Queen.
2 to 8 p.m.—Exhibition open to the public.
2.30 to 7.30 p.m.—Cinema Lectures by British and Allied Representatives. (For details see list)

Tuesday, 21st May.
10 a.m. to 12.45 p.m.—Section Meetings. (For details see list)
10 a.m. to 8 p.m.—Exhibition open to the public.
2.15 p.m.—Visits to Roehampton, Richmond and Walton-on-Thames by Allied Delegates, in three parties.
2.30 to 7.30 p.m.—Cinema Lectures by British and Allied Representatives.
7.30 p.m.—Dinner at the Mansion House to Allied Delegates.

Wednesday, 22nd May.
10 a.m. to 12.45 p.m.—Section Meetings. (For details see list)
10 a.m. to 8 p.m.—Exhibition open to public.
2.15 p.m.—Visits to St. Dunstans (Blind) and Golders Green (Shell-Shock Recovery Home) by Allied Delegates, in two parties.
2.30 to 7.30 p.m.—Cinema Lectures by British and Allied Representatives.

Thursday, 23rd May.
10 a.m. to 12.45 p.m.—Section Meetings. (For details see list)
10 a.m. to 8 p.m.—Exhibition open to public.
2.15 p.m.—Visit to Shepherd's Bush and Battersea War Pensions Committee by Allied Delegates, in two parties.
2.30 to 7.30 p.m. Cinema Lectures by British and Allied Representatives.

Friday, 24th May.
10 a.m. to 12.45 p.m.—Section Meetings. (For details see list)
10 a.m. to 8 p.m.—Exhibition open to public.
12 (noon).—Final closing of the Conference by H.R.H. the Duke of Connaught.
2.30 to 7.30 p.m.—Cinema Lectures by British and Allied Representatives.
Afternoon Entertainments to Allied Delegates by Sir William Younger.
7.15 p.m.—Official Dinner to Allied Delegates, Ritz Hotel.

Saturday, 25th May.
Visit to Brighton by Allied Delegates, leaving Victoria about 10 a.m.
10 a.m. to 8 p.m.—Exhibition open to public.
2.30 to 7.30 p.m.—Cinema Lectures by British and Allied Representatives.

Sailors, Soldiers, and Air Force, in uniform, admitted free, 6 p.m. to 8 p.m.

E. A. STANTON, Lieut.-Colonel,
Secretary-General.

Figure 2 Agenda of the second (1918) inter-allied conference and exhibition on the after-care of disabled soldiers. (Collection of Steve Forbes © All rights reserved. Image by Richard Holttum)

contributions to British and American periodicals. They will also find two of his contributions to as many British 'gift books' – anthologies of poetry, prose and illustrations – published in aid of Queen Mary's Auxiliary Convalescent Hospital and St Dunstan's Hostel for Blinded Soldiers and Sailors. Part II of this collection draws together six of Galsworthy's essays of fiction dating from the winter of 1915 to the spring of 1919. These essays are organized thematically in two sections, the first of which includes compositions that reflect key aspects of his wartime public service at home. The second section contains the major literary products of his service in France at the Hôpital Bénévole for French soldiers with rheumatic and neurasthenic diseases.

Nine of the ten compositions which appear in part one of this collection have not seen the light of day in any full form since their original publication during the war. The six pieces of fiction included in Part II of this collection have been reprinted infrequently since Galsworthy's death in 1933, and their historical contexts have simply never received the critical attention they deserve from historians of the Great War. While all of these texts have now entered the public domain, and a few have been made readily available through print-on-demand technology,[14] there has not been a commensurate growth of interest in studying Galsworthy's wartime activities generally and in particular with regard to his humanitarian support for and his compositions about soldiers disabled in the conflict. In seeding such interest by recovering Galsworthy's wartime life and creative work from the dustbin of history and literature, *John Galsworthy and Disabled Soldiers of the Great War* becomes the first 'new' collection of Galsworthy's writings to appear since the 1937 publication of his *Glimpses and Reflections*.[15] Indeed – following on his wartime essay collections entitled *A Sheaf* (1916) and *Another Sheaf* (1919)[16] – this book could be considered a posthumous 'third *Sheaf*' in Galsworthy's canon, one that not only rediscovers and reappraises his place in the history of the period of 1914–18 but also identifies his relevance to wider dialogue about soldiers disabled in subsequent wars.

Historiography

Great War studies and historical biography
As mentioned previously, this book advances several intersecting fields of scholarship. Among these are two branches of study related specifically to the Great War: sociocultural studies and related history of medicine projects on the one hand, and studies of propaganda on the

other. Scholars working within and across these arenas have at worst ignored Galsworthy entirely or at best given cursory attention to the historical significance of his humanitarian support for and his compositions about soldiers disabled in the Great War.

Galsworthy's absence is notable in much landmark scholarship of the Great War, including that of Jay Winter, who argues that bereavement of the period prompted a revival of traditional modes of aesthetic expression and thus revitalized classical, romantic and religious themes of the past. The resurgence of these modes of expression, Winter claims, was a means to reconnect a grieving generation with its familiar past.[17] My focus on Galsworthy draws partly on this perspective, as it reveals that while the war did bring dramatic change – particularly in the form of unprecedented slaughter and bodily damage – distinct patterns of social and cultural continuity persisted within this environment and, in doing so, helped contemporaries make sense of the very change taking place around them. In my study, the patterns of continuity suggested by Winter are represented by the persistence into the war years of Galsworthy's dedication to humanitarianism across a variety of categories, including animal rights, censorship, and reform of prisons, suffrage and divorce and labour laws.[18] In supporting these causes among many others Galsworthy therefore 'shared the faith of many Liberals . . . that English society could be made more equitable and humane',[19] although he preferred to call himself a humanist who possessed tremendous optimism. As he explained to one admirer in 1910, during the same year his play *Justice* appeared on the London stage:

> I am not a Socialist in the strict economic sense of the word, for I think Socialism should be limited to the securing of the decency, and healthy foundations of a State, and beyond that I believe it to be dangerous to energy and impracticable in point of fact. In spirit I am a Socialist, if Socialism means increase of brotherly and human feeling. I have seen a good deal of our submerged classes. I know at first hand something of conditions on which Capital and Labour meet and fight . . . I have read and thought a good deal on prisons and prison life, and have been over many prisons. I believe I may say that I hate cruelty and injustice . . .[20]

Galsworthy conveyed these sentiments in various ways throughout his adult life, but nowhere did he encapsulate them better than in *A Sheaf* and *Another Sheaf*. These companion volumes together represent the largest concentration of Galsworthy's humanitarian writings from before, during and immediately after the Great War.

A Sheaf connected Galsworthy's pre-war humanitarian concerns with those of the war years, as its profits aimed specifically to support St Dunstan's Hostel for Blinded Sailors and Soldiers. Its contents included forty compositions that spanned the subjects of animal treatment, the legal system, prisons and punishment, the position of women, wartime society and the post-war world; among these were two compositions – 'Totally disabled' and 'Remade or marred' – which appear here in Chapters 2 and 4, respectively. *Another Sheaf* reprinted a dozen of Galsworthy's compositions uniquely about the war, including his essay 'The sacred work', which appears in Chapter 7, and other compositions which addressed the effects of the conflict on industry, agriculture and relations among the citizens of allied nations.

Despite the window that *A Sheaf* and *Another Sheaf* open on to Galsworthy's humanitarianism, scholars have paid relatively little attention to these collections generally and specifically to their relationship to disabled soldiers of the Great War. As mentioned previously, with their contents recently arriving in the public domain, these collections have seen wide republication, but, again, they appear without the accompanying historical analysis they deserve. Such oversight aside, when scholars have addressed *A Sheaf* and *Another Sheaf* they have done so fleetingly, merely describing their content to show how Galsworthy sought to support the war, even while he despised it, not by promoting public hatred of the enemy but rather by engaging with events through his skills as a writer.[21] Other scholars either dismiss these collections as having less literary and historical value relative to the author's better-known novels and plays, or, like much of Galsworthy's material published between 1910 and 1920, due to their tendency toward sentimentality, which stood in direct opposition to the contemporary trend toward modernism. Indeed, this latter rationale echoes the very condemnation of Galsworthy by Virginia Woolf, who despised him for evoking late Victorian and early Edwardian tastes and 'inventing all kinds of trivia with which to fill [the pages of their novels]; and, in so doing, deprived their readers of a single insight into human character'.[22] As Woolf wrote in her essay *Mr Bennett and Mrs Brown*, Galsworthy, like Arnold Bennett and H. G. Wells:

> looked . . . out of the window; at factories, at Utopias, even at the decoration and upholstery of the carriage; but never at her, never at life, never at human nature . . . [Bennett, Galsworthy and Wells] have developed a technique of novel-writing which suits their purpose; they have made tools

and established conventions which do their business. But those tools are not our tools, and that business is not our business. For us those conventions are ruin, those tools are death . . .[23]

Woolf's criticism notwithstanding, modern biographers and critics of Galsworthy are correct in their own assessments of his wartime public pronouncements as ornate and evocative of late Victorian and early Edwardian style. However, such dismissal of these texts on literary grounds should not be a reason for historians to relegate them to the dustbin of history. Let us return to 'fitting' Galsworthy with arguments about social and cultural continuity in the face of social and cultural change. Put simply, like so many who lived through the Great War, Galsworthy drew upon what was familiar to make sense of unfamiliar, indeed unprecedented, events. This book therefore recovers a large number of Galsworthy's 'lost' texts related to disabled soldiers not from a purely literary perspective but rather historically and biographically – indeed, in context as historical and biographical documents – to reveal him as participating in personal and public patterns of continuity, as one who sought to make sense of an unfamiliar war not by relying on modernism as so many of his contemporaries did but rather by drawing on familiar literary conventions and established humanitarian perspectives on society. In achieving this goal and revealing the complex ways in which Galsworthy, like so many others of his generation, perceived the war after 1918, *John Galsworthy and Disabled Soldiers of the Great War* contributes to an ever-growing body of scholarship about how contemporaries engaged in the events of the Great War – both on the war front and the home front – and how those who survived the events of the day sought both to remember and to forget them and their aftermath.[24]

With regard to history of medicine scholarship that intersects with sociocultural studies of the Great War, this book advances a number of works which – even as they successfully examine how the war shattered and disabled men's bodies – offer only cursory analyses of Galsworthy's connection with this aspect of the period. Exemplary here are the projects of Seth Koven, Joanna Bourke and Sarah Cole, which address from various perspectives how the war eroded the ways men traditionally thought of themselves as men.[25] Koven and Bourke reveal important nuances in this process by highlighting the significance of pre-war medical and welfare programmes for wartime and post-war identity. Focusing on the curative programme at Chailey Heritage Hospital, Sussex, Koven shows how crippled boys, who were traditionally objects of rescue in orthopaedic healing programmes, became agents of healing during the Great War. By pairing a disabled soldier with a crippled boy the medical authorities at Chailey intended to help the soldier remember his duty in the face of adversity, and in doing so urge him to remain a brave 'soldier' and to fight to regain his role as a citizen, a breadwinner and a productive member of civilian society. Framing Galsworthy's inaugural editorial in *Reveille* as a historical document, Koven effectively reveals the strength of his support of disabled soldiers as well as his 'prophetic' vision of a nation faced with a generation of broken men. Bourke also references Galsworthy as she identifies the endurance of traditional masculine discourse in the attempts of both the public and the government to reconcile the damage wrought on the bodies of dismembered soldiers. Cole picks up where Koven and Bourke leave by presenting an excellent focus on Galsworthy and his 'unflinching' interest in disabled ex-servicemen as he articulated it specifically through his editorship of *Reveille*.[26]

John Galsworthy and Disabled Soldiers of the Great War extends all three perspectives by revealing the depth and breadth of Galsworthy's humanitarian support for and his compositions about soldiers disabled in the war. In so doing, it presents the most comprehensive history written to date of Galsworthy's engagement with the 'sacred work' of the day. Indeed, this book relocates Galsworthy from the periphery of Great War history and literature to a centre where he can be recognized critically alongside contemporaries like Wilfred Owen, Siegfried Sassoon, Robert Graves and others whose 'voices' have both spoken for and have been interpreted by scholars as best representing the 'generation of 1914'.[27]

The second branch of Great War historiography extended by this book is that involving propaganda of the period generally and the War Propaganda Bureau (WPB) in particular. Established in September 1914 as a secret unit of the Foreign Office and organized chiefly by Charles Masterman, the WPB was based in and known confidentially as Wellington House. Its initial mission was to assist the Allied effort by targeting overseas elite opinion, particularly in America, while coordinating various local and regional propaganda campaigns across the United Kingdom. Several scholars have ably reconstructed the history of this initiative, its changing course as the war unfolded and Galsworthy's attendance – with nearly two dozen of his contemporaries – at its inaugural meeting. convened by Masterman on 2 September 1914.[28] Among these, the projects of David Wright and Peter Buitenhuis are especially valuable for establishing the historiographical framework of this book.

In his article 'The Great War, government propaganda and English "men of letters," 1914–16', Wright documents the propaganda work that Galsworthy undertook during the weeks following the first meeting of Wellington House. At least a portion of this effort was commissioned directly by the unit – and without payment – through the novelist and playwright Anthony Hope Hawkins, with whom Galsworthy met in London in mid-October.[29] During this period, Wright correctly explains, Galsworthy 'poured out articles on recruiting, the German destruction of Louvain and the heroic resistance of the Belgians and French'.[30] And during the two years that followed he composed 'a mass of journalism on the need to support relief funds and on Anglo-American relations'. As Wright mentions briefly in his article, and as I detail in my own analysis, Galsworthy donated the income he earned from these compositions to various humanitarian efforts but in particular to those associated with disabled soldiers. Overlooking the significance of this fact about Galsworthy's life during the Great War, Wright concludes simply that this body of work by the author was 'poor quality pot-boiling stuff, but a pot which [he] did not find easy to bring to the boil, as it went so much against the grain'. But the fact that this work *did* exist 'so much against the grain' is precisely *why* it deserves our attention. To gloss over it as Wright does – and as so many other historians and literary biographers have done in their respective studies – translates to overlooking the historical and biographical meaning of Galsworthy's authorship that promoted the 'sacred work' of rehabilitating disabled soldiers and reintegrating them into post-war civilian society. I argue therefore that Galsworthy's very act of writing about, and his very actions connected with, disabled soldiers were as much about his self-empowerment in the face of perceived disability as they were about political propaganda.

Buitenhuis's book *The Great War of Words* extends Wright's invest-igation by conveying the broader the story of how, after the war, many former WPB writers and other authors became deeply embittered about the Allied propaganda machine and their role in the creation of patriotic pamphlets, heroic fiction and 'front line' but glamorized reporting.[31] At this time, Buitenhuis argues, there was a growing conviction among these writers that too many lies had been told and that, in propagating Allied myths, they had sacrificed the all-important rule of their craft, namely professional detachment. Buitenhuis therefore chronicles both the disillusionment of the former propagandists and the reaction against their elders by younger writers, many of whom had served in the trenches. The consequences for post-war literature were profound: the prestige and power of authorship dwindled significantly, while the old rhetoric based on a widely held consensus collapsed and was replaced by lean, ironic and often understated modes of writing. Becoming embittered about wartime propaganda long before most of his contemporaries, Galsworthy stands out in this history. As Buitenhuis concludes, he was 'on the whole a voice of sanity and moderation amid a din of exaggeration'.[32]

John Galsworthy and Disabled Soldiers of the Great War therefore offers a vast body of evidence in support of Buitenhuis's conclusion and in rethinking Wright's simplistic conclusion about Galsworthy's 'mass of journalism' associated with wartime humanitarian causes generally and disabled soldiers in particular. In essence, this book is an unprecedented investigation of why the 'sacred work' became such an intense focus of interest in Galsworthy's life and such a prominent theme of his writing during the Great War. Illustrative of this prominence and intensity are Galsworthy's manuscript notes and essay 'first pages' reproduced here.

My own investigation begins with an overview of key analytical frameworks developed within the field of disability studies. It continues with an examination of Galsworthy's perception of himself through his private diary and his correspondence as he considered the coming war in August 1914 and as the conflict dragged on for the next four years. These approaches combine to reveal critical connections between Galsworthy's sense of *himself* as disabled during the war and his contemporaneous support of disabled soldiers. They also provide background for a discussion of the material dimensions of the culture of disability in which Galsworthy engaged for deeply personal reasons.

Disability studies

Recent years have seen disability studies become a major force in scholarship, influencing nearly every major discipline and subdiscipline in the humanities and social sciences, and promoting dialogue among scholars in these areas as well as between them and the wider disability community.[33] This field has also helped to establish linkages between humanities/social science scholars and allied health professionals who engage the social model of disability, which key scholars define as 'the vast web of social, political, economic, medical and legal forces that create material and virtual barriers for individuals with physical or cognitive impairments'. This model stands in opposition to its 'medical' counterpart, which prescribes that disability is the result of a physical condition and is therefore intrinsic to the individual. Both frameworks are integral to examining critically Galsworthy's personal reflections on the war as it approached during the summer of 1914 and as its initial events unfolded through the autumn. Those reflections, as we shall see, suggested his sense of being paralysed by several forces: by the horror of the war (which he abhorred), by his marriage (which he viewed as 'paralysing'), by his physical ill health (which involved a 'game shoulder' and 'shortsightedness') and by his age (which, according to the military establishment, combined with his ill health to disqualify him from enlistment). At the same time, a careful reading of these reflections suggests that Galsworthy sought to overcome his sense of paralysis – indeed, to enable himself – through engagement in the occupation that he knew best, namely writing. Put another way, what he believed to be purposeful authorship – purposeful in light of what he believed to be the most pressing outcome of the war – he could mediate his hatred of the conflict with his desire to do his own 'bit' for King and Country in the most philosophically viable way.

Material culture studies

Like the field of disability studies, the field of material culture studies has come to define another area of cross-disciplinary inquiry which informs my recovery and reappraisal of Galsworthy and his writings about disabled soldiers of the Great War. Researchers who embrace the field of material culture studies generally argue that the range of narratives 'contained' in extant primary sources relating to a specific historical period – three-dimensional objects as well as posters, written and printed documents, photographs and films – are not fully retrievable by any single discipline. They argue further that studying the physical remains of a society and the individuals and communities which these remains reflect helps to decipher the past and to reveal in its course the interface of societies and objects, indeed how each has helped to define the other.[34] Examining Galsworthy and his writings through this lens therefore reveals not only a rich textual history but also unplumbed material and visual histories which during the time of their production combined with written media to reinforce heroic stereotypes, to promote the promise of artificial limbs and work therapy regimens, and to focus the vision – famously articulated by Prime Minister David Lloyd George in

1918 – of a home front 'fit for heroes to live in'. As detailed in separate but related sections of the following analysis, three intersecting themes frame this examination and, in doing so, open a window on to the constellation of objects and images that operated in conjunction with Galsworthy's words to reflect and shape the culture of caregiving surrounding disabled soldiers. The first of these themes involves the curative workshops and objects produced therein by soldiers, both of which, as I mentioned above, received considerable attention at the 1918 inter-allied conference and exhibition. The second theme involves wartime charity 'gift books' and distinctive material culture related to these publications. The final theme involves the distinctive clothing of the convalescent soldier disabled in battle, what Galsworthy described in his 1919 satire *The Burning Spear* as 'blue garments and red ties of hospital life'.

1914: 'The nightmare of it . . . I wish to Heaven I could work'

For Galsworthy, the run-up to the Great War was a time of personal depression and professional paralysis. 'These war-clouds are monstrous,' he wrote about the impending conflict. 'If Europe is involved in an Austro-Servian [*sic*] quarrel, one will cease to believe in anything'.[35] The following days were no better as he observed 'war-clouds still black' and 'the suddenness of this horror . . . appalling'. The first day of August dawned 'Blacker and blacker!' as Germany declared war on France and Europe's web of alliances continued to draw nations into conflict.[36] It was all '[t]oo ghastly for words', Galsworthy observed. '[T]he European war has come true. The nightmare of it.' In the days that followed he longed to return to writing as he rode in the countryside to distract his thoughts from the war. 'I wish to Heaven I could work,' he recorded in his diary.[37] On 3 August 1914, one day before Britain declared war on Germany, he experienced 'a miserably anxious day' as the nation stood 'on the verge of war' and 'the question of Belgium's neutrality' took on greater urgency. 'If Germany will not respect it,' Galsworthy surmised, 'we shall be in.' He concluded, 'I hate and abhor war of all kinds; I despise and loathe it. And the thought of the million daily acts of its violence and hateful brutishness keeps riving my soul . . .'.[38]

During the weeks that followed, Galsworthy had incessant 'thoughts on the war'. These, he explained, 'eventually caused a "strain" that 'simply wears away a little the capacity for feeling'. And '[E]very now and then,' he concluded, 'the horror of it sweeps one'.[39] Galsworthy's creative paralysis continued through August, his only project being a revision of his novel *The Freelands*, a story about social relations in and the effects of capitalism on England's rural economy.[40] As James B. Pinker, Galsworthy's literary agent, described the situation to Charles Scribner, Galsworthy's American publisher, '. . . Since the War broke out he has not, he tells me, written anything creative, but he is trying again now, and in a week or two he will know whether he can get on or not . . .'[41]

In fact, shortly before Pinker wrote to Scribner, Galsworthy did 'get on' by embracing the very *ability* he possessed despite the war (and no less *before* its clouds darkened Europe), namely that of writing. As he noted in his diary during the middle of August, '[I] settled down to finish *The Freelands* and make money (for the country)' in the form of 'relief funds'.[42] Scribner had promised him a 'big price' for the work in serial form, and so urgently did Galsworthy want to make the donation that he asked for the bulk of his earnings in advance. As his agent Pinker explained to Scribner:

> I have already suggested terms to you . . . in a letter which I have received from Mr Galsworthy this morning he asks me to make an arrangement by which you would pay a good part of the serial money, if not the whole of it, in advance on delivery of m.s., so that he can help relief funds substantially and at once. As a matter of fact, this is the spur of inducement which is keeping Mr. Galsworthy at work in these times, and you will, I am sure, understand his feeling . . .[43]

A long-time admirer of Galsworthy, Scribner understood the author well and agreed to offer the sum before the manuscript arrived in his New York office.[44] After nearly a year and a half of writing – and despite what he called a 'pull to concentrate on it since the War began' – Galsworthy finished *The Freelands* on 1 October 1914. As he explained in his diary, the £1,500 he earned from the work 'was the most substantial thing I could do for relief funds'.[45] Such was Galsworthy's approach to his occupation of writing during this traumatic period, engaging in it for moral reasons – to cure his personal dilemma about supporting 'King and Country' – and for professional reasons – to revive his creativity and purposefulness which the war threatened immeasurably.

This perspective informed Galsworthy's response to a telegram he received at his home in Wingstone, Sussex, on 2 September 1914. It was an invitation to join the WPB, which he accepted by travelling shortly thereafter to a 'meeting (in London) of chief literary men at Wellington House to concert measures of putting forward principles for which England is fighting'.[46] The writing projects he undertook during the period after this gathering – specifically the essay entitled 'Thoughts on this war' and others associated with Belgium and army recruitment – were the first of many he offered to the WPB for publication through its national and international networks.[47] However, of relevance here is not Galsworthy's engagement with the WPB *per se* but rather the humanitarian motivation which underpinned it. A letter from Galsworthy to Scribner, dated 8 September 1914 and addressing his essay 'Thoughts on the war', is revealing:

> Pinker tells me that he has sold you my war 'Thoughts' for £100 and I want just to say that if the length (it seems shorter than I thought) disappoints you, please propose a reduction of price. At the same time I sincerely hope [Scribner's] Sons will not have to do this, because I design to give every penny I get for it (and all I can possibly spare from any other proceeds of my work nowadays) to Relief Funds.[48]

Thus by early November – apart from the £1,500 he had earned during the previous month from *The Freelands* – Galsworthy had raised through additional writing another £1,250 for various relief funds.[49] He found purpose through such work, therefore, even as the 'horror' of the war and the extent of his 'disability' in the face of it finally 'swept' him a few weeks later. As he wrote then in his diary:

> The heartsearchings of this War are terrible, the illumination of oneself rather horrible. I think and think what is my duty, and all the time know that if I arrived at certain conclusions I shouldn't do that duty. This is what comes of giving yourself to a woman body and soul. [My wife Ada] paralyses and has always paralysed me. I have never been able to face the idea of being cut off from her.
>
> In cool blood I suppose what I am doing – that is, writing on – novels and stories – and devoting all I can make, especially from America – no mean sum – to Relief – is being of more use that attempting to mismanage Relief Funds, or stretcher-bearing at some hospital, or even than training my elderly unfit body in some elderly corps.
>
> I say to myself: 'If I were young and unmarried I should certainly have gone! There is no doubt about that!' But there is great doubt whether if I had been of military age *and married to A.* I should have gone. Luckily for my conscience I really believe my game shoulder would not stand a week's training without getting my arm into a sling. Moreover I suppose there is no one yet training as shortsighted as I am. Still, I worry – worry – all the time – bald and grey and forty-seven and worrying. Funny![50]

Thus for Galsworthy purposeful writing was the only possible means of overcoming his complex sense of himself as disabled, one that emanated from medical judgement of his body and his mind, and from society's judgement of 'elderly' men who could not fight like younger men. He embraced this hopeful perspective on writing despite the final depressing days of 1914. 'And so the year closes,' Galsworthy wrote in his diary. 'Very happy till August. Very unhappy since. Nor is there any use in deluding oneself into thinking that next year will be any better.'[51] Indeed, the next year *was* no better as the first wave of soldiers disabled in the war began to return home. When they did Galsworthy began to realize the full human damage being wrought by the conflict. He responded with compositions that were not merely descriptive of that damage and efforts to repair it but also semi-autobiographical, as they revealed his thoughts as an observer who, due largely to his own disability, was set apart from, but nonetheless wished to participate in, the events of the day.

1915: St Dunstan's and Roehampton

In June 1915, Galsworthy wrote to the American publisher Alfred A. Knopf with an intensely personal view of his occupation of writing, one that implied what his life would be like without his full engagement in it:

> Well, what I say is for your ears, or eyes rather, alone. It's a frank and very successful exposition of the old idea that men should work for the joy of working . . . that a man must do his job to the utmost pitch of polish for the love of it. I mean – take the idea away, and there's little or nothing left – no deep conception or treatment of life, or character – no blood and thickness of emotional texture; which is what the author with that particular thesis should have demanded of his own job – namely the painting of life . . .[52]

Such 'painting' occupied Galsworthy in a variety of ways between the spring and autumn of 1915, but especially so with regard to two essays he composed for as many 'charity books' associated with disabled soldiers.[53] In May, he completed work on a short story about a patriotic farm hand who, despite his lack of education and perception by others as being 'not all there', wishes to join the army to fight the Germans. Entitled 'The recruit', this piece appeared in *The Blinded Soldiers and*

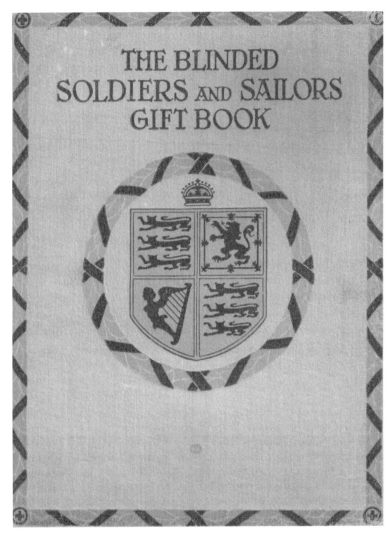

Figure 3   George Goodchild (ed.), *The Blinded Soldiers and Sailors Gift Book in Aid of St Dunstan's* (London: Jarrold & Sons, 1915), in which Galsworthy's short story 'The recruit' appeared. (Private collection. Image by the author)

Sailors Gift Book in aid of St Dunstan's Hostel (Figure 3). That autumn – near the same time when he wrote to Charles Scribner that 'the war absorbs us terribly . . . work is the only refuge, and moreover one's best way of being useful'[54] – Galsworthy visited Queen Mary's Auxiliary Convalescent Hospital at Roehampton and shortly thereafter wrote the foreword to its own charity book (Figure 4).

These two compositions are reprinted in this book not only to establish Galsworthy's association with St Dunstan's and Roehampton, but also to help reveal the constellation of images and objects which operated in conjunction with his words to define the culture of caregiving surrounding these institutions and their counterparts, indeed to transmit to the public awareness of and charitable giving toward them. To this end, the charity books of St Dunstan's and Roehampton were themselves significant objects of the day. Advertisements like this one in the *Times* (Figure 5) helped booksellers to sell hundreds of thousands of copies of these publications.[55]

Each sale – indeed, each book itself – represented a bridge between the battlefront experiences of soldiers, on the one hand, and the home front experiences of civilians, on the other. Through either contributing to charity books, as Galsworthy did, or purchasing them, those who did not serve at the front could demonstrate their appreciation of the bodily sacrifice of those who did as well as the material methods of repairing their wounds, whether through the artificial limbs and curative workshops of Roehampton or the retraining schemes of St Dunstan's.

Galsworthy and Roehampton

Established in 1915, Queen Mary's Convalescent Auxiliary Hospital at Roehampton was the flagship institution of Britain's network of sixteen orthopaedic facilities set aside by the military authorities to 'deal systematically with the question of [disabled] men's after-careers while [the men were] still undergoing treatment in hospital'.[56] Although its official motto – 'Hope welcomes all who enter here!' – emphasized an intangible of the environment, at its centre was the material manifestation of that hope, namely artificial limbs that could enable disabled soldiers to take up various kinds of therapeutic work. Galsworthy conveyed this scene precisely in his foreword to *The Queen's Gift Book*, emphasizing the hospital's 'green and fortunate haven' populated by 'four hundred men in their bluish hospital garb and their red neckties' and its 'real business . . . to fit [them] properly with new limbs, and with a new future'. Galsworthy's subsequent focus on those 'new limbs' – specifically through a dialogue with their maker at Roehampton – revealed his awareness of the promise which contemporaries associated with such medical *matériel*.

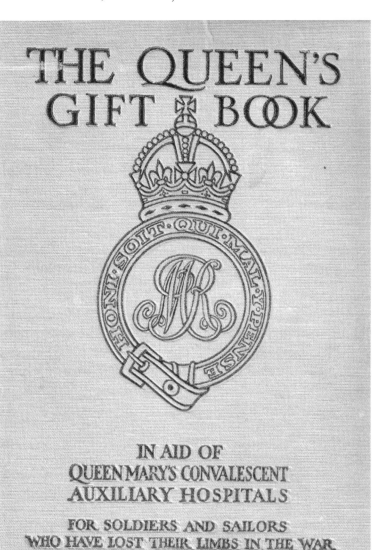

Figure 4   The Queen's Gift Book in Aid of Queen Mary's Convalescent Auxiliary Hospitals for Soldiers and Sailors who have Lost their Limbs in the War (London: Hodder & Stoughton, 1915), which included a foreword by Galsworthy. (Private collection. Image by the author)

Figure 5 'The royal gift book', display advertisement in the *Times*, 3 December 1915, p. 4. (From Gale, *Times Digital Archive*, © Gale, a part of Cengage Learning Inc., www.cengage.com/permissions. Reproduced by permission)

In part, Galsworthy's sketch of Roehampton and its limb makers echoed the optimism conveyed by media of other official funding appeals, including a poster (Figure 6) which emphasized Roehampton's soldier-patients to be 'wounded but working, down but not out', a photograph (Figure 7) from the Ministry of Pensions journal *Recalled to Life* which displayed the soldier-patients of Roehampton as active 'workers' as opposed to recipients of any charity and an image (Figure 8) from the *Illustrated London News*, which detailed the 'many types of wonderful mechanical arms and legs now on the market' for the maimed soldier. But, whereas the messages of these media were unequivocally positive and focused for the most part on the *immediate* mission of rehabilitation programmes, Galsworthy's concluding perspectives on Roehampton stood well apart as they pointed critically toward the future when 'the mountainous happenings of to-day will acquire a dream-like quality . . . the haloes round the maimed [will] grow dim to us . . .' and 'they will be limping monuments of a half-buried war . . .'. Here, therefore, was a complex nexus of realism, prophecy and autobiography. At its centre was Galsworthy seeking to accomplish several objectives: painting the landscape of the post-war world as it would be populated by a generation of lovers, brothers, husbands and fathers disabled for life; recognizing the gaps in experience between those who served and those who remained at home as well as his own identity in the latter category; and, despite that identity, wanting to make a personally viable and professionally meaningful contribution to the war effort. More than mere ephemera, therefore, Galsworthy's foreword to *The Queen's Gift Book* – and no less that publication itself – was a means by which he began to face a grim present and an uncertain future based upon a familiar past record of humanitarian concern.[57]

Galsworthy and St Dunstan's Hostel

St Dunstan's Hostel was established in early 1914 by the National Institute for the Blind, the British Red Cross Society and the Order of St John of Jerusalem. Located initially in a house in Bayswater, London, it moved during the following year to the Regent's Park property of Otto Kahn, the American banker and influential patron of the arts who supported the institution heavily during the war.[58] Here, as St Dunstan's chairman Sir Arthur Pearson stated in his address to the 1918 inter-allied conference, 'soldiers and sailors who have lost their sight at the war are taught to be blind, re-educated, and trained'.[59]

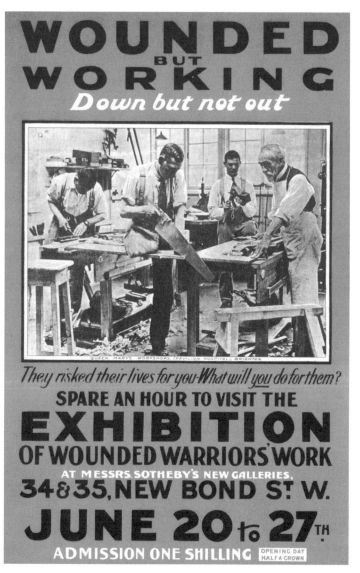

Figure 6 'Wounded but working. Down but not out.' Queen Mary's
Workshops, Pavilion Hospital, Brighton. 'They risked their lives for you.
What will you do for them? Spare an hour to visit the exhibition of wounded
warriors' work at Messrs Sotheby's new galleries', ca. 1914–18.
(Hoover Institution Archives, Stanford University)

Figure 7 'Roehampton workers', from *Recalled to Life* 1 (June 1917), following p. 64. (United States National Library of Medicine, National Institutes of Health)

In support of this mission, Jarrold & Sons of London published the English version of *The Blinded Soldiers and Sailors Gift Book* in 1915 and G. P. Putnam's Sons of New York published the identical American edition the following year.[60] While the narrative of Galsworthy's story 'The recruit' did not involve St Dunstan's *per se*, the composition nonetheless deserves attention for being a chapter in this publication, and therefore of a piece with this and other material means by which Pearson and his associates shaped the public image of their institution and its men, indeed much like their counterparts did at Roehampton. Such other material means unique to St Dunstan's included the production and circulation of picture postcards like that in (Figure 9), which conveyed the exterior of the site as a serene home fit for heroes, or, as the 1916 annual report of St Dunstan's described it, '. . . the Happiest House in London, for those blinded men who have learnt to live their lives anew with such gay courage know all that is worth the knowing about happiness'.[61] Complementing this perspective, official photographs of the workshops of St Dunstan's revealed its interior to be an environment of

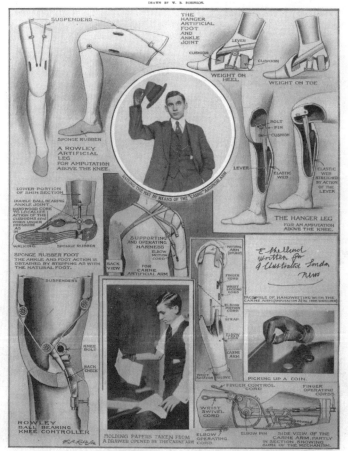

Figure 8   W. B. Robinson, 'Replacing lost limbs: marvellous artificial arms and legs', *Illustrated London News*, 13 November 1915, p. 633. (Robert W. Woodruff Library, Emory University)

Figure 9   Postcard, St Dunstan's Hostel for Blinded Soldiers and Sailors.
(Private collection. Image by the author)

productivity and purpose for men who deserved the best care as they
faced their future in the post-war world (Figure 10).

Other objects associated with St Dunstan's encouraged similarly positive messages. They did so in large part through iconography of the
distinctive blue uniform that military authorities required wounded
soldiers to wear in hospital and in public, after which they popularly
became known as 'convalescent blues' or 'blue boys'. These ill fitting,
bright-coloured and pocketless outfits had substantial precedents in pre-
war institutional culture as they functioned during the war to promote
a comradeship of healing among men.[62] Here was an obvious mark
of the contemporary war machine upon the body of the convalescent
soldier, one which substantially complicated the masculinity of soldiers,
underscored their sense of being a class apart from the rest of society
and established them as emblematic of a war-ravaged present and
an uncertain future. Illustrations drawn by hospitalized soldiers for
their institutional magazines plainly suggested that in the eyes of some
men their mandated outfit failed substantially to confer a deserved dig-
nity of personal appearance and sense of masculine independence
(Figure 11). Other soldiers likely shared this negative view but nonetheless found positive value in 'the blues' when – in a way comparable
to contemporary 'khaki fever' – they helped to attract public praise

Figure 10   The carpentry workshops of St Dunstan's Hostel for Blinded
British Soldiers and Sailors, London, from J. H. Rawlinson, *Through
St Dunstan's to Light* (Toronto: Thomas Allen, 1919), p. 30.
(Private collection. Image by the author)

generally and especially the attention of attractive young women (Figure
12).[63] Contemporary picture postcards like these clearly underscored the
mixed sentiments held by convalescent soldiers (Figures 13 and 14).

Taken together, these positive and negative images combined with
others – associated both with St Dunstan's and with other organizations
of the day, like the Stick-crutch Fund (Figure 15) – to promulgate the
iconic status of the 'convalescent blue' on the home front.

The administrators of St Dunstan's embraced the iconic status of
the 'convalescent blue' with particular enthusiasm. 'Happy St Dunstan's
men' – presumably content due to the camaraderie they experienced in
the serene environs of the institution – adorned objects like the coin
collection tin in Figure 16 and the tobacco container in Figures 17 and
18. Other objects like this match-book holder (Figures 19, 20 and 21)
emphasized not contentment but rather the stoicism of blue-clad St
Dunstan's men. And although the St Dunstan's lapel pin, or badge
(Figures 22 and 23), and the institution's annual report for 1916 (Figure

Figure 11 'Hospital Fashions: "The Bond Street Cut" by Private Vernon Lorimer – from the 3rd L.G.H. Style Book for 1916', *Gazette of the Third London General Hospital*, March 1916, p. 152. (Private collection. Image by the author)

Figure 12 'Patient: "You think I'm in blue – well, I'm really in 'the pink'"',' by Private E. S. Walker, *Gazette of the Third London General Hospital*, September 1917, p. 334. (Private collection. Image by the author)

Strafe the Tailor—A Bad Fit of the "Blues."

Figure 13 Postcard, 'Strafe the Tailor – A Bad Fit of the "Blues"'
(London: George Pulman & Sons, ca. 1914–18). (Private collection.
Image by the author)

Figure 14 Postcard, 'Sorry I can't get round – why don't you come here?'
(Holmfirth: Bamforth & Co., ca. 1914–18). (Private collection. Reproduced
with permission from Bamforth & Co. and the Bamforth Postcard
Collection, Leeds. Image by the author)

Figure 15 'The crutch we want. Subscribe liberally. Stick-crutch Fund, Kensington, London' (ca. 1918). (Department of Art, Imperial War Museum, London)

Figure 16   St Dunstan's coin collection tin, ca. 1914–18. (Private collection.
Image by Brian Spatola)

Figure 17   St Dunstan's tobacco
container, ca. 1914–18, front.
(Private collection. Image by
Brian Spatola)

Figure 18   St Dunstan's tobacco
container, ca. 1914–18, back.
(Private collection. Image by
Brian Spatola)

24) used remarkably similar imagery to suggest the vulnerability of a St
Dunstan's man as he receives guidance from a young girl, he nonethe-
less stands tall and faces the future with confidence as a result of his
St Dunstan's-sponsored retraining.

Figure 19 St Dunstan's match book holder, ca. 1914–18, front. (Private collection. Image by the author)

Figure 21 St Dunstan's match book holder, ca. 1914–18, back. (Private collection. Image by the author)

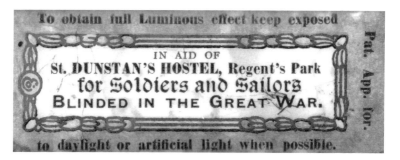

Figure 20 St Dunstan's match book holder, ca. 1914–18, side. (Private collection. Image by the author)

Thus through *The Blinded Soldiers and Sailors Gift Book* Galsworthy's story 'The recruit' was of a piece with the diverse material culture associated with St Dunstan's and with the 'convalescent blue' soldier. The fact that these iconic figures appeared in Galsworthy's other writings about disabled soldiers – initially in his foreword to *The Queen's Gift Book*, then in his essay 'Heritage' and once more in his novel *The Burning Spear* – opens a window on to his awareness of them and the

Figure 22 St Dunstan's lapel pin, ca. 1914–18, front. (Private collection. Image by the author)

Figure 23 St Dunstan's lapel pin, ca. 1914–18, back. (Private collection. Image by the author)

Report of St. Dunstan's Hostel for Blinded Soldiers and Sailors for the Year ended March 26th, 1916

ISSUED BY THE BLINDED SOLDIERS AND SAILORS CARE COMMITTEE.

Figure 24 *Report of St Dunstan's Hostel for Blinded Soldiers and Sailors for the year ended March 26th, 1916. Issued by the Blinded Soldiers and Sailors Care Committee.* (Department of Printed Books, Imperial War Museum, London. Image by the author)

challenges of personal and public identity which they faced upon their return from the front, both within the culture of caregiving and beyond it in civilian life.

1916: 'For the maimed – now!'

During the early months of 1916, Galsworthy composed 'Totally disabled' to benefit the Star and Garter Home for Disabled Soldiers and Sailors. The essay appeared in *The Observer* on 19 March 1916, evoked autobiography from its very opening and was a major success for the institution, as it helped to raise £3,000 in donations in one day.[64] 'If I were that!' Galsworthy wrote here. 'Not as one getting into the yellow leaf, but with all the spring running in me. If I lay, just turning my eyes here and there! How should I feel?' In response to his own question, Galsworthy turned not further inward but rather to the subjects before him. 'How do *they* feel – those helpless soldiers and sailors already lying in the old ballroom of the "Star and Garter"?' Later in the essay, Galsworthy plainly underscored his identity apart from these men even as he articulated his responsibility – with the rest of society – for their secure future. '. . . [W]e others approach them,' he wrote:

> with heads bowed, in as great reverence as we give to the green graves of our brave dead. And if pity – that pity which to some, it seems, is but ignoble weakness – be not driven from this earth, then with pity we shall nerve our resolve that never shall anything be lacking to support or comfort those who gave all for us and are so broken by their sacrifice . . .

Two months later Galsworthy again combined autobiography and prophecy in his essay 'For the maimed – now!' which he wrote following his visit to the Lord Roberts Memorial Workshops. Reprinted in Chapter 3, this essay appeared originally on 26 May 1916 in the *Morning post* and later, retitled as 'Those whom the war has broken', in the August 1916 issue of *Current History*. 'I don't know how other people feel,' Galsworthy began here,

> but when in the streets there passes some poor fellow who a few months ago was stronger and more active then one's self, had before him many more years of enjoyment and utility, almost a boy, perhaps, and who is now to be for ever like a bird with a broken wing or a ship with a mast gone and half its sails trailed down, there comes on one a sensation like no other that this war produces . . .

The future ahead, Galsworthy continued, was clear:

> The armless, legless, the blinded, the paralysed – all live on into the green years when the wilderness will bloom again and flowers grow where this storm once withered the face of the earth; on into the calm years when men will look back and rub their eyes. It is this which comes down on the heart of him who sees the maimed men go by – this sensation of watching, from far on in the future when there shall not be another trace left of that hurricane, thousands upon thousands stricken out of full life into a half-existence, thousands upon thousands who, but for the merest chance, might be ourselves . . .

'This is a queer world of ours,' he observed further, '[for] in those [Lord Roberts Memorial] workshops men who have been through hell and left part of themselves behind are making toys, and the toys are remaking them.' Remarkable for its emphasis on the restorative power of the very objects that were being produced by men disabled in the war, this portion of 'For the maimed – now!' suggested Galsworthy's awareness of the essential role of *matériel* in 'after-care' regimes and the value of that role in promoting these regimes to the public. Indeed, Galsworthy's observation about the toy products of the Lord Roberts Workshops was in tune with the message of this publicity poster (Figure 25) issued by the institution, which depicted the variety of its wooden toys available for purchase.[65]

Galsworthy's observation was also of a piece with the views of contemporaries who, like Galsworthy, enthusiastically supported these workshops. For example, in his own observations of the London facility and its provincial branches, Major Algernon Tudor Craig called attention to the objects as well as to their broader context, namely their design, publicity and sale.[66] 'Each branch is given its own speciality in the way of manufacture, and in such a way that it can be of service to each other branch, thereby co-ordinating the work as much as possible'. Craig observed further:

> For instance, the Yorkshire Branch at Bradford does all the printing for all the Workshops, while the West Midlands Branch at Birmingham does all the metalwork required. Take, for example one of the cheap and amusing table games which may be obtained in the showroom. The woodwork in it is made in the London Workshops, where the label is also designed; the latter is printed in the Bradford Workshops; the metalwork is produced in the Birmingham Workshops; while the game itself is completed, and the cardboard box to hold it, is made in the Brighton Workshops. In this way also advertising can be done more economically from the head Workshop,

Figure 25 Poster, 'Wooden toys. Lord Roberts Memorial Workshops for Disabled Soldiers & Sailors. Head office, Fulham, London', ca. 1914–18. (Hoover Institution Archives, Stanford University)

while material can be purchased more advantageously and in greater bulk. Each Workshop has its travellers, whose activities are confined to the provincial area concerned, but at the same time each branch pushes and disposes of the work of each other branch, receiving credit from the branch in question for any commissions on such sales . . .[67]

Combined with Galsworthy's insights, Craig's description of the manufacturing and supply networks developed by the workshops reveals an object-focused curative regime which was not unlike the one Galsworthy would observe two years later, in July 1918, when he visited the Chailey Heritage School, East Sussex, and which he described briefly in his associated essay – reproduced in Chapter 12 – entitled 'Heritage: an impression'.[68]

To be sure, 'Heritage' focused chiefly on the intangible 'sheer emotion of church sounds' that surrounded Chailey through its chapel, sounds which 'now and then steal away reason from the unbeliever, and take him drugged and dreaming'.[69] The tangible – indeed, material – aspects of the environment were nonetheless apparent to Galsworthy as he observed that 'the first thing each child cripple makes here is a little symbolic ladder' which enables him to '[climb] a rung on the way to his sky of self-support'.[70] And when this child leaves Chailey, Galsworthy wrote further, 'he steps off the top of it into the blue, and – so they say – walks there upright and undismayed, as if he had never suffered at Fate's hands'. However, he asked,

> what do he and she – for many are of the pleasant sex – think of the sky when they get there; that dusty and smoke-laden sky of industrialism which begat them? How can they breathe in it, coming from this place of flowers and fresh air, of clean bright workshops and elegant huts which they on crutches built for themselves?[71]

Galsworthy offered no answers to these questions but rather issued a condemnation that spoke directly to past abuses and suggested the new ones which had emerged with the return of so many men broken in battle. 'Masters of British industry, and leaders of the men and women who slave to make its wheels go round,' Galsworthy demanded, '. . . make a pilgrimage to this spot, and learn what a foul disfigurement you have brought on the land of England these last five generations! . . . Blind and deaf and dumb industrialism is the accursed thing in this land and in all others . . .'[72] Juxtaposed to official images of Chailey like this one (Figure 26), Galsworthy's condemnation therefore appeared ironic, since the very 'industrialism' of the institution's 'clean bright workshops' was the very hope – indeed, the focus of treatment – for children broken

Figure 26 'Crippled boy instructing a crippled soldier in the art of wood-turning', *American Journal of Care for Cripples* 3: 4 (December 1916), after p. 170. (US National Library of Medicine, National Institutes of Health)

by the Victorian Age and for soldiers broken by the war.[73] More remarkable here, however, was Galsworthy's prophetic vision. As he had done in his previous writings about the war-disabled, he looked to the future even while he was aware of the exigencies of the present.

Galsworthy's prophetic thoughts combined with his concerns about the present – indeed, with his purposeful role in the war effort – to inform his approach to *A Sheaf* during the spring of 1916. As he wrote to Charles Scribner:

> I am thinking of bringing out in the autumn a collection of my writings [to be entitled 'A Sheaf of Wild Oats'] which are in the nature of pleas (more or less humanitarian) divided into three parts 'Before the War'. 'The War'. 'And After'; and if I am ever to do it I suppose this is more or less the moment, seeing that the past is so past, and the future so blind . . .[74]

Galsworthy's sister, Mabel E. Reynolds, urged him to take up this project, and he seemed keen to do so, for the very reasons he had communicated Scribner, as well as to Knopf and to others. 'Did I tell you that I'm issuing a volume of "wild oats" – humanist writings – as you wanted – in September?' Galsworthy wrote to Mabel in July. '. . . I thought after all I might as well make what money I could out of them for funds.'[75] This correspondence to his sister is significant, as it reveals that while *A Sheaf* may have been conceptualized by Galsworthy during the period of his involvement with the WPB, the collection was not specifically published by the WPB, since the work did not appear among the nearly 1,200 books, pamphlets and miscellaneous publications that the unit actually issued during its existence.[76]

Scribner welcomed receiving *A Sheaf*, and, for specific reasons, he encouraged Galsworthy to emphasize the humanitarian subjects therein rather than the war itself. '. . . There have been so many war books,' Scribner explained,

> that we find it difficult to create much interest in a new one at present – even Mrs. [Humphry] Ward's book [*The War on all Fronts: England's Effort. Letters to an American Friend*], issued last week, and with a preface by Mr. [Joseph H.] Choate, makes its way slowly. Your volume is so different in many ways that I believe we shall do well with it though I would suggest that you do not place too much emphasis on the war element. The humanitarian plea would go much farther. This leads me to doubt whether the titles of the parts . . . are desirable the first one particularly might be changed but of course I leave that to your judgment . . .[77]

Galsworthy understood and embraced Scribner's point of view. 'I quite understand that Americans must be suffering under the shoals of war books,' he replied. 'The first section of my book is far the longest – longer considerably than the other two put together – and humanitarian throughout save for two or three sub-sections. The war writings are on the whole by no means of the partisan order. I will see if I can alter the title of the first section . . .'[78]

Galsworthy did change his framework along the lines suggested by Scribner, entitling the first section not 'Before the war' but rather 'Much cry – little wool', the second simply 'The war' and the third 'And – after?' In the preface to the volume Galsworthy referred to himself in the third person as he described what followed as 'a garnering of non-creative writings; mostly pleas of some sort or another – wild oats of a novelist, which the writer has been asked to bind up'. He continued, again in the third person, fending off an unattributed accusation of profiteering and identifying the charitable beneficiary of the collection:

> He cannot say that he had any wanton pleasure in sowing any of [these writings]; and, lest there be others of the same opinion as the anonymous gentleman who thus joyously addressed him last July: – "But there – I suppose you are getting a bit out of it. Men of your calibre will do anything

for filthy lucre – you old and cunning reptile!" – he mentioned that he has not, personally, profited a penny by anything in this volume, and that the future proceeds therefrom will be given to St Dunstan's, and the National Institute for the Blind, London . . .

Galsworthy offered no such note in *Another Sheaf*, which he began to conceptualize during the early summer of 1918. Moreover, no evidence suggests that the proceeds of this second volume supported a specific cause.[79] Nonetheless, the positive public reception of both collections on both sides of the Atlantic reaffirmed his long-standing humanitarian reputation and growing public association with disabled soldiers of the current war. As the *New Statesman* declared following the publication of *A Sheaf*, [Galsworthy is] a 'watch-dog of civilization . . . expending as much energy upon the advocacy of public causes as upon his creative work'.[80] According to the *Times Literary Supplement*, 'what is valuable in [*Another Sheaf*] is the insistence on our present opportunity, and the vision of the goal which Mr. Galsworthy . . . displays before us'.[81] On the other side of the Atlantic, the *Boston Evening Transcript* described Galsworthy's essays in *A Sheaf* as 'contributions to the literature of humanitarian reform [that] show [his] skill as debater and as a commonsense literary man'.[82] The *Springfield Republican* punctuated these positive observations by reporting that 'John Galsworthy backs up his direct arguments with statistics and personal investigations, creating in *A Sheaf* an "ethically significant" work'.[83] And the *Boston Evening Transcript* stated that 'John Galsworthy speaks frankly in *Another Sheaf*, questioning seriously the road England must take as she and the citizen-soldiers readjust to life' after the war.[84]

1916: Hôpital Bénévole and Kitchener House

On 8 September 1916, a few weeks before *A Sheaf* appeared in bookshops, Galsworthy visited the London office of the Red Cross to offer his family house as a war hospital. His inspiration for doing so stemmed not only from his expanding concern about disabled soldiers – indeed, his desire to offer something more from which they could benefit – but also from his appreciation of humanitarian work being undertaken by his long-time friend, the American painter Julie Helen Heyneman, who had established California House for wounded Belgian soldiers in Lancaster Gate, London. Galsworthy's family home, located not far away, at 8 Cambridge Gate, would eventually take a similar form during the spring of 1917, and be known as Kitchener House, a club for wounded

British soldiers and sailors, with Galsworthy chairing the executive committee of the institution.

Galsworthy's vision of his home being used in this purposeful way coincided with his composition of 'Remade or marred: a great national duty', which appears in Chapter 4. It also coincided with his chance meeting on 8 September 1916 with an old friend, Dorothy Allhusen, who proposed the 'idea of going out to work at her French hospital', Hôpital Bénévole, for 'rheumatic and neurasthenic solders'.[85] Shortly after this meeting, Allhusen joined Galsworthy and his wife, Ada, for tea at their home and the three arranged for the couple 'to go out to her hospital at Die, near Valence, on Nov. 8', as Galsworthy wrote in his diary, 'I as a bathman and masseur, Ada as linen superintendent'.[86] Only one day after his meeting with Allhusen, in preparation for his work abroad, Galsworthy enrolled in a course on Swedish Massage.[87]

Thus during the autumn of 1916, Galsworthy embarked on two major humanitarian endeavours, one at home and another in France. Both would substantially inform the 'national duty' about which he wrote in his essay 'Remade or marred' and pave the way to other projects – both national and international – which would address the 'sacred work' of rehabilitating disabled soldiers and reintegrating them into post-war society.

Hôpital Bénévole

In October 1916 Galsworthy wrote to his friend, the French essayist André Chevrillon, about his intention to volunteer at Allhusen's Hôpital Bénévole and his thought that the work would re-energize his writing. '. . . It seems a little absurd, and I'm afraid I shan't be much good,' Galsworthy explained, 'but I badly want a rest from the head and pen, and one can only rest from that by working with the hands. It will be a joy, anyway, to see France, and your soldiers. . . .'[88] Although he did achieve the break he desired, Galsworthy's experiences on the ground were largely the opposite of his own expectations, as he continued to think about his numerous writing projects and engage in substantial correspondence about the establishment of Kitchener House and the welfare of soldier-patients at Hôpital Bénévole itself. Put simply, Galsworthy's time in France was not an interlude to advocacy on behalf of disabled soldiers, but rather a substantial augmentation of his efforts along this trajectory.

Shortly after his arrival at Hôpital Bénévole, Galsworthy recorded in his diary several positive reflections on the institution, on his initial work therein, and on its staff and patients: 'Men very nice (neurasthenic, shell-shock, and rheumatic, about 35 of them),' he wrote on 19 November. '. . . Staff very genial; atmosphere good,' he continued. The following day he '[b]egan [his] massage; well-installed; interesting; Ada all sorts of odd jobs. Weather better. Place beautiful in a strange way.' And on 21 November, alongside the observation 'I like the work', Galsworthy offered an outline of his daily routine:

Breakfast,	8.15.
Massage,	9.30 to 11.30.
Luncheon,	12:30.
Walk.	
Muller exercises with men,	3.30 to 4.
Tea,	4.
Massage,	4.45 to 5.15.
Dinner,	7.
Massage,	8.30 to 10.

This outline, Galsworthy's cursory impressions thereof and a contemporary group photograph (Figure 27) together belie the significance of

Figure 27   Galsworthy and his wife, Ada (seated in front row, first and second from left, respectively), with staff and soldier-patients of Hôpital Bénévole, Martouret, France, ca. December 1916. (Special Collections Department, University of Birmingham)

Galsworthy's experiences at the institution. Within weeks of his arrival he began to advocate for the welfare of the soldier-patients under his care.

'All is well here,' he wrote initially to Dorothy Allhusen on 30 December 1916,

> except that Y— [one of the hospital's patients] has disappeared. He went into Die after lunch yesterday (Friday) and was seen at the Café du Progrès ordering black coffee, and at a tobacconist's ordering cigarette papers at 2.30, since then, nothing at present. The gendarmerie has been given details of him. We shall probably have news soon, it being market day. I fear we oughtn't to have given him money . . .[89]

Shortly after the New Year, on 3 January 1917, Galsworthy wrote again to Allhusen with news of 'Y—,' specifically that he had returned safely but not before 'he was arrested by gendarmes at Beaurières, beyond Luc, about 37 km from here, on Sunday morning, and sent back to us by train, arriving that evening'.[90] Galsworthy explained further, taking a remarkably personal interest in the situation of this soldier:

> He persists that he was lost, and that he had what he calls *a coup de tête* – but as a matter of fact the poor fellow took the expedition out of sheer ennui. He has suddenly produced a pocket-book with heaps of letters which he has had on him all this time, and which contain several addresses of relatives – one in Lyons and one in Paris. I have written to his father-in-law in Paris and his uncle in Lyons, to tell them that we have him here. All the letters from his wife and others are affectionate, so that he is not by any means a cast-off. We must find him something steady to do, and try and talk to him more. I was awfully sorry, and rather upset, I'm afraid, that Z— was sent off (even though he was so outrageous). He is in hospital at Valence, and I shall hope to see him there when we go in to-morrow in the car and get some money . . .[91]

Galsworthy wrote further to Allhusen with thoughts about ending his stay at the hospital and, once more, about the closing of the institution due to troop movements. Here, in raising the issue of 'things pressing at home', he also suggested the anxiety he was experiencing:

> It seems that towards the end of this month (unless fresh men arrive) we shall probably be reduced to five or six men, and I suppose the question of closing will come up. Apart from this contingency, and from the possibility that you will have become 'fed-up' with my very peculiar nature, and be glad for us to go, I ought to tell you now that I find March 5 (Monday) will be the very end of the time I can spare. While you are at Ceret you

may be wanting to rearrange things in some way, so that I want you to know exactly how you stand with us. I'm very sorry that we can't manage the full four months, but there are things pressing at home. We much hope they are not worrying you much at Ceret, and that you will come back rested. All is well here . . .'[92]

Galsworthy sealed his letter in an envelope but later opened it to 'say that last night two new arrivals were telephoned to us. They, too, will come up for their prolongations, presumably at the beginning of February, or rather will end their month then.'[93] He continued, offering Allhusen his thoughts on the future of the hospital, based upon his observations about impending German troop movements. 'Everything seems to point to the first week in February as the psychological moment for closing,' he wrote. 'If you should be seriously considering this, would it not be as well to telegraph to Miss Russell not to accept any further men till you have taken your decision? You know, better than I, that there is always a moment in affairs when foresight can be exercised, and that if that moment is let pass, things are out of one's hands, and drift to anyhow conclusions.'[94]

By 'things pressing at home' Galsworthy was likely referring in early January not only to Kitchener House, which was taking shape for its formal opening that spring, but also to his numerous writing projects for Charles Scribner and, as he would reveal later, to debate over the National Service Bill which would eventually make military service compulsory for all single men aged eighteen to forty-one. Aside from these various concerns, no evidence suggests that Allhusen was in fact 'fed up' as Galsworthy had conjectured. Nonetheless she could well have harboured such sentiments, given Galsworthy's persistent opinion on the future of the hospital and no less his advocacy for the well-being of its soldier-patients. On 5 January 1917, Galsworthy wrote to Allhusen yet again about both matters:

I have been into the dates with Trouslard, and it appears that the future situation is as follows: La Roche (Chasseur d'Afrique) goes up for prolongation Jan. 8 and may get one. Raphanel, Forney, and Nogue go up Jan. 11; the first two are sure not to get them and Nogue is doubtful. Favoreau goes up on Jan. 18, and is most likely to get one. Amour on Jan. 22 (very doubtful). Trouslard, Perrin, and Raous go up on Feb. 1, and are pretty sure not to get them. La Roche, if he gets prolongation this time, will be due to go up again about Feb. 6.

So that after the first week in February (barring new arrivals, of which there is no sign – the wounded man has not been sent, and there is no news of him) you will have only Robert, who might just as well – and better – be at home; Vian, the pale boy, who is picking up fast; and Y—.[95]

Galsworthy continued, again revealing his concern about the future of the hospital, based on circumstances well beyond its environs:

I talked to one or two people in Valence, and have been reading the French papers; and I'm bound to tell you that I think the Germans *will* probably make an attempt to strike into France through Switzerland, very likely in February, if not before. It seems to be freely spoken of in Berlin. If they do, this part of the world will become the last to which men will be sent, and moreover there will be such a blockage on the railway lines that the hospital will become unworkable.[96]

He concluded with the opinion that:

Under all these circumstances I give you the very strong advice (unasked) to close this hospital before you go back to England early in February. I really don't think you will be justified in hanging on to it. It will take some little breaking up, so your decision ought to be made quickly.[97]

Through these letters and others that followed, therefore, Galsworthy played a role well beyond that of masseur. He was nothing less than a tenacious advocate for the *poilus* at Hôpital Bénévole.

The most notable example of this concern took shape in late January 1917, when he wrote privately to Clarisse Chevrillon, wife of André Chevrillon, about alleged mistreatment of *poilus* during their stay at the institution. 'Some time ago,' he began, 'you kindly wrote to my wife saying that if one would give you details of any cases of wrong treatment of *poilus*, a friend of yours might get an inspector to "open an eye." There are two cases of men, who have been in this convalescent hospital . . .' Galsworthy continued, describing both of these cases in significant detail, the first being 'Y—, Infan: 2de Classe' from Grenoble. 'Injury commenced 20 March 1916,' he explained:

Éclat d'obus [shellshock]: Commotion: Entered on hospital books as having cerebral disturbance: Conduct here very nervous, worries, and distressed, but no serious mental trouble. Read, and wrote normally; when on permission he came back to time. Has a wife and two children whom he adores. Home address is Saint-Symphorion d'Ozon (Isère). After leaving here he returned to his depot at Grenoble (having been refused prolongation, though improving here in the quiet and liberty of this place), Dec. 1st. Was then sent to Hôpital de la Tronche, Grenoble, and thence transferred about Christmas time to the Asile Sr. Robert, *près* Grenoble, which is apparently a lunatic asylum. Everybody here who knew him agrees that though highly nervous, his reason, if properly treated, was not in danger. *If he is now mad he has almost certainly been driven so by the decision to place him in an asylum.* The cure for this man was to send him home for a good long time, without fear hanging over him, and the *probability is that he could still be saved by that course.* He was a man of fine physique and handsome; it seems that he took drugs, probably because of the fear hanging over him. A letter from his wife is enclosed, and another from himself, both to our Directrice, Mrs. Allhusen.[98]

Galsworthy continued his correspondence to Clarisse Chevrillon, describing the second case of alleged mistreatment involving 'a Breton fisherman (deep sea cod fishery), called Z—', who arrived at Hôpital Bénévole from 'Hôpital C 38, Lyon, on November 25, and left . . . on December 28 for the Hôpital Général, Valence'. Galsworthy explained that this man suffered from 'Petit état de dépression mélancolique [a state of melancholic depression]':

He was, while here, silent, and utterly solitary, spent most of his time climbing the trees, and pretending, I think, that they were masts. He would reply intelligently to anything you asked, but never spoke to anyone, and could hardly be induced to stay still for his meals, and would get up at night and wander out two or three times. He broke out once and got rather badly drunk. In my view he suffered from the most acute form of nostalgia for his home *and the sea*; and from a sort of claustrophobia, or dread of being shut-up, which is just what is now happening to him in hospital at Valence. The cure for this man is also to send him home for a good long spell; and I should say the only cure. I asked a celebrated doctor of Lyon (who saw him here one day) whether it was not a case for 'réforme' and he answered 'Yes'. He agreed that the man was suffering from acute nostalgia. He lives at Charenix, *près* Dol, Ille et Vilaine. If an inspector could be asked to carefully examine these men it would be a great relief to several minds. Can it be done, however, without mentioning names?[99]

Galsworthy concluded humbly yet with unwavering concern:

I need not tell you that my position here (a mere masseur who has no dealings with either of the men in question) is too unofficial to count; and that great discretion is required in view of the special position of such a hospital as this. But it is really terrible to feel that these men are probably being wrecked by wrong treatment. Will you consult your husband and your friends and let us know what can be done without embroiling the hospital with the authorities. I also enclose a letter to myself from the poor Breton's poorer mother – one has sent her some assistance. It seems to be much more awful to see men being destroyed behind the front than at the front itself. There are so many for whom the only cure is a good long spell of home again . . .[100]

Galsworthy's suggestion of a 'spell' was in part evocative of his own situation by early March 1917. After a period that fell just short of four months he felt the need to return home to look after his own physical well-being and psychological sense of purpose as the war continued to unfold. 'As to ourselves', he wrote to Mrs Allhusen on 3 January, 'I'm beginning to feel I'm not pulling my weight. I expect the National Service Bill will pass early in February, and I'd like to be back before it gets into action, unless I'm doing much more good than I am at present.'[101] Situated in the broader context of his support for soldiers disabled in the war, the good which Galsworthy achieved on behalf of the *poilus* of Hôpital Bénévole was undoubtedly a significant chapter in his wartime life and, as we shall see, one which would directly inform his further writing about the 'sacred work'.

From Hôpital Bénévole to Cassis
Following their stay at Hôpital Bénévole, Galsworthy and Ada travelled through Marseilles, Valence and Arles on their way to Cassis-sur-Mer, where they spent eleven days touring the countryside and tending to their respective ailments, Ada 'a bad shin, caused by a fall at Martouret' and Galsworthy a case of 'mild sciatia'.[102] The serenity of Cassis enabled Galsworthy to reflect on his experiences of the previous months. There he composed 'Flotsam and Jetsam: a reminiscence', a story about two shellshocked soldiers – the 'flotsam and jetsam' of the war – which was clearly inspired by the men he met at Hôpital Bénévole and about whom he wrote in his correspondence to Clarisse Chevrillon.[103] Reproduced in Chapter 14 of this book, the piece appeared originally in *Scribner's Magazine* and again in Galsworthy's *Tatterdemalion* (1920).

Hôpital Bénévole and its *poilus* also inspired Galsworthy to compose 'Cafard' and 'Poirot and Bidan: a recollection'.[104] These stories appear in Chapters 15 and 16, respectively. Galsworthy wrote 'Cafard' in early July 1917 and 'Poirot and Bidan' around the same time.[105] 'Cafard' – whose French title literally means 'cockroach' or 'melancholy' – is a sentimental story about a shellshocked soldier with 'the little black beetle in the brain, which gnaws and eats and destroys' his hope as he 'returns to the front in fear and despair'. The soldier, however, is eventually 'restored to hope by his contact with a little dog'.[106] This story appeared during the final year of the war in *Scribner's Magazine* and thereafter in *The Nation* and *Current Opinion*. *Tatterdemalion* also contained the piece, and Galsworthy included it in another of his post-war short-story collections, *Caravan* (1925).

'Poirot and Bidan' tells the story of 'two contrasting and mutually hostile types of French soldier, the old, ruddy, stocky, talkative northerner and the young, pale, long-faced, silent southerner, both restored to health from shell-shock and to friendship by the gentle ministrations of the hospital'.[107] The piece appeared originally in the first issue of *Reveille* (August 1918), the Ministry of Pensions magazine edited by Galsworthy, which is discussed at length below. It was reprinted two years later in *Tatterdemalion*.

Cassis, Lyon, Paris and return to England

On 16 March 1917, Galsworthy and Ada departed Cassis for Lyon. There he visited both the École Joffre – whose toy-making workshop (Figure 28) likely reminded him of the Lord Roberts facility in London – and

Courtesy Red Cross Institute for Crippled and Disabled Men
TOY MAKERS AT THE ÉCOLE JOFFRE, LYONS, FRANCE, EACH MAN LACKING AN ARM THROUGH EITHER AMPUTATION OR PARALYSIS

Figure 28 'Toy makers at the École Joffre, Lyons, France, each man lacking an arm through either amputation or paralysis', from Garrard Harris, *The Redemption of the Disabled: A Study of Programmes of Rehabilitation for the Disabled of War and of Industry* (London: D. Appleton & Co., 1919), p. 81.
(Wilma L. West Library, American Occupational Therapy Foundation)

'the establishment at Tourvielle for training of disabled soldiers' – whose artificial-limb workshops likely recalled in his mind those of Roehampton, which he visited two years earlier and subsequently wrote about in his foreword to *The Queen's Gift Book*.

From Lyon, Galsworthy travelled with Ada to Paris, where he toured the 'St Maurice institutions for disabled soldiers', an experience which also likely evoked his experiences at and observations of counterpart institutions in England.[108] Soon after this visit, on 27 March, Galsworthy and Ada departed Paris for Southampton, via Le Havre, and returned to England the following day.

Shortly after that return, Galsworthy reflected on his experiences at Hôpital Bénévole in a lengthy letter to Allhusen:

> Now that I have seen with my own eyes . . . and worked with my own hand . . . and known it – as a summer hospital – surmount all the difficulties of winter in these difficult days, I can give you an impression that has some value. There is no doubt whatever in my mind that the French authorities look on it with a favouring eye, and appreciate this help, and that is perhaps the main thing from the general point of view. But what I can testify to more intimately is the appreciation and gratitude of the French soldier. It would warm the hearts of your subscribers to see that, as I have seen it. The human sympathy and individual care that your hospital gives them is beyond that which they expect, beyond that which they receive elsewhere. Le Martouret has an atmosphere of home. How many times have I not watched men coming there, strange and driven-looking, yield to that atmosphere and become different beings within three days! It has been a rare privilege to work among the poilus. They are salt of the earth! It's impossible not to like them with all one's heart – Bless them one and all!

Galsworthy continued:

> There is another work that your hospital does. It teaches the French people something of England, and the goodwill and admiration approaching reverence that England now has for France. It is a little centre from which radiates, with every soldier that goes forth from its care, real knowledge and appreciation of the English, even now strange birds to the French – a star from which travels light to many French eyes, not only of the soldiers, but of their friends and families. It spreads far and wide the good seed of that comradeship between our two peoples, which ever more and more becomes essential to the future of the world. A rare good work your hospital is doing. Thank you for letting us come to it and help . . .

'To leave it was a grief,' Galsworthy concluded, but such sentiment did not dull the inspiration he plainly drew from his time in France overall.

The advocacy he undertook at Hôpital Bénévole and the subsequent visits he paid to the École Joffre, Tourvielle and St Maurice institutions framed his growing interest in supporting disabled soldiers. Moreover, it provided important context to the related non-fiction writings Galsworthy would compose during the final eighteen months of the war. The first of these, entitled 'The need for reality', appeared during the summer of 1917 and explicitly recalled his observations of French rehabilitation centres as he offered thoughts on voluntary versus compulsory retraining programmes. Reprinted in Chapter 5, this essay was published – significantly unillustrated – on both sides of the Atlantic in 1917, first in the British War Pensions gazette and then in the *American Journal of Care for Cripples*. Shortly before the end of the war it appeared again in America – this time illustrated – in *Carry on: A Magazine on the Reconstruction of Disabled Soldiers and Sailors*. Three photographs accompanied the piece. The first depicted disabled American soldiers at Fort McHenry, Baltimore, Maryland, learning the 'profitable trade' of automotive mechanics (Figure 29), and the second depicted disabled Canadian soldiers on a farm in Calgary, Alberta, learning how to operate a tractor. The third photograph depicted the Office of the Surgeon General of the US Army, Washington, DC. Taken together, and juxtaposed to Galsworthy's words, these images conveyed his growing international reputation as an advocate for the war wounded. Another 'internationalized' illustration of Galsworthy's words – specifically his essay 'The gist of the matter', which appeared in the January 1919 issue of *Carry on* – underscored his stature in this regard.

Galsworthy and Kitchener House

'About 8 Cambridge Gate,' Galsworthy wrote to his sister, Mabel, during his stay at Hôpital Bénévole, 'I certainly wouldn't like it called Galsworthy House, and I really don't see how I can let it be described as lent by me when it's lent by all of us.'[109] Here, then, was the second initiative orchestrated by Galsworthy in 1916–17 to support soldiers disabled in the war. He wrote further to Mabel, 'I'll pay the rates, and shall be able to send a hundred or two towards the fitting up.' Galsworthy's wealth and generosity were certainly not the only forces behind what would become Kitchener House for wounded British soldiers and sailors. Financial support of the Joint War Committee was essential to preparing the institution for opening on 6 February 1917, approximately one month and a half before Galsworthy returned from France. By October, Kitchener House was well on the way to fulfilling its

Figure 29 'Our future engineers', from *Carry on: A Magazine on the Reconstruction of Disabled Soldiers and Sailors*, August 1918. 'A good many handicapped automobiles are being rehabilitated,' explains the caption of this photograph, 'while disabled soldiers learn a profitable trade at Fort McHenry [Baltimore, MD]. The future demand for skilled mechanics is drawing men partially handicapped into this promising field, where the wages are high and the work steady.' (US National Library of Medicine, National Institutes of Health)

mission through the guidance of Julie Heyneman, who, as mentioned previously, had established California House for disabled Belgian soldiers (Figure 30).[110]

According to Heyneman, California House provided 'rational and absorbing occupations for paralysed and other badly disabled men, and had created for them an atmosphere of cheerful industry which [promoted] excellent results in [their] physical, moral and mental development'.[111] Kitchener House operated on the same model, as the *British Journal of Nursing* reported:

[It] supplies a crying need for the wounded soldier. The spacious, beautiful, recreation room overlooks the park, and is provided with very easy chairs, newspapers and games. Here every man is welcome who chooses to take advantage of its hospitality. Here he may obtain good dinner free of charge with half an hour's notice; here he can have free tea without notice of any kind. Sometimes as many as a hundred guests are present. But though the men are quite at liberty to use the house for recreative purposes only, this is not its primary object. The aim of Kitchener House is more far reaching that the mere social side of the men's lives. The top floors of the house are devoted to the educational side, and the men are encouraged to take full advantage of this most important scheme.

Miss Heyneman is most anxious to break new ground in this direction, and with this end in view, she is creative in her aims, seeking to introduce branches of trade that have practically never been practised, or have become lost arts in this country.

Wood carving, gilding, frame making, bookbinding are among the industries taught. Boxes and picture frames are modelled in Gesso. Classes for French and Spanish are being held, and one for Dutch has recently been demanded . . .[112]

Despite these accomplishments, Heyneman sought to achieve what she described as the fullest form of 'after-care' possible through the co-operation of 'Sisters and nurses who have charge of the wounded . . . [and who] . . . do not perhaps all sufficiently realise the all-important "after-care" of their [patients'] destinies'. The *British Journal of Nursing* explained this approach in detail:

The real tragedy of these men's lives comes when they are discharged from the hospital and have to face life as it will be for them in the future. They are then no longer the centre of unremitting attention and often spoiling, but from that moment they are thrown on their own resources. No longer able to follow their own calling, they have learned no other craft to take its

Figure 30   Poster, 'California House for Disabled Belgian Soldiers', by Stan
Van Offel, ca. 1916. (Department of Art, Imperial War Museum, London)

place. What can Sisters and nurses do in this matter? The can tell the men about Kitchener House, and so far as is in their power remove every obstacle to their becoming members of it. The authorities of the Club leave no stone unturned to make it easy. If it is signified from a hospital that two or three badly disabled men are anxious to take advantage of the Club a conveyance is sent for them free of charge. In many cases the less helpless have their 'bus fares paid. Distance, therefore, is no hindrance, and the men come from long distances. The younger and more disabled the man the more welcome he is. Men who come for the purposes of recreation only, frequently catch the spirit of their more enterprising comrades, and are induced to join one of the classes. It cannot be argued that a short stay in hospital will render attendance at the Club useless. Often the seed of future success is sown even if the fruit is not brought to maturity at once . . .[113]

Galsworthy immersed himself in the culture of Kitchener House through the autumn of 1917, taking up the chairmanship of its executive committee and working closely with Heyneman to oversee operations of the institution and its replication in other cities. The knowledge and experience that he had acquired at Hôpital Bénévole and elsewhere plainly informed his efforts as he took up his leadership of the institution and carefully documented his thoughts about its operations (Figure 31). With regard to the 'main direction which we are going to follow', Galsworthy asked the executive committee during one of its first meetings, '[a]re we to aim only at mental and intellectual instruction', including languages, fine arts, commercial training and science, 'or are we to include lay Carpentry [*sic*] in the orthopedic sense . . . and manual crafts[?]'[114]
Galsworthy continued, as his manuscript notes reveal, setting out a variety of practical questions for consideration by the group:

2. The second point is: How is the house to be run? Free? Or on a system of small entrance & class fees? Or a combination of the two. 3. The third point is: Shall the house have a social side? There must obviously be a good reading room; and we think there should be a luncheon & tea room [and] passes [to] give officers the opportunity of using it for brunch? The fourth point: What days & hours shall the house be open? And what will be the best hours for classes? The fifth point is the question of management. We propose a small house committee of ladies as the present Kitchener House for the actual practical details of house work and food etc. *And* a small Executive Committee to arrange the classes etc. Should there be wounded officers on this Committee? . . .[115]

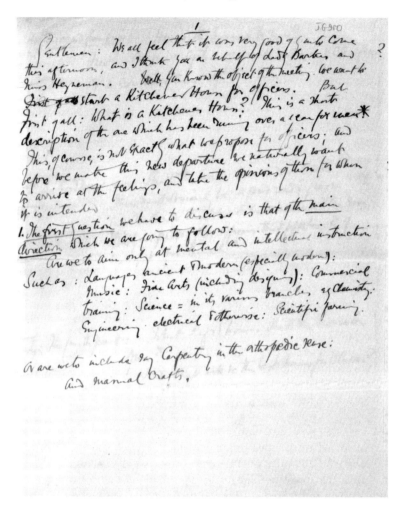

Figure 31 First page of Galsworthy's manuscript notes on Kitchener House. (Collection of Steve Forbes © all rights reserved. Image by Richard Holttum)

Complementing these questions, Galsworthy drew up the following twelve aims for consideration by like-minded humanitarians who wished to join the cause:

1 Secure the loan of a good sized house rent free for the period of the war, and if possible six months after.

2 Having . . . the promise of it apply to your mayor or the local authorities for their financial co-operation. In thirteen months Kitchener House has cost £940 to keep up. This sum includes: furniture, equipment, repair, transport of soldiers, meals, salaries, wages, teaching tools, books, telephone cost, gas and electricity. 9866 meals have been served. Failing co-operation of the local authorities, raise the money by voluntary subscription. *Possibly* the Red Cross may give you a small grant.

3 Secure an honorary secretary of proved ability and some experience with wounded soldiers.

4 Furnish and let in your staff.* (Here add requisite staff, and furniture requirements, piano, bagatelle board . . . for amusement.)

5 Form an Executive Committee and an Honorary Committee.

6 Circularize your neighbouring hospitals to draw your wounded soldiers.

7 Approach any Arts & Crafts guild in your locality; or any local firms engaged in the following industries, to give you aid in forming your classes.* (Here add suggested industries.)

8 Secure teachers of modern languages; & of the following small crafts.* (Add.)

9 Secure all possible voluntary transport.
   Subjoined are the other conditions which prevail at the first Kitchener House 8 Cambridge Gate Regent's Park London NW. who will welcome any application for further information or advice.

10 Disabled and retired officers and professional men should have control over the management and organization of the scheme.

11 There should be affiliated a representative to approach the Pensions with a view to granting discharged officers a subsidiary pension to enable them to meet their liabilities while completing their studies for so long as that particular profession requires.

12 Leading members of the professions should be approached and their sympathies enlisted in the scheme.

While Hynemann 'heartily approve[d]' of these aims, she drew on her own experience at Kitchener House and California House – and no less on contemporary understandings of the nascent field of occupational therapy – to suggest that the classes be recategorized and conceptualised as 'Arts and Crafts instead of recreations'.[116] After further deliberation, and following receipt of 'suggestions from different officers',[117] Galsworthy delivered the proposal to the Red Cross for its consideration. Claude Douglas-Pennant offered him a lukewarm response, due chiefly to financial pressures on the organization. 'I have shown [Arthur] Stanley and [Robert] Hudson your letter and proposed appeal,' he wrote to Galsworthy:

> The former is all in favour of the extension scheme but said it was entirely a matter for the latter to decide whether it could be supported by Red Cross Funds and accordingly I saw Hudson, who does not agree to the insertion of the words underlined.[118] He is quite agreeable to a statement that the Red Cross have helped with the initial house to give it a start but are not prepared to pledge themselves to support financially the extension. During the next few months he says we shall have all our work cut out to supply the needs of our men in France and feels we must concentrate our Funds on that purpose and not dissipate them on further ventures. I think that if any sum was wanted for any particular place Hudson would approve a small grant for that purpose for equipment or some such object, but I do not think that we can get them to subsidize any general scheme. As Hudson points out, if you are appealing to the public for help your appeal would have a better chance of success if it were pointed out to the public that the Red Cross Funds were not available . . .[119]

Ultimately, and likely with some reluctance, Galsworthy deferred to this opinion. On 19 April 1917, the *Times* published the final version of his appeal, entitled 'Kitchener Houses: occupation and convalescence', the text of which appears in Chapter 6. While the piece acknowledged that the existing Kitchener House had been maintained 'under the auspices of the Red Cross', it made no mention of any future support. But Galsworthy did not give up. As late as June he continued to press the Red Cross via Pennant to support a Kitchener House for officers, and official documents seems to suggest that his efforts were successful.[120]

1918: (I) the beginning of the end

The final year of the war brought Galsworthy three more opportunities to support disabled soldiers. However, each contributed in its own way to promoting his disillusionment with the very efforts which he had originally hoped would give him a sense of purpose. The first and most substantial of these opportunities was his editorship of the Ministry of Pensions journal *Reveille*. The second, which also involved the Ministry of Pensions, was Galsworthy's authorship of the foreword to, as well as his editorship of, the proceedings of the aforementioned second inter-allied conference and exhibition on the after-care of disabled men. The third opportunity, and the one that was of the shortest duration, was Galsworthy's official representation of Britain on the management committee of the *Revue interalliée pour l'étude des questions intéressant les mutilés de la guerre*, the official journal of the inter-allied conference on the after-care of disabled men.

Reveille *and proceedings of the inter-allied conference and exhibition*

Galsworthy became editor of *Reveille* in April 1918, but his ascendancy to this position – and no less his overall involvement with the Ministry of Pensions during this period – can be traced to events of the previous autumn and winter when he engaged the military medical authorities on at least two occasions about 'the sluggishness of the Pensions Committee'.[121] While the precise outcome of these conversations is unclear, they likely combined with Galsworthy's reputation to make him an attractive advocate for Ministry efforts on behalf of disabled soldiers.

One of those efforts, the quarterly journal *Recalled to Life*, was languishing under the editorship of Godfrey Rathbone Benson (Baron Charnwood).[122] The mission of the publication, as Charnwood stated in his introductory editorial, was to:

> diffuse as widely as possible among those who are in any way concerned with the welfare of our sailors and soldiers returning disabled from the War, and not less among such sailors and soldiers themselves, knowledge as to the means by which they may be restored, as nearly as the nature of their injuries permits, to full participation in, and full enjoyment of, the activities of civil life.[123]

Despite this promise, the journal was ultimately a failure. As Galsworthy later described its demise, '[T]he quarterly was beginning to fall between two stools. Its substance was too technical for the Public, and not perhaps technical enough for the experts.'[124] Faced with these reviews, and perhaps also with pressure from the Ministry to reconstitute the journal and tie its contents to the upcoming inter-allied conference and exhibition on the after-care of disabled men, Charnwood turned to Galsworthy on 20 December 1917 with an offer of 'joining him over *Recalled to Life*' and in co-editorship of the envisioned conference proceedings. That same day Galsworthy agreed to both co-operative arrangements, but neither of them emerged fully.

Two weeks later and apart from this face-to-face discussion and agreement, a Ministry official approached Galsworthy directly about 'help[ing] with the publishing' of the inter-allied conference proceedings.[125] This separate approach – one which significantly did not mention Charnwood in any way – could well have suggested not only a rift between Charnwood and the Ministry, but also stark recognition on the part of its officials that Galsworthy's engagement in and reputation for supporting disabled soldiers held much greater promise than the efforts of Charnwood, who, as editor of *Recalled to Life*, was seen as responsible for the failure of the publication. A further approach from the Ministry, in which Galsworthy was again invited to compose a foreword to the conference proceedings, revealed the hope that officials placed in his contribution and overall participation:

> A foreward [*sic*] from yourself will find a cachet on this work which will be representative not only of our own specialists but also those of our Allies & Dominions . . . P.S. The content of your foreword I leave entirely to your judgement . . .[126]

Soon thereafter Galsworthy offered his essay entitled 'The sacred work', which he described to the surgeon Robert Jones as 'contain[ing] an expression of my feeling that the whole process of restoration must be looked at as one organic whole from start to finish'.[127] Upon receiving this piece the Ministry official responded that it was 'Simply Perfect . . . Your foreward [*sic*] does indeed give a wonderful "human sole" [*sic*] to what I fear may otherwise be a somewhat dreary volume & will stand out as a jem [*sic*] in a setting of steel.'[128] The essay appeared not only in the proceedings, but also shortly thereafter across the Atlantic in the *American Journal of Care for Cripples* under the slightly altered title 'So comes the sacred work', and in *The Living Age*, under the title 'The stricken'.[129] The original version, from the proceedings of the inter-allied conference, appears in Chapter 7.

While Charnwood was involved to some degree in organizing the conference proceedings, he received no recognition in the final publication, which bore Galsworthy's name alone as both editor and author of its foreword.[130] As for Charnwood's journal *Recalled to Life*, Galsworthy held specific views on its publication which he shared privately with Robert Jones. '[W]hat is required,' Galsworthy wrote to Jones, is a change of feeling[,] no – a stirring up of – (a) The Public. (b) The wounded & disabled man. (c) The various Departments. Now "Recalled to Life" can have no chance of reaching a and b; and it does not stir up c because it has no public opinion at the back of it. My suggestion therefore is that instead of revising it I should get a mandate from the War Office and Pensions Ministry to organize a campaign in the Dailies and Weeklies. Charged with this mandate I should approach say: John Bull; the D.M. [Daily Mail] & D.N. [Daily News], to deal with (a) & (b) and The Times and Observer to deal with (c). I should say to the editions: This is the state of affairs, and here is my mandate. Give me space – say a column every three weeks for articles on this vital subject, either by myself or by recognized authorities, or well-known writers, such as Colonel Sir Robert Jones, or, Mr. Jerome K. Jerome. It would be my business to get people to write, and to myself to write terse and vigorous and informative stuff and place it where it would hit the right public. I feel that no real change can be made through a magazine such as "Recalled to Life" with a very limited circulation – a tiny circulation; or with technical articles, which will only be read by experts already more or less conversant with their contents. The lack of *apparent* coherence in this scheme will be all the good, because the Public etc. won't see the force which is guiding it unconsciously, and therefore won't be able to kick against it; and with a little care one ought to be able to achieve a real coherence of direction. And of course the enormous advantage would be the huge circulation of John Bull etc. etc. One has got to come right down to the men's level and the men's point of view, and to get hold of the public's fancy, to do any real good. I feel however that unless the government will give me some sort of magic wand to open the Edition's hearts and columns with I shouldn't be able to get the space. I think the present 'condition of things' is jolly bad . . .[131]

Recalled to Life ceased publication after its third issue of April 1918 (Figure 32), shortly after Galsworthy offered these thoughts to Jones and within weeks of Galsworthy formally becoming its new editor.[132] He quickly recast the publication along the lines he envisioned. The title became *Reveille*, as he later explained in his introductory editorial, 'The gist of the matter', because 'though we look as if our eyes are open, we are not awake; and because while Death still blows his bugle in those fields, we would blow a call against him'.

Galsworthy's ascendancy to the editorship of *Reveille* marked the beginning of a remarkable literary initiative. Through the summer, and with careful planning that is evident in his personal papers (Figures 33 and 34), he solicited from a host of notable authors and artists a variety of prose, poetry and illustrations to include in the inaugural issue that was slated to appear in August. Galsworthy's requests were noticeably

Rediscovery and reappraisal

RECALLED TO LIFE.

A Journal devoted to the Care, Re-education, and
Return to Civil Life of Disabled Sailors and Soldiers.

Editor, LORD CHARNWOOD.

No. 3.

LONDON :

JOHN BALE, SONS & DANIELSSON, LTD.
OXFORD HOUSE
83-91, GREAT TITCHFIELD STREET, OXFORD STREET, W. 1.

Price Two Shillings net.

Figure 32   Recalled to Life No. 3 (April 1918), the final issue of this journal,
which was edited by Lord Charnwood and which preceded Galsworthy's
Reveille. (US National Library of Medicine, National Institutes of Health)

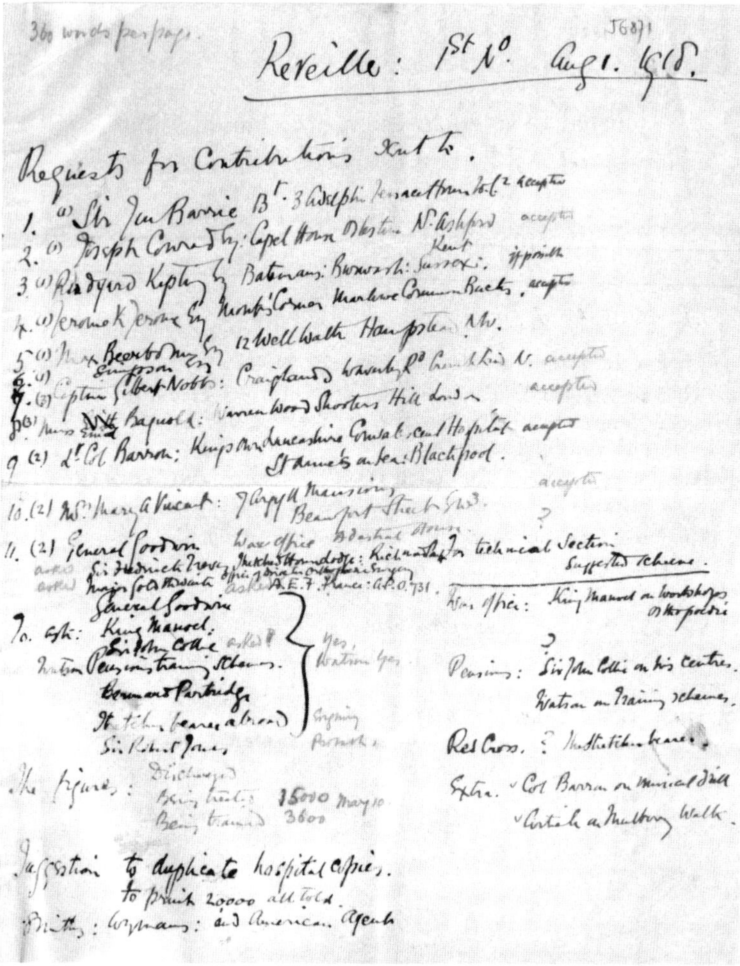

Figure 33 Galsworthy's manuscript notes entitled '*Reveille*: 1st No. Aug. 1, 1918'. (Collection of Steve Forbes © all rights reserved. Image by Richard Holttum)

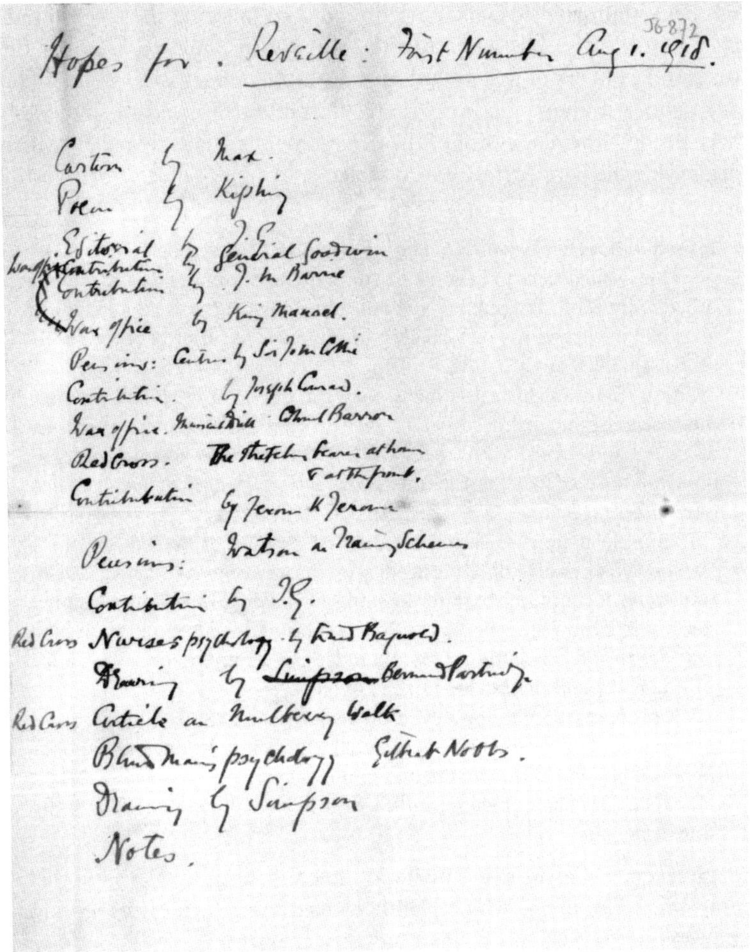
Hopes for . Reveille : First Number Aug. 1. 1918.

Cartoon by Max.
Poem by Kipling
Editorial by J.G. General Goodwin
Contribution by J. M. Barrie
War office by King Manuel.
Pensions: Contribution by Sir John Collie
Contribution by Joseph Conrad.
War office. Musical Drill Colonel Barrow
Red Cross. The stretcher bearers at home & at the front.
Contribution by Jerome K Jerome
Pensions: Dalton on Training Schemes
Contribution by J.G.
Red Cross Nurses psychology by Enid Bagnold.
Drawing by ~~Simpson~~ Bernard Partridge.
Red Cross Article on Mulberry Walk
Blind man's psychology Gilbert Nobbs.
Drawing by Simpson
Notes.

Figure 34 Galsworthy's manuscript notes entitled 'Hopes for *Reveille*: First Number Aug. 1, 1918'. (Collection of Steve Forbes © All rights reserved) (Image by Richard Holttum) uniform, stating basic facts outright and then tailoring the correspondence accordingly. His letter to the artist Byam Shaw represented the tone and content of a standard approach that nonetheless conveyed a deep concern about the present and the future of disabled soldiers. 'I have become the new editor of the Government's quarterly review which deals with the care & future of disabled soldiers & sailors,' Galsworthy wrote to Shaw:

> It used to be called *Recalled to Life* but will now be called *Reveille*, and will be reconstituted so as to have an artistic & literary human side and a much broader appeal to the public. No contribution is paid: it is all a labour of love, and a work of the very greatest importance, for at present the future of our disabled men is under all the surface appearances . . . very black owing to the want of realisation among the public at large and the men themselves of the vital necessity . . . [to] . . . continue treatment after their discharge and special training for work which they can keep in competition with the able man. Not so much now, *but on demobilization, and later, when times get bad.*
>
> I am very anxious to secure for the first number of *Reveille* a striking cartoon which will embody the idea of the review – the single call of awakening & summons back to the ranks of *civil* life. I wondered whether you would be so very generous as to make this drawing for me, entirely to your desire and conception. It would indeed be a bit of national work for on it may depend the catching of the public eye.
>
> We propose to use it not only in the review as frontispiece, but also as a show-card at bookstalls etc. I ought to tell you that in the opening number there will be some of the first names in our literature. The drawing should of course be in black & white, and I ought to have it by the middle of June, if possible . . .

Shaw accepted Galsworthy's invitation to contribute, and he soon thereafter offered an image which plainly evoked the return of the working-class soldier to post-war civilian industry (Figure 35).

Twenty individuals in all accepted and contributed to the inaugural issue of *Reveille*. Among them, besides Shaw, was Rudyard Kipling, whose response to Galsworthy stood among the most impassioned for reasons that perhaps stemmed from Kipling's loss of his only son in September 1915:

> Up to the present the cripples have been mostly in hospitals and, as you say, people don't at all realize what a number of them there are. And, besides physical disability, there are multitudes of men knocked out as to their nerves & physique who try to pick up civil employment again and find that they break down . . .[133]

Figure 35 Sketch by the artist Byam Shaw, which appeared in *Reveille* No. 1 (August 1918), following p. 37. (Private collection. Image by the author)

With regard to the work of rehabilitation that lay ahead, Kipling concluded that 'It's going to be an awful job . . .'.

In close co-operation with Galsworthy, officials of the Ministry of Pensions and His Majesty's Stationary Office (HMSO) crafted a public announcement of the inaugural issue of *Reveille*. Based on a long-established model of communication with the press, yet one that had taken on new urgency due to the need for wartime propaganda, officials transmitted to magazines and newspapers across the country at least one general announcement that Galsworthy wrote himself.[134] Editors either published this text outright or modified it slightly to suit their views and their readers' tastes:

> A feast of good things is provided in this first number of the new Government quarterly 'Reveille,' a review devoted to the disabled soldier and sailor and edited by Mr. John Galsworthy. Among the literary contributions are a poem by Rudyard Kipling entitled 'The Pilgrim's Way', an article by Joseph Conrad, describing the author's experiences in Poland at the beginning of the War; a play by Sir J. M. Barrie; a French hospital sketch by John Galsworthy; an essay on the Epistolary Art by E. V. Lucas; and a description of a night in the life of an ambulance driver at the Front by Jerome K. Jerome. Miss Enid Bagnold, author of 'A Diary without Dates,' contributes a striking impression entitled 'Outside Hospital.' The frontispiece is the first of a series of colour cartoons entitled 'Artists at the Front', by Max Beerbohm, and there are drawings by Byam Shaw and Edmund J. Sullivan. Articles on various aspects of the treatment and training of disabled soldiers are contributed by the Minister of Pensions [John Hodge], Sir John Collie, Major Robert Mitchell, Colonel Sir Robert Jones, King Manoel, Lieut. Colonel Goldthwait, and Colonel Netterville Barron, who describes a new system of musical drill. 'Reveille' will be published by H.M. Stationery Office next Thursday, price 2s. 6d. net, and can be ordered through any bookseller.[135]

When editors elaborated on this stock announcement, the result was typically a critical statement in support of the effort generally and Galsworthy's contributions in particular:

> Lord Charnwood's quarterly, *Recalled to Life*, dealing with the problems of the disabled sailor and soldier, has after three numbers suffered a sea-change, to reappear as *Reveille* under the editorship of Mr. Galsworthy, with the imprint of the Stationery Office. The aim is the same – to concentrate public attention on the nation's duty to our disabled heroes, and to show how they may best be trained and fitted for permanent situations in civil life. The editor's method is, however, very different. We might say

that, while Lord Charnwood offered a pill, Mr. Galsworthy administers the pill with a large spoonful of jam. *Recalled to Life* was solely informative; *Reveille* is informing too, but it opens with a whimsical caricature by Mr. Max Beerbohm of Sir William Orpen sketching at the front, and follows it with a poem by Mr. Kipling, a little play by Sir J. M. Barrie, and articles by Mr. E. V. Lucas and Mr. Conrad. Having read these admirable literary achievements, with the war as a common motive, we are prepared for the articles by Mr. Hodge, Sir John Collie, Major Robert Mitchell, ex-King Manoel, and others, that deal with various aspects of the real business at hand. Mr. Galsworthy in an excellent article entitled 'The Gist of It' puts the case for generous, well-considered, and immediate action on behalf of the disabled. It is false kindness, he urges, to encourage a maimed man to take the first job that offers. In the present scarcity of labour, an employer will engage almost any man, however unfit, but it does not and cannot follow that he will keep the man when peace returns. We must not let the disabled men drift; we much encourage them to believe in themselves, and we must help them to become skilled workers whose services will always be required. 'At present,' says Mr. Galsworthy, 'possibly not one in three of our discharged soldiers who needed further physical treatment has taken it; and perhaps not one in ten who really require to be re-educated to special work is being trained for it. The System is helpless without a great awakening of the Public, and through the Public of the disabled man.' *Reveille* will help the public to realise the nature and urgency of the problem, and it should render much direct and indirect help to a move-ment in which everyone may play a part, however small. We may call attention to the lists of occupations suitable for disabled men, based on actual cases, and of the very numerous courses of training now available in all districts.[136]

There would be little repetition of contributors during the seven-month life span of *Reveille*. Only Beerbohm, Hodge and Galsworthy contributed to all three issues. Another essay by Collie appeared in the second issue, published in November 1918, and Mitchell contributed new material to the third and final issue that was published in February 1919.[137]

Even as Galsworthy himself contributed regularly to *Reveille* he did not neglect his editorial duties. In co-operation with his assistant, C. S. Evans, he took a direct hand in managing communications related to the printing and distribution of the journal by HMSO.

While Galsworthy regretted the delay in the publication of the inau-gural issue of *Reveille*,[138] he found more disturbing the fact that HMSO, and likely also the Ministry of Pensions, intended to meddle with the Net Book Agreement, a retail price maintenance arrangement estab-lished in 1900 which gave booksellers a guaranteed margin through a discount on the selling price of publications.[139] Specifically, Galsworthy learned that the government did not make it fully clear at the outset of supporting *Reveille* that the 'consent' of the Treasury was required to allow booksellers to receive the publication on consignment, or 'on sale and return'. This arrangement placed any overall loss on the publisher, as it enabled booksellers to return the agreed-upon sum earned through sales in addition to unsold copies of the publication. If government officials did not grant consent for 'sale and return', any overall loss would be borne by the bookseller.

'I greatly regret not having been made aware that [requiring permission for "sale and return"] were the Stationery Office's usual terms,' Galsworthy wrote to unspecified officials at HMSO on 27 July 1918:

> I venture however to think that the [sale-and-return] terms we have granted are the only possible terms which will secure hearty co-operation on the part of wholesalers in the case of a new review, and that without such co-operation we cannot hope to reach the Public successfully. I most earnestly beg that the Treasury's ratification be obtained forthwith; for there is no doubt whatever that the Treasury will gain money thereby; and if it is not obtained I fear the worst consequences to an enterprise conducted on behalf of the Government itself, for an object which every department of the Government has at heart . . .

Galsworthy continued adamantly:

> *We must have wide publicity for this Review*, or it might just as well not be published. May I with all respect speak quite frankly on this matter. I am not giving my time – nor is any other voluntary contributor – to the production of an amicable futility, or of a work buried as soon as it is born. The War Office and Pension Ministry wish and expect *Reveille* to reach and stir the large public on behalf of our disabled sailors and soldiers. Without hearty co-operation by everyone, that is not, and will not be, possible. I surely cannot be wrong in believing that H.M. Stationary Office will do their utmost to help on such a work? I enclose one of the circulars sent by Mssrs. W. H. Smith & Son to their 1,000 manager [*sic*], to show you the kind of spirit with which they, amongst others, are prepared to back this effort. And I would take this opportunity of reiterating my belief that we shall be met with a demand far in excess of the 15,000 copies we are printing, and of urging that material may be on hand ready *for printing another large edition at once* if wanted. If it is not wanted this material will come in for the second number. It is now or never with the future of our disabled. This Review with a clear run can do a great work within a year; but if it is starved or thwarted, it cannot, and might just as

well not be issued. Considered what the case is you will forgive me, I am sure, for putting things plainly, for begging H.M. Stationery Office to have faith in their publication, and to do their very best for it, and for our disabled men.[140]

Galsworthy's plea on behalf of *Reveille* was successful, but the Treasury refused to modify the traditional terms upon which it conducted business with booksellers. As Evans wrote to Galsworthy in early August 1918, '[the] Treasury have very reluctantly ratified the terms we arranged with W. H. Smith, Boot & Kennedy, but their determination to keep to their antiquated scale of terms for the Booksellers in general remains unaffected'.[141]

While regulations of HMSO created one set of frustrations for Galsworthy, the Ministry of Pensions created another through its policy of censorship. On 30 May 1918, during the course of preparing the inaugural issue of *Reveille*, the secretary to the Ministry of Pensions, Matthew Nathan, wrote to Galsworthy that 'I think before we agree to the publication of [the table of officers and men pensioned for disability] I should get the formal approval of the Adjutant General, and I am writing to him for the purpose'.[142] On the following day Nathan notified Galsworthy of the approval, but the issue of censorship emerged again before *Reveille* appeared.[143] That policy of censorship was most succinctly conveyed by Nathan when he stated as a matter of fact to Galsworthy that 'I will do the censoring of the magazine with as little delay after . . . its receipt as possible'.[144] And Nathan did censor the inaugural issue, which eventually appeared on 10 August. Shortly thereafter, Nathan wrote to Galsworthy urging caution on a specific portion of the issue while praising other sections – including a piece by Galsworthy himself – that apparently passed muster:

I have send to [*Reveille* assistant editor] Mr Evans the proof of '*Reveille*' calling his attention to a minor alteration Sir John Collie has made in his article, and to another verbal correction which seemed to me necessary. I am also asking him to have printed in some fairly prominent position, a note that the authors are alone responsible for the view expressed in their articles. I do this because I notice in one place there is a reference to National Factories for employment of disabled men after the War, and I am not at all sure that these would be in accordance with the Minister's views. The only matter of any importance with regard to which Sir John Collie and I were in some doubt, is the advisability of there appearing in the review such a depressing note – depressing is not quite the right word – as the second one under the heading of 'Experiences'. I am not sure as to the effect of reading such an article on a disabled man or on an ordinary member of the public, but you have no doubt very carefully considered this. 'The Gist of the Matter' seems to me to be excellent and the poem immediately before it is a fine specimen of Kipling's work.[145]

On 15 July, Galsworthy responded to Nathan, expressing 'concern about the censorship and the publication being seen as propaganda':

Thank you very much for sending back the proofs so quickly. The correction has been made, and a note is being put at the top of page 39, which is the beginning of the technical section, 'The authors alone are responsible for the views expressed in their articles.' I am so very glad that you like 'The Gist of the Matter'. Yes, the Kipling piece is a fine thing, especially the last stanza about the Second 'Experience'. Yes, I very carefully considered the point you raise, and very deliberately included it, for this reason: There is a great danger that a Review of this sort will however undeservedly get the reputation of being camouflage. I have already heard the word used in connection with the idea. For the sake of the Ministry, and still more for the sake of the cause, I think such a reputation would be most undesirable. I feel that something not all 'couleur de rose', felt reality, is essential, and gives a truer ring to the whole effort. Moreover, no disabled man, I think, reading that experience, which probably goes no further than his own feelings, will say anything but: 'Yes, that's true.' I see no reason why it should depress or militate [*sic*] against your efforts. On the contrary. About the 'National Factories', which is hardly perhaps the right expression for my thrown-out prophecy: it's so very far in the future that it will hardly be the present Minister of Pensions who deals with it. What I feel is that some five to ten years hence some measure of the sort will be found necessary, for the residue which cannot or will not absorb itself in industry through the means now afforded. I will make that clearer in the next number . . .[146]

Galsworthy did attempt to clarify his position in the second issue of *Reveille*, specifically through his essay 'Looking ahead'. However, ongoing censorship of the publication ultimately prompted Galsworthy to resign his editorship. As he wrote in late January 1919 to Lady Alice Rothenstein, wife of Sir William Rothenstein, the English painter and writer, 'I have decided to resign the editorship of Reveille from after the appearance of No. 3 now in the press. It's a question of censorship . . . I don't expect the quarterly to be kept on'.[147] Galsworthy elaborated in his private notebook that he had been facing

a certain trouble over the censorship of articles in *Reveille*, which criticized the methods of the Ministry of Pensions, had come to a climax in the unbénévolent hands of the permanent official who had taken Sir Matthew

Nathan's place at the Ministry,[148] and had always been inimical to the magazine. Feeling that not to retain some critical and independent attitude in the review was to seriously mislead the Public, I decided to resign the editorship after the third number had appeared. This I did at the beginning of February, and thereafter the Ministry discontinued the magazine. According to general opinion, as far as once could judge, it had done some good work in its way. It more than paid for its production commercially, and died regretted by a good many people . . .[149]

To be sure, Galsworthy was correct about the 'general opinion' of *Reveille*. Reviews throughout its short, three-issue run were consistently positive.

Reproduced in the second part of this book is the complete body of non-fiction which Galsworthy contributed to *Reveille*. Chapter 8 contains the aforementioned essay 'The gist of the matter', in which Galsworthy introduced his editorship, stated the purpose of the new publication, and confronted the present challenge of 'a Britain daily more and more peopled by sufferers of this war' and the future question of 'what sort of a Land it will be, if, five and ten years hence, tens of thousands injured in this long tragedy are drifting unhappy amongst us, without the anchorage of permanent, well-paid, self-respecting work?' American officials were quick to learn the value of Galsworthy's critical perspectives. In January 1919, the Office of the Surgeon General of the US Army printed an abbreviated version of 'Gist' in its publication *Carry on: A Magazine on the Reconstruction of Disabled Soldiers and Sailors*, juxtaposing to its previously unillustrated words photographs of men receiving after-care at St Dunstan's as well as disabled American soldiers undergoing various forms of rehabilitation at Fort Des Moines (Iowa), Letterman General Hospital (San Francisco, California), No. 3 General Hospital (Plattsburg, New York) and Evergreen Red Cross Institute for the Blind (Baltimore, Maryland). Such cross-Atlantic images plainly underscored what was by this time Galsworthy's international reputation as a champion of the war-wounded.

Chapter 9 contains 'Looking ahead', which appeared in the second issue of *Reveille* of November 1918 and continued Galsworthy's investigation of the nation 'hanging over the edge of an abyss' with respect to 'the problem of our disabled'. This essay is especially noteworthy for articulating Galsworthy's critical view of the reasoning and means by which the British government had finally 'adopted . . . the decentralized and democratic way' of discharging disabled soldiers 'as soon as reasonably possible, to their own homes; and their continued treatment and training are left to Local War Pensions Committees to arrange so far as may be, in local hospitals and local institutes and workshops'. This approach, Galsworthy continued, 'is more organic, better in accord with our British instincts, and though modifications are in the wind, we appear to be at this time of day irrevocably committed to the main lines of it'. At the same time, Galsworthy warned with attention both to statistical evidence and to prophetic vision that the locally focused plan was:

> inevitably slower than a drastic highly centralized method. Take the most recent figures: Fresh pension claims of disabled soldiers dealt with between April 1 and September 17 number 134,013; men admitted to training in that period, about 6,200. The percentage of discharged men back in their old employment is estimated at about 50. Making that and other allowances, men are still being discharged *into the open labour market* at a much greater rate than that at which they are being specially refitted for civil life. We have not only to equalize those rates, but great arrears to make up, and shall have ultimately to deal with many men, now back in old jobs, who, later on, will be shouldered out of them by competition – in fact, a balance of disability which will not be disclosed till industrial conditions are normal again . . .

He continued, emphasizing immediate concerns as well as future challenges:

> We confess to being haunted by a fear more solid than ever was ghost. From the time these words are read we may have but a year and a half at most to make our peace with the Honour of our Country. To speak quite frankly, we fear disgrace and disaster. Do people realize what a dreadful thing it will be, if all the butter of fair words about 'our heroes' melts into one vast disfiguring grease spot; and instead of men honoured and contented we have an army of broken wanderers with such curses on their lips? The beginnings of it are here already . . . The situation demands not only all our energy and co-operation now, but *far sight into the future*. It demands that we should for once falsify our British happy-go-luckiness, our ingrained habit of waiting till we're forced; for once go ahead of disgrace and trouble, which otherwise will come so surely as these words are put on paper . . .

Chapter 10 reprints Galsworthy's essay 'Spirit and letter', which appeared in the third and final issue of *Reveille*, dated February 1919, and which reflected his frustration with the Ministry of Pensions and his resulting cynical view of his efforts on behalf of the unit. Here Galsworthy's seems not only to foretell his resignation from the editorship of *Reveille* but also the appearance of the novel he was writing during the same period – *The Burning Spear: Being the Experiences of Mr John Lavender in time of war* – in which he satirizes his experience as a supporter of disabled soldiers. 'How difficult it is to keep the breath of life in any large work of public utility,' he began in 'Spirit and letter':

> How fatally easy to become bureaucratic and treat creatures of flesh and blood as if they were autonomous. To change from keen folk only too ready to help, into formal persons carrying on from a sense of duty, is an unconscious process only too rapidly accomplished.

Expressing sharp criticism of the very sense of purposefulness which empowered him from the early days of the war, he continued:

> Slow petrifaction of eager humanity by the drip thereon of forms is a minor tragedy being played all the time on thousands of tiny stages. Nor is that drip the only petrifying agency. Those of us who have dabbled in philanthropy know well what paralysis can come over sympathy out of mere damnéd iteration . . .

Bureaucracy as much as philanthropy was Galsworthy's target here as he encouraged his readers to:

> think what lies behind every letter written by a disabled man to the Ministry of Pensions or to his Local Committee, and of what has gone on in the soul of him before he forces his body to enter precincts where his future shall be wrapped into filled-up forms and bandied from one to another. We never realize how passionately we prize our independence and how deeply interesting we find our own futures until we have to submit them to be delved into, docketed and doled out. And to have to submit them at the end of four years of risk and hardship and pain which have saved the country must indeed seem like insult added unto injuries . . .

As before, his explicit subject here was the life of the disabled soldier. But implicitly it was his own life as he had conducted it through purposeful writing during the previous four years and as he was becoming disillusioned not only by the most critical challenges of the day (and, as he had written previously, of the future) but also by the very immediate reality of his own work with the Ministry of Pensions being 'delved into' through censorship. Thus as bureaucratic 'forms' were not helping disabled soldiers, they were also not helping him (and others) to help them. '[The] fact remains,' Galsworthy wrote,

> that in departments generally 'forms' tend to bury human sympathy, as falling leaves to bury babes; they mean delays, and delays are dangerous

... Without 'forms' confusion would, of course, be worse confounded, but between that confusion and delays which produce in the minds of countless sufferers from the war a rankling sense that justice is being grudged them, there is a mean which, if not golden, is at all events far better than either of those extremes. It is worth while to take many risks to save sending men away with the feeling that they were owed bread and have been given stones. Now that we have the measure of this great problem at last, we hope it may be possible to open the money bags wider, to bring forth their contents quicker. We hope the time has come, too, to see whether 'forms' can be reduced in number, simplified in phrase, and issued faster. A sense of injustice among silver-badge men is ill balanced by a few millions saved to the pockets of us taxpayers.

Galsworthy's expression of cynicism in 'Spirit and letter' points to the final chapter of his wartime support of disabled soldiers.

The inter-allied review

Two circumstances combined to prompt Galsworthy's participation on the editorial board of the *Revue interalliée*, the official journal of the inter-allied conference and exhibition (Figure 36). The first was his reputation for writing about and supporting disabled soldiers. The second circumstance evidently involved another failure on the part of Lord Charnwood. As Edward Stanton, of the Ministry of Pensions, explained to Galsworthy in a letter dated 13 August 1918:

Charnwood hasn't helped the Editor [and rehabilitation specialist] Dr [Jean] Camus with anything. I am wondering if you would. Dr Camus has asked me to send him some material from England or find some myself for as he rightly says otherwise the Revue will devolve into a purely French publication with only French news and he is very anxious to have something from us. I unfortunately am not blessed with any litterary [*sic*] abilities and my time is very much taken up at the Ministry ...[150]

Suggesting that Charnwood's failure to assist Camus, if not his outright uninterest in the *Revue*, had prompted Charnwood's own dismissal, Stanton appealed more directly to Galsworthy the next day:

I am requested by the Minister of Pensions [John Hodge] to ask you if you would be willing to take the place of Lord Charnwood as British Representative on the Committee of Management of the Inter-Allied Revue ... Lord Charnwood is off to America and besides has not had time to give the Inter-Allied Revue any notes which they would so much like to have from Great Britain. The Ministry do so hope you will agree to take on this extra work, which, however, need not give you much worry. Expenses to

REVUE INTERALLIÉE

pour l'étude des questions intéressant

Les Mutilés de la Guerre

Physiothérapie = Prothèse
Rééducation Fonctionnelle = Rééducation Professionnelle
Intérêts Économiques et Moraux

Figure 36   Revue interalliée pour l'étude des questions intéressant les mutilés de la guerre (September 1918), on whose editorial board Galsworthy sat during the summer and autumn of 1918. (Library of Congress)

and from Paris when it is necessary to attend a meeting are paid up to the regulation scale by Government . . .'[151]

Galsworthy accepted the appointment on the condition that he would serve only for the duration of the war. When Stanton failed to recognize this fact in the written thanks he offered on 17 August,[152] Galsworthy wasted no time in penning a blunt reply: 'You do not make any reference in [your letter] to my undertaking the work for the period of the war only, in case you have overlooked the point I write to remind you of it. So if you will kindly let Dr Jean Camus know that I am undertaking the work for the period of the war I will go ahead and get into communication with him.'[153] Stanton replied the next day, 'I note your restriction and will notify the Paris Committee accordingly.'[154] Thus when the war ended three months later so did Galsworthy's involvement with the *Revue interalliée.*

1918: (II) disillusionment

By the end of 1917, the war along the western front had reached a stalemate as fighting increased and Allied casualties mounted. The following spring saw Germany make significant gains, and in an effort to cope with staggering losses the British government passed the Man-power Bill to draft men between the ages of eighteen and fifty-six. Galsworthy, then 'at the age of 50 years and 343 days', qualified for consideration. That summer he reported to the National Service Medical Board of Exeter, where, as he noted in his diary, a doctor 'totally rejected [him] on score of sight'.[155] Following the examination Galsworthy '[returned] to Bovey station [and there] learned of a fresh German offensive against the French'.[156] His concluding observation of the day suggested his certain feeling of relief from the 'black clouds of war' – indeed, from his own sense of disability – that had plagued him since the summer of 1914 and despite the purposeful writing and humanitarian actions he undertook on behalf of disabled soldiers.[157] 'This day,' he observed, 'the turning point of the war, was the day I came nearest to taking fighting part in it.'[158] From a psychological perspective, so significant was this moment of 'total rejection' that Galsworthy took pains to create and include in his personal papers an 'exact copy' of his discharge certificate.[159]

Yet Galsworthy's mind was not wholly at rest following his visit to the medical board. Where enthusiasm had characterized his support of disabled soldiers, disillusionment set in. And while Galsworthy plainly suggested this new outlook through the non-fiction essays he composed during the final year of the war – in particular the piece entitled 'Spirit and letter' – he also suggested it through a major work of fiction, namely his Don Quixote-inspired 'comedic satire' and semi-autobiographical novel *The Burning Spear: Being the Experiences of Mr John Lavender in Time of War* (Figure 37).

Remarkable are the similarities between Galsworthy's background and wartime experiences and those of the main character of this novel, the 'gentleman' Mr John Lavender. Like Galsworthy, Lavender 'had been brought up to the Bar, but like most barristers had never practised, and had spent his time among animals and the wisdom of the past'.[160] Also like Galsworthy, Lavender wondered about the contribution he could make to his nation at war – beyond any 'unsuspected balance' of his 'bank-book'. In doing so, Lavender decided to volunteer his talents – specifically his public-speaking abilities – to the government's 'Ministry of Propagation'. As he explained to his housekeeper, 'I am going down about it to-morrow . . . [as] . . . I feel my energies are not fully employed.' Recalling Galsworthy's own journey to London in early September 1914 when he joined the War Propaganda Bureau, Lavender 'went down to the centre of the official world', where he met a Minister who accepted his voluntary services. These opening scenes of *The Burning Spear* suggest a similarity between Galsworthy and Lavender that is made all too clear in the thirteenth chapter of the novel – entitled 'Addresses some soldiers on their future' – which is reproduced fully here in Chapter 13.

In this excerpt we find Lavender on a 'pleasant afternoon', taking a 'seat on one of the benches which adorned the Spaniard's Road' and reading 'a periodical' that could well be *Reveille*, as it 'enjoined on everyone the necessity of taking the utmost interest in soldiers disabled by the war'. Lavender agrees immediately with the contents therein, which state that 'it is indeed our duty to force them, no matter what their disablements, to continue and surpass the heroism they displayed out there, and become superior to what they once were'. Such thinking informs his subsequent encounter with 'three soldiers in the blue garments and red ties of hospital life'. During the course of this interaction Lavender consistently misunderstands their humour and their perspectives, especially when they suggest that he is blind, if not insane, and that he has escaped from a nearby institution. The soldiers' sarcasm meets Lavender's aloofness at every turn and, in the end, with no sense of the reality surrounding him, Lavender bids the soldiers farewell. 'I consider it a great privilege . . . to have been allowed to converse with you. Goodbye,

THE BURNING SPEAR

Being the Experiences of Mr.
John Lavender in Time of War

Recorded by A.R.P—M.

The Publishers are not at liberty
to give the name of the Author of
this new 'Don Quixote.' They can
say, however, that he is one of the
most distinguished of living writers
whose only reason for anonymity is
that it has enabled him to picture
with free satire certain contradictions
and whimsicalities of modern life.

Figure 37   Galsworthy's The Burning Spear: Being the Experiences of Mr John
Lavender in Time of War, recorded by A.R.P.–M. (London: Chatto &
Windus, 1919). (Private collection. Image by the author)

and God bless you!' To this one of the three soldiers replies, 'Blimey . . . some of these old civilians'ave come it barmy on the crumpet since the war began. Give me the trenches!'

Galsworthy completed *The Burning Spear* during the autumn of 1918, and he published it in April the following year under the pseudonym 'A.R.P.–M.' When he admitted authorship of the book in 1923, he explained that his choice of pseudonymity in the first instance was 'for reasons concerned with others'. Herein Galsworthy was presumably referring to the novel addressing the subject of interning Germans – specifically in its fourteenth chapter – and to his German nephew Rudolf Sauter, who remained interned at the Alexandra Palace when the novel was originally published.[161] However, given the themes of 'Addresses some soldiers on their future', it would seem that Galsworthy also chose to publish *The Burning Spear* pseudonymously for reasons related to the state of his own support of disabled soldiers. After all, how could such an internationally respected champion of these men satirize the 'sacred work' in the novel, as he seemed to do? The fact that Galsworthy did precisely this underscores the disillusionment that inhabited his mind by 1918, as well as the complex process he undertook thereafter of both forgetting and remembering the war and his support of its human returns.

Conclusion: forgetting and remembering

Following the appearance of 'Spirit and letter' in the final issue of *Reveille*, Galsworthy did not publicly address the subject of disabled soldiers again until 1921, when the Disabled Society published his foreword to its *Handbook for the Limbless*. Although it consisted of only nine paragraphs, the piece was nonetheless a significant coda to Galsworthy's wartime support for and his compositions about soldiers disabled in the war, as it represented for him a desire to forget the psychological and physical damage wrought by the conflict, yet also an obligation to remember the men that it returned home broken for life. Suggesting the very therapeutic value of his words and the *Handbook* itself – both for himself and for the nation – Galsworthy wrote that 'It will do a lot of us, who still have all our limbs, good to read this *Handbook*, and be reminded of what so many thousands are now up against, and of how sturdily they are withstanding discouragement.' Turning explicitly to artificial limbs, and eluding wryly to his wartime engagement with that subject, Galsworthy continued:

There is one practical point, to which, as a layman, I suppose I ought not to refer, and am therefore going to: the Light Leg. The evidence collected here in its favour, and against the heavy wooden limb, is most striking and exhilarating. The only real argument, now, against the leg would seem to be expense. If that is so, one can only urge that every effort be made, officially and otherwise, to overcome that difficulty. We may be bankrupt, but not so bankrupt as all that, where a great boon to the limbless is concerned . . .

Galsworthy footnoted this observation with a gesture toward the future that paled in comparison to his sweeping prophetic visions of the war years. He explained simply that since he wrote the foreword 'a Committee of Enquiry appointed by the Ministry of Pensions has recommended the issue of the light leg; its cost has been reduced, so that, over a period of years, it will even be less expensive than the heavy limb'.[162]

The fact that this piece was by all accounts Galsworthy's last original public statement relating to disabled soldiers should not be surprising. Like so many individuals of his generation who lived through the war as noncombatants, and especially those who were simply unable or too old to fight, Galsworthy eventually sought to forget the trauma of the period and the rhetoric of the culture of caregiving that surrounded disabled soldiers, including the promises of artificial limbs like those of Roehampton, the curative workshops like those of Chailey Heritage and the Lord Roberts facility and the retraining programmes like those of Kitchener House. Put simply, by 1918 Galsworthy had had enough of the war. As correctly prophetic as his wartime compositions were, the empty rhetoric of heroism and the false promises of the day prevailed. Galsworthy's ability to write – the only true ability he possessed in the face of being 'disabled' by his marital circumstances and by medical judgement – undoubtedly enabled his participation in the tumultuous events of the day. Ultimately, however, he judged that participation as being no better than a drop in the flood of propaganda which overtook the nation from the earliest days of the conflict. As he assessed the situation in 1919:

. . . I have often thought, during these past years, what an ironical eye Providence must have been turning on National Propaganda – on all the disingenuous breath which has been issued to order, and all those miles of patriotic writings dutifully produced in each country, to prove to other countries that they are its inferiors! A very little wind will blow those ephemeral sheets into the limbo of thin air. Already they are decomposing, soon they will be dust . . .[163]

Four years later, in a new preface to *The Burning Spear* which he composed for the Manaton edition of his collected works (1923–24), Galsworthy acknowledged that the novel had helped him to confront the reality that emerged just after the war. The story was, he explained, 'a revenge of the nerves'. Through it he asked:

> Was it not bad enough to have to bear the dreads and strains and griefs of the war without having to ready day by day the venomous or nonsensical stuff which began pouring from tongues and pens soon after the war began and never ceased till months after the war stopped? They said we couldn't do without it. But our fighting men undoubtedly despised that flood of lies and rhetoric. It discouraged far more than it inspired them. The Englishman does not like to play his games or fight his battles to a running accompaniment of insult to the enemy. The English nation is grown up, it can hear the truth. Our press and public men underestimated us. That war is war we know; but that the war spirit and the endurance which war needs can only be inspired by hymns of hate and suppressions of truth we deny. The last thing the English lose is their ironic humour. They saw through all those windy distortions and writings to the order of a spirit far beneath their own. May we never again have to be lost to such braying![164]

Thus so disillusioned was Galsworthy with the war – and so interested was he to forget his contributions to it – that from 1921 down to his death in 1933 he never again took up the subject of disabled soldiers in any original way. To be sure, his post-war collections of essays included several of the pieces reproduced in this book, but these collections encompassed chiefly his works of fiction, not his non-fiction that addressed directly the current and future state of Britain's war-wounded. In this respect the Manaton edition is particularly significant for the very way it suggested Galsworthy's desire to forget the war by excluding material from *Reveille* and including merely the wartime *titles* of *A Sheaf* and *Another Sheaf*, not their corresponding *contents*.[165] Such breaking up of these two landmark collections, in other words, resulted in the exclusion of his wartime essays 'Remade or marred: a great national duty' and 'The sacred work'.[166] And in the preface to Manaton volume seventeen, where Galsworthy reprinted 'Totally disabled', his justification for including this essay alongside a handful of others that were unrelated to the subject of disabled soldiers and their future in society evoked more his desire to forget the war than to remember: 'I have let [these works] stand because, though their immediate issues are mercifully dead the fundamental issue between Might and Right – as we call

the springs of a human conscience – will never be dead.'[167] Thus even as
the Manaton edition stood as a means to remember an overarching
career as a writer, it operated simultaneously for Galsworthy on a personal level as a means to forget the painful chapters of his wartime life,
and no less the war itself, which, as Galsworthy observed shortly before
his death, 'killed a terrible lot of – I don't know what to call it – self-
importance, faith, idealism, in me . . .'[168]

Postscript

On 10 December 1932 – a little more than one month before Galsworthy's
death – Anders Österling, member of the Nobel Committee of the Swedish Academy, presented British diplomat Clark Kerr with Galsworthy's
Nobel Prize in Literature. Due to illness, Galsworthy was unable to
attend the ceremony and receive the award personally.[169]

From the perspective of the events described above, and documented
through Galsworthy's wartime writings which follow, the Nobel ceremony was tinged with irony. Galsworthy won the award chiefly for *The
Forsyte Saga*, but his broader view as a socially conscious writer plainly
informed the choice of the selection committee. As Österling stated in
his presentation speech, Galsworthy 'never tired of fighting against all
that seemed narrow and harsh in the national character, and the persistence of his attacks on social evil indicates his strong impressions and
deeply wounded feeling of justice'. Österling did not enumerate the
variety of social causes supported by Galsworthy, and he made no specific mention of Galsworthy's wartime support of and compositions
about disabled soldiers. Galsworthy himself was likely satisfied – if not
outright content – with the Österling's generalization, not least because
he knew that he did tire of fighting, both against the mobilized state at
war and against the traumatic aftermath of the conflict which mitigated
'the sacred work' of looking properly after a generation of men returned
home disabled for life. Indeed, read in the context of Galsworthy's wartime service to the Ministry of Pensions, the acceptance of his Nobel
Prize by an official of the British government was itself ironic, since
Galsworthy's official service ultimately contributed significantly to
destroying his sense of self and his professional identity as a writer.

Gathered together here for the first time, the compositions that follow
are as much about that self and that professional identity as they are about
disabled soldiers of the 'war to end all wars'. I hope that these texts and
the contexts revealed in the preceding historical analysis will pave the

way to new inquiries about Galsworthy's humanitarian concerns, about the complex purpose of writing and publishing during wartime, about the 'sacred work' of rehabilitation during the immediate aftermath of battle and about longer-term efforts to care for disabled veterans of all wars.

Notes

1 These novels and interludes include *The Man of Property* (1906), *Indian Summer of a Forsyte* (1918), *In Chancery* (1920), *Awakening* (1920) and *To let* (1921).

2 Charles Scribner's Sons published the American edition on 24 March 1922, while William Heinemann published the English edition two months later, on 25 May. Harold Vincent Marrot, *A Bibliography of the Works of John Galsworthy* (London: Elkin Mathews & Marrot, 1928), reprinted, New York: Burt Franklin, 1968. Hereafter the latter is cited.

3 Respectively, *That Forsyte Woman* (1949), directed by Compton Bennett, Metro-Goldwyn-Mayer; *The Forsyte Saga*, directed by James Cellan Jones and David Giles, British Broadcasting Corporation (BBC); *The Forsyte Saga*, narrated by Dirk Bogarde, BBC Radio 4; *The Forsyte Saga*, directed by Christopher Menaul and Dave Moore, Granada Television.

4 Jeffrey S. Reznick, *Healing the Nation: Soldiers and the Culture of Caregiving during the Great War* (Manchester: Manchester University Press, 2005).

5 John Galsworthy, foreword, in Great Britain, Ministry of Pensions, *The Inter-allied Conference on the After-care of Disabled Men: Second Annual Meeting, held in London, May 20 to 25, 1918. Reports presented to the Conference* (London: HMSO, 1918), 13.

6 Ann-Marie Einhaus and Barbara Korte, eds, *The Penguin Book of First World War Stories* (London: Penguin Books, 2007), 214–223. 'Told by the schoolmaster' appeared originally in *The Argosy* (May 1924). It was reprinted subsequently in *The Forum* (December 1926) and in Galsworthy's posthumous collection of essays entitled *Forsytes, Pendyces and Others* (London: William Heinemann, 1935). Galsworthy's 1917 short stong *Defeat* appeared in the 1930 collection *Great short stories of the War* (London: Eyre and Spotriswode), and later in the reprint of that collection, entitled *Great First World War Stories* (London: Chancellor Press, 1994), but his work of the period is noticeably absent in what is perhaps the most important modern anthology of war literature, Jon Glover and Jon Silkin, eds, *The Penguin Book of First World War Prose* (London: Viking, 1989).

7 'About *The Skin Game*' at www.offwestend.com/index.php/plays/view/544, accessed 25 March 2007.

8 Lawrence Van Gelder, 'When old money meets new, it's wartime all over again', *New York Times*, 11 July 2005, at http://theater2.nytimes.com/2005/

07/11/theater/reviews/11skin.html?ei=5070&en=9f1cfb9, accessed 19 March 2007.

9 Catherine Rampell, 'John Galsworthy's *The Skin Game*', *Village Voice*, 19 July 2005, at http://villagevoice.com/theater/0529, sightlines,66010,11.html, accessed 25 March 2007.

10 Simon Saltzman, 'A CurtainUp review of *The Skin Game*', at www.curtainup.com/skingame.html, accessed 22 March 2007.

11 Sam Marlowe, '*The Skin Game*', *The Times Online*, 26 March 2007, at http://entertainment.timesonline.co.uk/tol/arts_and_entertainment/stage/theatre/article1572382.ece, accessed 27 April 2007.

12 John Thaxter, '*The Skin Game*', *The Stage*, 26 March 2007, at www.thestage.co.uk/reviews/review/php/16330/the-skin-game, accessed 27 March 2007. London theatre reviewer Timothy Ramsden offered a similarly positive opinion of this play 'that theatre forgot'. See Timothy Ramsden, '*The Skin Game*', *Reviews Gate*, 3 April 2007, at www.reviewsgate.com/index.php?name=News&file=article&sid=3373, accessed 6 June 2008.

13 'Worth the detour: *The Skin Game*', *The First Post: The Daily Online Magazine*, www.thefirstpost.co.uk/index.php?menuID=4&subID=1277, accessed 25 March 2007.

14 See, for example, John Galsworthy, *A Sheaf* (Classic Books, 2000) and *Another Sheaf* (Classic Books, 2000) and (Kessinger Publishing Co., 2007), among other editions.

15 John Galsworthy, *Glimpses and Reflections* (London: William Heinemann, 1937).

16 William Heinemann published the English edition of *A Sheaf* on 12 October 1916 and Charles Scribner's Sons published the American edition on 30 September of the same year. Three years later Heinemann published the English edition of *Another Sheaf* and Scribner's published the American edition. *Another Sheaf* was reprinted within weeks after its release in January 1919 but evidently not again until 2001, after it entered the public domain. See note 14 above.

17 Jay M. Winter, *Sites of Memory, Sites of Mourning: The Great War in European Cultural History* (New York: Cambridge University Press, 1995). This scholarship fits generally within a school of thought which argues that despite its unprecedented slaughter the Great War was not necessarily a watershed event after all. See Modris Eksteins, *Rites of Spring: The Great War and the Birth of the Modern Age* (Boston, MA: Houghton Mifflin, 1989), and George Mosse, *Fallen Soldiers: Reshaping the Memory of the two World Wars* (New York: Oxford University Press, 1990).

18 Harold Vincent Marrot, *The Life and Letters of John Galsworthy* (London: William Heinemann, 1935; New York: Charles Scribner's Sons, 1936), 215–216. Hereafter the latter is cited.

19 James Gindin, *John Galsworthy's Life and Art: An Alien's Fortress* (Ann Arbor: University of Michigan Press, 1987), 207.

20 Galsworthy to Oscar Leonard, of St Louis, Missouri, 3 May 1910. Princeton University Library, Archives of Charles Scribner's Sons.

21 See Gindin, *John Galsworthy's Life and Art*; Dudley Barker, *The Man of Principle: A View of John Galsworthy* (New York: London House & Maxwell, 1963), 170 ff., and Alec Fréchet, *John Galsworthy: A Reassessment*, trans. Denis Mahaffey (London: Macmilllan, 1982), 30–35. Comparable oversights are found in other biographies of Galsworthy, including Robert H. Coats, *John Galsworthy as a Dramatic Artist* (New York: Charles Scribner's Sons, 1926); Natalie Croman, *John Galsworthy: A Study in Continuity and Contrast* (Cambridge, MA: Harvard University Press, 1933); Gilbert Henry Fabes, *John Galsworthy, his First Editions: Points and Values* (London: W. & G. Foyle, 1932); David Holloway, *John Galsworthy* (London: Morgan-Grampian Books, 1968), 56; Sheila Kaye-Smith, *John Galsworthy* (London: Nesbit, 1916); Leon Shalit, *John Galsworthy: A Survey*, trans. Ethel E. Coe and Therese Harburg (London: Heinemann, 1929); V. E. Simmrell, 'John Galsworthy: the artist as propagandist', *Quarterly Journal of Speech Education* 13 (1927): 225–36; Jan Hendrik Smit, *The Short Stories of John Galsworthy* (Rotterdam: D. Van Sijn, 1947), and Sanford Sternlicht, *John Galsworthy* (Boston, MA: Twyne Publishers, 1987). See also Anthony West, ed., *The Galsworthy Reader* (New York, Charles Scribner's Sons, 1967). Additionally, the few scholars who have studied Galsworthy's identity as a social reformer have not engaged the author's wartime work. See, for example, Mike Nellis, 'John Galsworthy's *Justice*', *British Journal of Criminology* 36 (1996): 61–84. Maarten Willem Knoester, 'Faith of a Novelist: Religion in John Galsworthy's Work', doctoral thesis, Leiden University, 2006.

22 Mitchell A. Leaska, ed., *The Virginia Woolf Reader* (London: Harcourt, 1984), 192.

23 Virginia Woolf, 'Mr Bennett and Mrs Brown', as quoted in Leaska, ed., *The Virginia Woolf Reader*, 192–212, 205.

24 On this subject see especially Martin Evans and Kenneth Lunn, eds, *War and Memory in the Twentieth Century* (Oxford: Berg, 1997), Adrian Forty and Suzanne Küchler, eds, *The Art of Forgetting* (Oxford: Berg, 1999), Pierre Nora and Lawrence D. Kritzman, eds, *Realms of Memory: Rethinking the French Past* (New York: Columbia University Press, 1996) and Michael Rowlands, *Remembering to Forget: Sublimation as Sacrifice in War Memorials*, in Forty and Küchler, eds, *The Art of Forgetting* (Oxford: Berg, 1999), 127–145, and Sonia Batten, 'Forgetting the First World War', *Journal of the Centre for First World War Studies* 2: 2 (2005), at www.js-ww1.bham.ac.uk/fetch.asp?article=issue4_batten.pdf, accessed 18 July 2008.

25 Seth Koven, 'Remembering and dismemberment: crippled children, wounded soldiers, and the Great War in Great Britain', *American Historical Review* 99: 4 (1994): 1167–1202; Joanna Bourke, *Dismembering the Male: Men's Bodies, Britain, and the Great War* (London: Reaktion Books, 1995); Sarah Cole, *Modernism, Male Friendship and the First World War* (Cambridge:

Cambridge University Press, 2003). These studies complicate existing histories of disabled soldiers in both Western Europe and North America, including Antoine Prost, *In the Wake of War: les Anciens combattants and French Society*, trans. Helen McPhail (Oxford: Berg, 1992), and Robert Whalen, *Bitter Wounds: German Victims of the Great War, 1914–1939* (Ithaca, NY: Cornell University Press, 1984). See also Beth Linker, 'For life and Limb: The Reconstruction of a Nation and its Disabled Soldiers in World War I America', doctorial thesis, Yale University, 2006, and Heather Perry, 'Recycling the Disabled: Army, Medicine and Masculinity in World War Germany, 1914–1922', doctoral thesis, Indiana University, 2002.

26 Cole, *Modernism*, 200ff.

2/ Robert Wohl, *The Generation of 1914* (Cambridge, MA: Harvard University Press, 1979). See also Peter Buitenhuis, *The Great War of Words: British, American and Canadian Propaganda and Fiction, 1914–1933* (Vancouver: University of British Columbia Press, 1987), 148.

28 Other literati who joined Galsworthy at this unprecedented gathering were H. G. Wells, Arnold Bennett, John Masefield, John Buchan, Edith Wharton and Henry James. On the WPB and Wellington House see especially Jonathan Atkin, *A War of Individuals: Bloomsbury Attitudes to the Great War* (Manchester: Manchester University Press, 2002); Lucy Masterman, *C. F. G. Masterman: A Biography* (London: Nicholson & Watson, 1939); Gary S. Messinger, *Propaganda and the State in the First World War* (Manchester: Manchester University Press, 1992); Nicholas Reeves, *Official British Film Propaganda during the First World War* (London: Croom Helm, 1986); M. L. Sanders and Philip M. Taylor, *British Propaganda during the First World War* (London: Macmillan, 1982). See also Lord Beaverbrook, *Men and Power, 1917–1918* (London: Hutchinson, 1956) and A. J. P. Taylor, *Beaverbrook* (London: Hamish Hamilton, 1972). On British and Allied propaganda generally during the period see Stewart Halsey Ross, *Propaganda for War: How the United States was conditioned to fight the Great War of 1914–1918* (London: McFarland & Co., 1996); Bernard Waites, 'The government of the home front and the "moral economy" of the working class', in Peter H. Liddle, ed., *Home Fires and Foreign Fields* (Washington, DC: Brassey's Defense Publishers, 1985), 175–193, and Jay M. Winter, 'Propaganda and the mobilization of consent', in Hew Strachan, ed., *World War I: A History* (Oxford: Oxford University Press, 1999), 216–226.

29 David Wright, 'The Great War, government propaganda and English "men of letters," 1914–1916', *Literature and History* 7 (1978), 70–85.

30 Wright, 'The Great War, 70–85.

31 Peter Buitenhuis, *The Great War of Words: British, American and Canadian Propaganda and Fiction, 1914–1933* (Vancouver: University of British Columbia Press, 1987).

32 Buitenhuis, *The Great War of Words*, 43.

33 On the current and future dominance of disability studies see Teresa Meade and David Serlin, eds, *Disability and History*, special issue of *Radical History Review* 94 (winter 2006), Durham, NC: Duke University Press. See also Neil Pemberton, 'Enabling the past: new perspectives in the history of disability', *History Workshop Journal* 61 (autumn 2006), 292–295, which reports on the first UK-based history of disability conference, entitled 'Enabling the Past: New Perspectives in the History of Disability', held at the University of Manchester in June 2005 and sponsored by the Wellcome Trust, the University of Manchester Centre for the History of Science, Medicine and Technology and the Centre for the Cultural History of War.

34 Victor Buchli, ed., *The Material Culture Reader* (Oxford: Berg, 2002); Steven Lubar and David Kingery, eds, *History from Things: Essays on Material Culture* (Washington, DC: Smithsonian Institution Press, 1993); David Kingery, ed., *Learning from Things: Method and Theory of Material Culture Studies* (Washington, DC: Smithsonian Institution Press, 1996). See also Thomas Schlereth, *Material Culture: A Research Guide* (Lawrence. KS: University Press of Kansas, 1985). On the related subject of visual culture see Peter Burke, *Eyewitnessing: The Uses of Images as Historical Evidence* (London: Reaktion Books, 2001), Ludmilla Jordanova, 'Medicine and visual culture', *Social History of Medicine* 3: 1 (1990): 89–99, and 'Material models as visual culture', in S. de Chadarevian and N. Hopwood, eds, *Models: The Third Dimension of Science* (Stanford, CA: Stanford University Press, 2004). Scholars of the Great War have only recently begun to give contemporary material culture the attention it deserves. See especially Mark Levitch, *Panthéon de la guerre: Reconfiguring a Panorama of the Great War* (Columbia, MO: University of Missouri Press, 2006); Reznick, *Healing the Nation*; Nicholas J. Saunders, *Trench Art: Materialities and Memories of War* (Oxford: Berg, 2003); Nicholas J. Saunders, ed., *Matters of Conflict: Material Culture, Memory and the First World War* (London: Routledge, 2004); Nicholas Saunders and Paul Cornish, eds, *Contested Objects: Material Memories of the Great War* (Abingdon: Routledge, 2009).

35 Galsworthy, diary entry of 29 July 1914, as quoted in Marrot, *Life and Letters*, 395.

36 Galsworthy, diary entry of 1 August 1914, as quoted in Marrot, *Life and Letters*, 395. While Galsworthy notes that these circumstances prompted him to attend a 'nursing fund meeting' and 'to enquire about ambulance classes', extant evidence offers no indication that Galsworthy actually took up this instruction.

37 Galsworthy, diary entry of 2 August 1914, as quoted in Marrot, *Life and Letters*, 395.

38 Galsworthy, diary entry of 3 August 1914, as quoted in Marrot, *Life and Letters*, 395.

39 Galsworthy, diary entries of 7–13 August 1914, as quoted in Marrot, *Life and Letters*, 408–409.

40 Marrot, *Life and Letters*, 408–409.
41 James B. Pinker to Charles Scribner, 28 August 1914, Princeton University Library, Archives of Charles Scribner's Sons.
42 Galsworthy, diary entry of 25 August 1914, as quoted in Marrot, *Life and Letters*, 409. During this period Galsworthy also contributed his recently written play *The Little Man* 'gratis to a volume issued by Methuen to help P[rince] of Wales' Fund'; ibid., p. 409. That volume was *Methuen's Annual, 1914.*
43 Pinker to Scribner, 10 September 1914, Princeton University Library, Archives of Charles Scribner's Sons.
44 Galsworthy, diary entry of 25 August 1914, as quoted in Marrot, *Life and Letters*, p. 409.
45 Galsworthy, diary entry of 1 October 1914, as quoted in Marrot, *Life and Letters*, 410.
46 Galsworthy, diary entry of ca. 2 September 1914, as quoted in Marrot, *Life and Letters*, 409.
47 Marrot, *Life and Letters*, 409–410. 'Thoughts on this war' appeared initially in the November 1914 issue of *Scribner's Magazine* and subsequently in *A Sheaf*. Related pieces included 'An appeal to the youth of Britain' in the *Daily Chronicle* (30 September 1914), 'What we must do for Belgium' in the *Daily News* (31 August 1914) and 'A "credo" for keeping faith' in the *Current History of the War*, published by the *New York Times* (September 1914).
48 Galsworthy to Scribner, 8 September 1914, Princeton University Library, Archives of Charles Scribner's Sons. In May 1915 Galsworthy wrote to the publisher Alfred A. Knopf about a preface he offered for W. H. Hudson's novel *Green Mansions*. 'If the war were not on,' he explained, 'I would not have taken anything for [it], but since all I can earn goes to Red Cross or other war funds, I will take what you like to give.' Galsworthy to Alfred A. Knopf, 25 May 1915, Princeton University Library, Archives of Charles Scribner's Sons.
49 Galsworthy, diary entry of 7 November 1914, as quoted in Marrot, *Life and Letters*, 411. The sources of these amounts included Galsworthy's income from the aforementioned three essays written following the first WPB meeting as well as the essay 'Reveille' for *King Albert's Book*, published by Hodder & Stoughton on behalf of the *Daily Telegraph* and the *Daily Sketch*, 'France' 'for the D[aily] M[ail]', and any French papers' and a poem entitled 'Belgium, hail!'
50 Galsworthy, diary entry of ca. 13 December 1914, as quoted in Marrot, *Life and Letters*, 411–412. Galsworthy turned forty-seven on 14 August 1914. Both Dudley Barker and Alec Fréchet highlight this entry, as well as those of August, in their character assessments of Galsworthy at the outset of the war, but in doing so they fail to realize the full significance of this self-perceived and medically defined disability in the author's life. See Barker, *The Man of Principle: A Biography of John Galsworthy* (New York: Stein &

Day, 1969 [ca. 1963], 172 and Fréchet, *John Galsworthy: A Reassessment*, trans. Denis Mahaffey (Totowa, NJ: Barnes & Noble Books, 1982), 30–31.

51 Galsworthy, diary entry of 31 December 1914, as quoted in Marrot, *Life and Letters*, 412.

52 Galsworthy to Alfred A. Knopf, 9 June 1915, Princeton University Library, Archives of Charles Scribner's Sons.

53 These compositions stood among several which Galsworthy offered to wartime 'charity books' in support of their respective causes. His other contributions included the essays 'Reveille' in *King Albert's Book* (London: Daily Telegraph, Daily Sketch and Hodder & Stoughton, 1914); 'Harvest', in William C. Edgar, ed., *How Belgium is Fed* (London: National Committee for Relief in Belgium, 1915); 'A strong character', in *Princess Marie-Jose's Children's Book* (London: Cassell, 1916), and 'Harvest', in Edith Wharton, ed., *Book of the Homeless* (New York: Charles Scribner's Sons, 1916). Biographers have largely overlooked Galsworthy's contributions to these publications, and scholars of the Great War have only begun to explore wartime charity books in the context of contemporary print culture. See especially Amanda Laugesen, 'Australian soldiers and the world of print during the Great War', in Many Hammond and Shafquat, eds, *Publishing and the First World War: Essays in Book History* (Basingstoke: Palgrave, 2007), 93–110.

54 Galsworthy to Scribner, 23 October 1915, Princeton University Library, Archives of Charles Scribner's Sons.

55 John Attenborough, *A Living Memory: Hodder & Stoughton, Publishers, 1868–1975* (London: Hodder & Stoughton, 1975), 78.

56 John Hodge, *et al.*, *The Inter-allied Conference on the After-care of Disabled Men: Second Annual Meeting, held in London, May 20 to 25, 1918. Reports presented to the Conference* (London: HMSO, 1918), 101–102.

57 On the subject of gift books generally and pre-war roots, see especially Andrew Piper, *Dreaming in Books: The Making of the Bibliographic Imagination in the Romantic Age* (Chicago: University of Chicago Press, forthcoming), 'The art of sharing: reading in the Romantic miscellany', in Paul Keen and Ina Ferris, eds, *Bookish Histories* (New York: Palgrave, 2009), and 'Korpus. Brentano, das Buch und die Mobilisierung eines literarischen und politischen Körpers', in Matthias Buschmeier and Till Dembeck, eds *Textbewegungen 1800/1900* (Würzburg: Königshausen & Neumann, 2007), 266–286.

58 Theresa M. Collins, *Otto Kahn: Art, Money, and Modern Time* (Chapel Hill, NC: University of North Carolina Press, 2002). See also John Kobler, *Otto the Magnificent: The Life of Otto Kahn* (New York: Charles Scribner's Sons, 1988). See also Julie Anderson ' "Spare your tears": Representing and narrating Blind Bodies in Britain, 1915–1925', presented at the Fifth Global Conference on 'Making Sense of Health, Illness and Disease' held

at Mansfield College, Oxford, 12–15 July 2006, and available on line at www.inter-disciplinary.net/mso/hid/hid5/s3.html, accessed 22 May 2007.

59 Sir Arthur Pearson, 'The blind', in Great Britain, Ministry of Pensions, *The inter-allied Conference: Reports*, 277–282. Pearson eventually articulated his vision for St Dunstan's more fully in his book *Victory over Blindness: How it was won by the Men of St Dunstan's and how others may win it* (London: Hodder & Stoughton, 1919).

60 Galsworthy's story 'The recruit' also appeared in America in the January 1916 issue of *Everybody's Magazine*. For evidence of Galsworthy's support for St Dunstan's before the war see Galsworthy, 'Books for the blind: the multitude staring at the dark: Mr Galsworthy's appeal', *Times*, 13 April 1914, p. 10.

61 *Report of St Dunstan's Hostel for Blinded Soldiers and Sailors for the Year ended March 31st, 1917* (London: Blinded Soldiers and Sailors Care Committee, 1917), 1.

62 Reznick, *Healing the Nation*, chapter 5, and Reznick, with Sophie Delaporte, Paul Lerner, Peter Leese and Jay Winter, 'Metropolitan hospitals', in Jay Winter, ed., *Capital Cities at War: Paris, London, Berlin, 1914–1919* (Cambridge: Cambridge University Press, 2007).

63 On the phenomenon of 'khaki fever' see especially Angela Woollacott, '"Khaki fever" and its control: gender, class, age and sexual morality on the British home front in the First World War', *Journal of Contemporary History* 29: 2 (April 1994): 325–347. See also Woollacott, 'Dressed to kill: clothes, cultural meaning and World War I women munitions workers', in Moira Donald and Linda Hurcombe, eds, *Gender and Material Culture* II, *Representations of Gender from Prehistory to the Present* (New York: St Martin's Press, 2000), 198–217.

64 Marrot, *Life and Letters*, 418. On the success of the appeal see Cohen, *The War Come Home*, 137.

65 For another excellent example of such object-focused publicity, see the poster 'Xmas toys. The Lord Roberts Memorial Workshops for Disabled Soldiers & Sailors (ca. 1914–18), Hoover Library and Archives, Stanford University.

66 Major Algernon Tudor Craig, 'Lord Roberts Memorial Workshops for Disabled Soldiers and Sailors', *American Journal of Care for Cripples* 5: 2 (1918), 309–311.

67 Craig, 'Lord Roberts Memorial Workshops', 309–311.

68 Galsworthy, 'Heritage', *Reveille* 2 (November 1918), 302–305.

69 Galsworthy, 'Heritage', *Reveille* 2 (November 1918), 302.

70 Galsworthy, 'Heritage', *Reveille* 2 (November 1918), 304.

71 Galsworthy, 'Heritage', *Reveille* 2 (November 1918), 304.

72 Galsworthy, 'Heritage', *Reveille* 2 (November 1918), 304.

73 Galsworthy, 'Heritage', *Reveille* 2 (November 1918), 304.

74 Galsworthy to Scribner, 8 May 1916, Princeton University Library, Archives of Charles Scribner's Sons.

75 Mabel Edith Galsworthy Reynolds. *Memories of John Galsworthy* (London: Robert Hale, 1936), 93.

76 See *Schedule of Wellington House Literature. Confidential*, London: HMSO, n.d., but likely 1917–18, Imperial War Museum, London, Department of Documents. Additional Wellington House literature is listed in the official document entitled *Library. Foreign Office News Department. Subject Catalogue of the English Section* (London: HMSO, 1918), 2nd edn. Details of the origins, printing and distribution of this literature are found in the second and third *Reports on the Work conducted for the Government at Wellington House. Very Confidential*, February 1916 and September 1916, respectively, Imperial War Museum, London, Department of Documents. See also Mary Sprott, 'A Survey of British Wartime Propaganda in America Issues from Wellington House', M.A. thesis, Stanford University, 1921.

77 Scribner to Galsworthy, 2 June 1916, Princeton University Library, Archives of Charles Scribner's Sons.

78 Galsworthy to Scribner, 15 June 1916, Princeton University Library, Archives of Charles Scribner's Sons.

79 Galsworthy to Scribner, 6 June 1918, Princeton University Library, Archives of Charles Scribner's Sons.

80 *New Statesman*, 'Mr Galsworthy as propagandist', 11 November 1916, Vol. 8 (1916–17), 140–141.

81 'England's opportunity', *Times Literary Supplement*, 6 February 1919, p. 66.

82 Edgett Edwin Francis, 'John Galsworthy hurls his lance', *Boston Evening Transcript*, 4 November 1916, section 3, p. 7.

83 '*A Sheaf* by Galsworthy: sketches and arguments that stimulate thinking', *Springfield Republican* (Springfield, MA), 7 November 1916, p. 6.

84 Dorothea Lawrance Mann, '*Another Sheaf*: a collection of John Galsworthy's wartime reflections', *Boston Evening Transcript*, 12 February 1919, section 2, p. 8.

85 Galsworthy, diary entry of 8 September 1914, as quoted in Marrot, *Life and Letters*, 422. Allhusen was the wife of Augustus Henry Eden Allhusen, MP. See Samuel J. Rogal, *A William Somerset Maugham Encyclopaedia*, 263.

86 Galsworthy, diary entry of 11 September 1914, as quoted in Marrot, *Life and Letters*, 422.

87 Galsworthy to Allhusen, 12 September 1914, as quoted in Marrot, *Life and Letters*, 758.

88 Galsworthy to Chevrillon, 3 October 1916, as quoted in Marrot, *The Life and Letters*, 759.

89 Galsworthy to Allhusen, 30 December 1916, as quoted in Marrot, *Life and Letters*, 760–761.

90 Galsworthy to Allhusen, 3 January 1917 as quoted in Marrot, *Life and Letters*, 761–762.
91 Galsworthy to Allhusen, 3 January 1917, as quoted in Marrot, *Life and Letters*, 761–762.
92 Galsworthy to Allhusen, 3 January 1917, as quoted in Marrot, *Life and Letters*, 761–762.
93 Galsworthy to Allhusen, 3 January 1917, as quoted in Marrot, *Life and Letters*, 761–762.
94 Galsworthy to Allhusen, 3 January 1917, as quoted in Marrot, *Life and Letters*, 761–762.
95 Galsworthy, diary entry of 5 January 1917, as quoted in Marrot, *Life and Letters*, 762–763.
96 Galsworthy, diary entry of 5 January 1917, as quoted in Marrot, *Life and Letters*, 762–763.
97 Galsworthy, diary entry of 5 January 1917, as quoted in Marrot, *Life and Letters*, 762–763.
98 Galsworthy to Chevrillon, 20 January 1917, as quoted in Marrot, *Life and Letters*, 763–764.
99 Galsworthy to Chevrillon, 20 January 1917, as quoted in Marrot, *Life and Letters*, 763–764.
100 Galsworthy to Chevrillon, 20 January 1917, as quoted in Marrot, *Life and Letters*, 763–764.
101 Galsworthy to Allhusen, 3 January 1917, as quoted in Marrot, *Life and Letters*, 761–762.
102 Galsworthy, notebook entry of ca. 5 March 1917, as quoted in Marrot, *Life and Letters*, 427.
103 Marrot, *Life and Letters*, 427. Galsworthy offered this piece very shortly thereafter to Charles Scribner's Sons. See James B. Pinker (Galsworthy's literary and dramatic agent) to Charles Scribner's Sons, 5 April 1917, Princeton University Library, Archives of Charles Scribner's Sons. See also James Gindin, *John Galsworthy's Life and Art: An Alien's Fortress* (Ann Arbor, MI: University of Michigan Press, 1987), 381.
104 Galsworthy composed a fourth composition – entitled 'Impressions of France, 1916–1917 – based upon his time in France. This piece is not included here simply due to its chief focus being on the wartime 'French character', not specifically the disabled soldiers with whom Galsworthy interacted at Hôpital Bénévole.
105 Marrot, *Life and Letters*, 429.
106 Gindin, *John Galsworthy's Life and Art*, 381.
107 Gindin, *John Galsworthy's Life and Art*, 380.
108 Marrot, *Life and Letters*, 428. The St Maurice institutions were known formally as the Institut national professionnel des invalids de la guerre.
109 By 'all of us' Galsworthy's meant his entire family.

110 Born in California, Heyneman eventually lived in London and San Francisco and was a pupil of John Singer Sargent and herself mentored the sculptor Arthur Putnam. Her creative accomplishments undoubtedly informed her interest in and approach to the occupational therapy that was administered at California House. See 'Guide to the Julie Helen Heyneman papers, 1886–1942' in the Online Archive of California, http://oac.cdlib.org/, ACCESSED 18 July 2008. During his time at Hôpital Bénévole, Galsworthy wrote to Heyneman repeatedly about Kitchener House, offering not only to help 'fit up the house' but also critical thoughts on its emvisioned 'advisory committee' – 'In fact this word . . . is of doubtful advantage. Why not call them vice-presidents or simply patrons?' – as well as ideas for the formalname of the institution (Galsworthy to Heyneman, correspondence dated 13 December 1916, 12, 17 January, 2 March 1917, Julie Helen Heyneman Papers, BANC MSS C-H 152 / Box 1, Bancroft Library, University of California, Berkeley).

111 Heyneman, undated report lodged in Galsworthy papers, Collection of Steve Forbes.

112 'Kitchener House: a club for wounded sailors and soldiers', *British Journal of Nursing*, 27 October 1917, p. 270.

113 'Kitchener House: a club for wounded sailors and soldiers', *British Journal of Nursing*, 27 October 1917, p. 270.

114 Untitled and undated (but likely ca. March 1918) manuscript, Collection of Steve Forbes.

115 Untitled and undated (but likely ca. March 1918) manuscript, Collection of Steve Forbes.

116 Heyneman to Galsworthy, 3 April 1918, Collection of Steve Forbes.

117 These suggestions, several of which Galsworthy captured in the first instance in his initial plan, included 'Courses in . . . Agriculture. Architecture. Engineering. Law. Languages'. These categories were broken down as follows: '(a). Technical Training to increase efficiency in future professional work. (b). Lectures on Natural Science. History. The Arts. Political Science. (c). German should be included among languages taught. (d). Accounts. Literature. Handwriting. Foreign Languages. Arts & Crafts. (e). That scholarships should be offered. (f). Carpentering'. One hundred and forty-six officers from nine institutions offered suggestions to the proposed scheme. 'Suggestions from different officers', undated (but likely late April 1918) Galsworthy manuscript, Collection of Steve Forbes.

118 Galsworthy's original typescript reveals these words to have been 'The Red Cross will be ready, to some extent, with monetary help'. Ultimately, due to the organization being unwilling to commit its funds to the enterprise, these words were not included in the final version of the appeal which appeared in the *Times* on 19 April 1917.

119 Pennant to Galsworthy, 4 April 1918, Collection of Steve Forbes. Pennant returned Galsworthy's draft appeal with this correspondence. Therein, clearly

underlined in blue pencil, was the contentious phase to which he referred: 'The Red Cross will be ready, to some extent, with monetary help.' See 'Kitchener Houses', undated Galsworthy typescript, Collection of Steve Forbes.

120 A Kitchener House for officers, located at 34 Grosvenor Place, appears in War Office, *Funds, Associations, and Societies, &c., for the Assistance of Officers and Men and their Dependants'* (114/Gen.No./6198) (December 1919), p. 3, and in the subsequent 1920 and 1921 editions. See p. 4 of both editions.

121 Galsworthy, diary entry of 14 December 1917, as quoted in Marrot, *Life and Letters*, 434–435.

122 Published on behalf of the Ministry of Pensions by John Bale, Sons & Danielsson Ltd, of London, its complete title was *Recalled to Life: A Journal devoted to the Care, Re-education, and Return to Civil Life of Disabled Sailors and Soldiers.*

123 Godfrey Rathbone Benson, Lord Charnwood, 'Introductory', *Recalled to Life* 1 (June 1917): 1.

124 Galsworthy, 'The gist of the matter', *Reveille* 1 (August 1918): 176–182. Douglas C. McMurtrie later reiterated the problems with *Recalled to Life*, stating simply that the publication 'was neither scientific nor popular'. See McMurtrie, 'A campaign of public education in the interests of the disabled soldier', *American Medicine* (October 1921): 534–540, 538.

125 See Colonel E. S. Stanton (Ministry of Pensions) to Galsworthy, 2 January 1918, Collection of Steve Forbes, as well as Galsworthy, diary entry of 20 December 1917, as quoted in Marrot, *Life and Letters*, 435.

126 Stanton to Galsworthy, 23 March 1918, Collection of Steve Forbes.

127 Galsworthy to Robert Jones, 7 April 1918, Collection of Steve Forbes.

128 Stanton to Galsworthy, 12 April 1918, Collection of Steve Forbes. Despite Stanton's initial and ultimate praise of the foreword he did find one significant fault with it, indicating to Galsworthy that he had 'taken the liberty of adding Newfoundland (a Dominion!) and India to your other mentioned British Possessions and I added etc etc because little places like Jamaica Western Africa & other small Crown Colonies too numerous should also be included in your praise and they might find hurt if manifestly excluded . . .'

129 John Galsworthy, 'So comes the sacred work', *American Journal of Care for Cripples* 7: 2 (1918): 88–91, and 'The stricken', *The Living Age* 11: 3868 (1918): 454–458.

130 Stanton to Galsworthy, 23 March 1918, Collection of Steve Forbes.

131 Galsworthy to Robert Jones, 7 April 1918, Collection of Steve Forbes.

132 While Galsworthy noted in his diary on 17 April 1918 that 'Charnwood came to see me about editorship', he did not detail the conversation that followed. On this day, Galsworthy noted further, he 'was appointed editor of *Recalled to Life*, renamed *Reveille*'. Galsworthy, diary entry of 17 April 1918, as quoted in Marrot, *Life and Letters*, 441.

133 Kipling to Galsworthy, 4 May 1918, Collection of Steve Forbes.

134 This conclusion is based upon an assessment of more than three dozen such announcements lodged in the Galsworthy papers held within the Collection of Steve Forbes.

135 *Jewish Chronicle*, 2 August 1918, n.p., one among many 'Durant Press Cuttings' lodged in the Galsworthy papers of the Collection of Steve Forbes. Evidence of Galsworthy's authorship of this text is based upon a typescript version lodged in his personal papers, specifically the document catalogued JG 894. In late July and early August 1918 this standard text appeared in various similar forms in many other publications, including the *Aberdeen Journal* (1 August 1918), *Grocers' Journal* (10 August), *Huddersfield Examiner* (30 July), *Irish News* (26 July), *People* (28 July) and *Southampton Times* (27 July). Similar coverage appeared during the same period in the *British Medical Journal, Church Bulletin, Family Newspaper, Daily Mail, Dublin Express, East Anglican Daily Times, Electrical Industries, Evening Standard and St James's Gazette, Field, Folkestone Herald, Glasgow News, Globe, Hull Daily Mail, Liverpool Daily Courier, Middlesex and Buckinghamshire Advertiser, New Witness, Newcastle Chronicle, Newspaper World, Observer, Punch, Scotsman, Sheffield Daily Telegraph, Spectator, Times, Western Daily Press, Westminster Gazette* and *World*. A similar standard announcement also appeared on the front page of Canada's *Manitoba Free Press* on 17 October 1918. Additional contributors not mentioned in the text quoted but in other versions included an anonymous 'Civilian', Edmund J. Sullivan, Gilbert Nobbs, A. G. Baker and A. Seymour Jones, JP. The very format of all three issues of the journal reflects a common constraint in publishing of the period, namely shortage of paper. The names of contributors were listed on the cover of each issue, an indexing measure that saved paper while reserving space for additional material to be included.

136 Review entitled 'Reveille', published in an unknown newspaper, n.p., n.d., but likely late July or early August 1918, lodged in the Galsworthy papers held within the Collection of Steve Forbes.

137 Other contributors to the second issue included Thomas Hardy, OM, John Masefield, Stacy Aumonier, G. K. Chesterton, Owen Seaman, Raven Hill, Lieutenant General Goodwin, CMG, DSO, Major Herbert Jones, P. C. Varrier-Jones, MD, Dudley Myers, OBE, Major A. F. Hurst, RAMC, Daniel Robinson, Major Alane Coupland, Allan V. White, Frank Brangwyn, ARA, W. H. Hudson, Maurice Baring, G. Rostrevor, John Drinkwater, Major H. H. C. Baird, DSO, Herbert Ward, G. Buckley, F. J. Passmore, Mary Stocks, Julie Helen Heyneman, Margaret Eleanor Sale, Robert Nichols and Leon de Smet. Other contributors to the third issue (as listed) included Robert Bridges, Edith Wharton, H. Granville Barker, Hilaire Belloc, Elizabeth Robins, Siegfried Sassoon, Will Dyson, Lieutenant Colonel Sir Arthur Griffith-Boscawen, MP, Lieutenant Colonel G. M. Long, Lieutenant C. A. Morton, Howard Angus Kennedy, Colonel H. M. Tory, DES, H. B. C.

Pollard, Lieutenant Colonel Frederick Mott, MD, FRS, Douglas McMurtrie, USA, James R, Kerr, Major C. Reginald Harding, T. H. Mawson, Dr Fortescue Fox, William Nicholson, Robert Graves, Chris Massie, Ralph Mottram, A. Neil Lyons, Roger T. Smith, T. Hilditch, Dr R. M. Walmsley, James Savidge, Clive Hamilton and Jean de Bosschère.

138 HMSO published the first issue of *Reveille* on 10 August. The delay was due in part to late delivery of Max Beerbohm's illustration (Galsworthy to HMSO, 27 July 1918, Collection of Steve Forbes, JG708).

139 Thanks to Jane Potter of the Oxford International Centre for Publishing Studies, Oxford Brookes University, for her expert guidance in understanding this aspect of wartime print culture.

140 Galsworthy to HMSO, 27 July 1918, Collection of Steve Forbes. Typescript copies of the W. H. Smith 'circulars' to which Galsworthy refers are also held in this collection, catalogued as JG 891 and JG 887–890.

141 Evans to Galsworthy, 8 August 1918, Collection of Steve Forbes.

142 Nathan to Galsworthy, 30 May 1918, Collection of Steve Forbes.

143 Nathan to Galsworthy, 31 May 1918, Collection of Steve Forbes.

144 Nathan to Galsworthy, 10 July 1918, Collection of Steve Forbes.

145 Nathan to Galsworthy, 12 July 1918, Collection of Steve Forbes.

146 Galsworthy to Nathan, 15 July 1918, Collection of Steve Forbes.

147 Galsworthy to Alice Rothenstein, 23 January 1919, Papers of Sir William Rothenstein, Houghton Library, Harvard University, bMS Eng 1148 (541). By permission of the Houghton Library, Harvard University.

148 Due to the timing of a staff change-over in the Ministry of Pensions as a result of recommendations of the Committee on Staffs (Bradbury Committee), it is unclear to whom Galsworthy was referring here, but the 'permanent official' succeeding Matthew Nathan was likely George William Chrystal, not his interim replacement J. A. Flynn. See National Archives, T 1/12405, Minute. Reorganisation of senior staff of the Ministry of Pensions: Recommendations of the Committee on Staffs (Bradbury Committee), and Hansard, 22 October 1918 and 18 November 1920.

149 Galsworthy, undated notebook entry, as quoted in Marrot, *Life and Letters*, 470.

150 Stanton to Galsworthy, 13 August 1918, Collection of Steve Forbes. Camus was a leading French authority on the rehabilitation of disabled soldiers.

151 Stanton to Galsworthy, 14 August 1918, Collection of Steve Forbes.

152 Stanton to Galsworthy, 17 August 1918, Collection of Steve Forbes.

153 Galsworthy to Stanton, 19 August 1918, Collection of Steve Forbes.

154 Stanton to Galsworthy, n.d. but determined to be 20 August 1918 due to reference to 'your [Galsworthy's] letter of yesterday's date', Collection of Steve Forbes.

155 Galsworthy, diary entry of 22 July 1918, as quoted in Marrot, *Life and Letters*, 443.

156 This news was the result of German forces opening their fifth offensive of the year on the western front.

157 Dudley Barker, *The Man of Principle: A Biography of John Galsworthy* (New York: Stein & Day, 1969), 182.

158 Galsworthy, diary entry of 22 July 1918, as quoted in Marrot, *Life and Letters*, 443.

159 The manuscript copy of this significant document is reproduced between p. 442 and p. 443 of Marrot, *Life and Letters*. The location of the original document – and thus its copyright status – is unknown, so its reproduction here was unfortunately not possible.

160 A.R.P.–M [John Galsworthy], *The Burning Spear: Being the Experiences of Mr John Lavender in Time of War, recorded by A.R.P.–M* (London: Chatto & Windus, 1919).

161 Gindin, *John Galsworthy's Life and Art*, 403.

162 John Galsworthy, 'Foreword', in G. Howson, ed., *Handbook for the Limbless* (London: Disabled Society, 1921), vi.

163 Galsworthy, 'At the Lowell centenary', in *Addresses in America, 1919* (London: Heinemann, 1919), 8–9.

164 Galsworthy, preface to *The Burning Spear* in *The Collected Works of John Galsworthy*, Manaton Edition Volume XVI (London: Heinemann, 1923), ix.

165 In fact, despite contemporary praise of these collections, their respective lives in print were short. While Heinemann reissued *Another Sheaf* only once and within days after its appearance in January 1919, it never reissued *A Sheaf* after its appearance in October 1916. Marrot, *Bibliography*, 100–101.

166 Marrot, *Bibliography*, 121–129.

167 Preface to Manaton Edition Volume XVII, pp. x–xi.

168 Galsworthy to Gilbert Murray, 6 March 1932, as quoted in Marrot, *Life and Letters*, 803.

169 *Nobel Lectures: Literature, 1901–1967*, ed. Horst Frenz (Amsterdam: Elsevier, 1969).

PART I

Select Non-fiction by John Galsworthy

~1~

Foreword to *The Queen's Gift Book in Aid of Queen Mary's Convalescent Auxiliary Hospitals for Soldiers and Sailors who have Lost their Limbs in the War*

Written shortly after Galsworthy's visit to Roehampton in the autumn of 1915, this composition appeared in *The Queen's Gift Book* alongside contributions by J. M. Barrie, John Buchan, Joseph Conrad and Arthur Conan Doyle, among others. It marked the first appearance of the iconic 'convalescent blues' in Galsworthy's wartime canon of writing about disabled soldiers and thus the first suggestion of his awareness of their challenges of personal and public identity both within the culture of caregiving and beyond it in civilian life. These figures appeared again in Galsworthy's essay 'Heritage', which is reproduced in Chapter 12, and once more in his novel *The Burning Spear*, one of the most significant chapters of which appears in Chapter 13.

The place I came to seemed a green and fortunate haven for the battered. Ah! Ships you can refit, making them as good as new; but these four hundred men in their blueish hospital garb and their red neckties can never be made as good as new. You can only make shift for them, and do your best. Legs and arms, legs and arms – they all want one or the other, and some want both.

They have just passed to dinner – a long procession – in wheelchairs, on crutches, or walking strangely, the freshly fitted leg thrown out a little apart, stiffly as yet; or seemingly quite whole and active men, till you observe they have only one arm. One of them has lost two legs and an arm, another an arm and a leg and an eye. So they go, young, pathetically strong – cheerful fellows, wonderful fellows, stoics. Someone says: 'They're not worrying; that's Tommy all over – never thinks of to-morrow.' Well, it would seem the better ground-philosophy for armless men, legless men, who by no measure of thought for to-morrow will ever have two arms or legs, or even perhaps one, again.

And yet – they must and shall have a to-morrow! That is the object and policy of this Haven called Queen Mary's Auxiliary Convalescent Hospitals, in Roehampton. Certainly crippled men could hardly have better quarters, attention, and grub than they get here (the Staff eat exactly what the patients do – such is the matron's admirable plan); but these one-legged, one-winged birds of passage stay but a few weeks or days. An ever-lengthening flock of the maimed waits for empty perches; and so, as soon as 'to-morrow' is fairly in sight, each passes out and on, to make way for a waiting comrade. The real business is to fit them properly with new limbs, and with a new future, while they are here.

How far can this be done?

An instrument-maker shows me legs – not very heavy, much lighter actually, but of course heavier in effect, than the lost limbs.

'How far does it show – say, with an amputation below the knee?'

The instrument-maker walks a few paces and comes back.

'You can judge for yourself – I've got one on.'

'I should never have known it.'

'No? It depends on the man. Some will always show it – others –'

'A matter of temperament!'

'That's right.'

'But – above the knee?'

'Charlie, just walk across, will you?'

A young man walks. You would say he had a bad corn, or a weak knee – no more.

'That,' says the instrument-maker, 'comes of getting the limb exactly right. And for that it's vital to have the man right here with you a bit at the start, so as you can watch it, pare away what's wrong, and get it to fit him O.K. Another thing I'll tell you: The better the instrument – and, unfortunately, the more expensive – the more comfortable it'll be.'

'It's not mere polish, then, that adds to the expense?'

'No, *sir*; it's extra efficiency – skill and time spent on it.'

'And does it worry a man much when it's first put on?'

'Well, it's not just an addition to his comfort; but he soon gets to feel all right with it. This is what we cover them with – calf-skin. I should like you to see the officer that's going to have this leg; he wears it A1.'

This then is the importance of precisely the 'just' limb.

And the second part of the work here – the placing of the maimed on the path of a new utility and hope, the fitting of him with his to-morrow?

It goes very well, they say – very well, so far. It is up to the public to see that it goes well to the end.

Passing back through the new wooden wards, twenty or thirty beds in each, and two stoves – very scrupulous, comfortable, airy; through the recreation rooms – small billiard tables, chess, dominoes, plenty of books, and heaps of papers, I sit down in a wheel-chair vacated by one with left leg gone and right leg badly damaged, who has got into a more solid chair alongside, to read a magazine. Here is a bit of irony – perhaps the only bit of its kind in the whole of the two hospitals. This one was damaged not by man, but by the act of God – the falling of a rock; and the very next week his battalion went to the front, and he was the only man left behind. He cannot be more than twenty-five, in radiant health, eyes full of light and life, and that expression of perfected patience which, above everything, touches the heart. He has read a good deal, he says, since he was in hospital. He will have his leg on Monday; but as to his future, he does not know as yet.

I go out to the lawn. Under a light-grey sky, between the terrace of the big house and some cedar trees whose dark branches lie so still and flat on the windless autumn air, they are punting a football. A little man in a Scotch cap, with a pale brown, keen-jawed face, prefers to lift his crutches, jump clean off the ground with his one leg, kick the ball hard, and return to earth. He looks as if he has been a good player in his time – a half-back, probably. They have very likely all been good players; and now a kind of incredulous amusement at their infirmity seems to possess them, whether they play or whether they look on. Watching the spread, the quick intricate flourish, and trail of their crutches, their laughing utter abandonment to the moment, one cannot help thinking of winged and lamped jackdaws sporting together; but no cheerful jackdaw ever had such pluck as this.

The tales that might be heard here would fill many volumes, if one had but the gift of expression. Here, for instance, is a man who, with arm and leg broken and one eye blinded, lay out on the field two days, and having just missed being prodded to death by one of Culture's children, was thrown into a barn with ten others, till our men came along and rescued them. Yes, that everlasting fellow is here now, waiting for his limbs and his 'to-morrow,' making less of his past suffering and his future fate than many a man in old days when a penny was added to the income tax.

Here is one who, having lost a leg and been wounded I forget where besides, lay, together with two other maimed and helpless fellows, nine days in a ruined farm with no food, and for water a puddle with a dead sheep in it, to which one of the three only was able to crawl. As the doctor put it: 'The puddle was sustaining – full of body.' Anyway, he lived, and is waiting for his limb and his future.

Beside me, watching the football, is a man in a wheel-chair with both feet gone – frost-bite. He knows as little as I whether all that frost-bite was necessary in our latitudes, even in the conditions that prevailed last winter . . . However, here he is in his wheel-chair, waiting for feet, and his future, and laughing when the man in the Scotch cap leaves the earth to kick the ball.

The doctor, the lady superintendent, the matron, the nurses, all tell us that these four hundred are not down-hearted, not even in their spare and lonely moments. Cockney and Yorkshireman, Celt and Canadian, West-countryman and Midlander, sailor or soldier, hardly a man of them downhearted. It's very wonderful, very grand, very touching. They draw strength, no doubt, from all being in the same boat, from their county's gratitude, from the admiring interest they feel they are inspiring; but allowing for all this, their hearts must be of oak right through.

But this is what I would be saying: True, that for the moment, and for the long coming months, perhaps years, that the war will last, even for a spell after Peace has come, the hearts and minds of all – crippled or not – will be filled and sustained by the thought of the danger to be overcome, the duties to be fulfilled, and the issues at stake. But Time strides on, and Time is a great leveller, making all things small to eyes turned backward, laying low the past, however high, with the pressure of the present's poignancy and of the future's hopes and fears. To us, who do not in this war leave behind some actual part of ourselves, our limbs, our sight, our speech, our hearing – to us, looking back, the mountainous happenings of to-day will acquire a dream-like quality and sink in the distance, or in new lights attain quite different shapes and values. Then will the haloes round the maimed grow dim to us, the consoling, grateful glow in hearts die down, and a cold wind blow round these half-wrecked lives. But in the hearts of the maimed memory will not fade nor from their seared fibre disablement depart. They will be limping monuments of a half-buried war, no longer upheld by the admiration of their countrymen, nor much by their own consciousness of duty done, but having to make good as best they can with an unremarked gallantry greater than an they showed in the wet, shell-searched trenches, or charging a storm of bullets – greater, because it must last so long – all the rest of their lives. To us others this war will in due time come to be but a terrific episode; but *they* will pay a perpetual price. After the first flush of honour and attention, it is hard to see what pennyworth of real compensation fate has in store for the maimed. Pensions? Yes, pensions! Into that paradise of beer and skittles the legless or armless no doubt enter; and a low-geared imagination will try to tell them that they are blessed, or to assure them that they are 'spoiled'; but something in them will ever say, and something in you and me will ever echo – 'No number of shillings a week, not even twenty-five, can make up this loss'; no more than daily hempseed makes up to the caged bullfinch for the loss of his wings, or guaranteed free meals to a leopard for his imprisonment. It is the spirit of a man that suffers when he can no longer express the bounding energy within him. And yet, perhaps, after all there is one deep compensation for those who can attain to it. For surely to have to conquer day by day a hundred little difficulties that one with all his limbs knows not, to have to bear stoically year by year the loss of full expression, must fortify the will-power; and by will-power men attain full stature. Is it a forlorn hope that sees these maimed comrades transfigured – with heads up, marching down the years in spite of Fate, finer-spirited, stronger-souled than ordinary men? That is, at any rate, the vision before this Haven where they have put in to be refitted.

To give the maimed back the best equivalent for what they have lost, the best mechanical substitutes for shattered limbs, and such openings in life as shall suit their altered outlook, keep hope and self-respect in them, keep them eager and full-lived men in that far future when the drums and fifes have long been still, and their very echo is but a ghost of unreal sound – to do all this in so far as it can be done, is the problem and the task before Queen Mary's Convalescent Auxiliary Hospitals.

And this book is designed to help the work. 'Tis in the nature of a hat passed round, into which, God send, many hundred thousand coins may be poured! But a book can only hope to raise a portion of the money wanted. More, more, and – alas! – ever more will be needed, not of our generosity, but of our consciences, till no single one of those who, by giving of their flesh and bone, have helped to save the flesh and bone of Britain and the fair name of Britain, can say with truth: 'I gave that bit of me, and I'm crippled for life. I thought they'd do what they could for me, after. But you see – they didn't.'

In the name of the Lady, dear to England, who watches over this work, it is my privilege to ask that we fail not our honour in this matter. However little these Stoics make of it now – theirs is an abiding sacrifice, an abiding grief. We are deep in their debt. All that we can, shall we not cheerfully repay?

2

Totally disabled

This composition appeared originally in *The Observer* on 19 March 1916. Within one day, it helped to raise £3,000 in donations to the Star and Garter Home for Disabled Soldiers and Sailors. Galsworthy later reprinted it in *A Sheaf* (1916) and in the twenty-one-volume Manaton Edition of his collected works, specifically in Vol. XVII and as part of the section entitled 'Concerning the war', where it was the only piece related directly to the subject of soldiers disabled in the Great War.

If I were that! Not as one getting into the yellow leaf, but with all the spring-running in me. If I lay, just turning my eyes here and there! How should I feel?

How do *they* feel – those helpless soldiers and sailors already lying in the old ballroom of 'Star and Garter'? The ghostly officer is ever crying in that hospital ward:

'Stick it, men! Stick it! Only for life! Stick it!'

Only for life – how many years! In the year only three hundred and sixty-five awakenings; only all those returns to merciful sleep!

'Stick it, men! Stick it!'

Totally disabled – incurably helpless! No! One can't realize what it feels like to be caught young and strong in such a net; to be caught – not for your own folly and excesses, not through accident or heredity, but as reward for giving yourself body and soul to your country. Better so, more easily borne; and yet how much more ironically tragic!

Who knows what the freedom of limbs means, till he has lost it? Who can measure the ecstasy of vigour, till every power of movement has been cut off? Who really grasps what it's like to lie like a log dependent

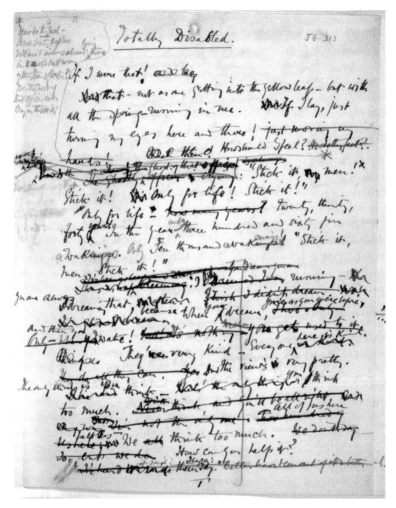

Figure 38 First page of Galsworthy's manuscript for 'Totally disabled'.
(Collection of Steve Forbes © all rights reserved. Image by Richard Holttum)

for everything on others – save those who have to? Think of the trout in the streams, of the birds in the air, the winged creatures innumerable, think of each beast and creeping thing – can one even imagine them without movement? Men, also, are meant to be free of their world, masters of their limbs and senses. They who lie helpless are no longer quite bodies, for the essence of body is movement; already they are almost spirits. It is as if, in passing, one looked at minds, nearly all in the heyday of consciousness and will.

Sometimes I vaguely fancy that after violent death a man's spirit may go on clinging above the earth just so long as his normal life would have run; that a spirit rived before its time wanders till such date as consciousness would have worn itself out in the body's natural death. If that random fancy were true, we to-day would all be passing among unseen crowds of these rived spirits, watching us, without envy perhaps, being freer than ourselves. But those who lie hopelessly disabled, having just missed that enfranchisement, are tied to what still exists, and yet in truth have died already. Of all men they have the chance to prove the mettle of the human soul – that mysterious consciousness capable of such heights and depths; no, not a greater chance than men tortured by long solitary confinement, or even that those who through excess or through heredity lie for ever helpless – but yet so great a chance that they are haloed for all of us happier ones who are free of our limbs and our lives. Some among those prisoned spirits must needs shrink and droop, and become atrophied in the long helplessness of a broken body. But many will grow finer – according to their natures – some pursuing the ideal of recompense in another world; some, in the stoic belief that serenity and fortitude are the fine flowers of life, unconsciously following the artist's creed – that to make a perfect thing, even if it be only of his own spirit, is in itself all the reward.

Whichever it may be, slow decay or slow perfecting, we others approach them with heads bowed, in as great reverence as we give to the green graves of our brave dead. And if pity – that pity which to some, it seems, is but ignoble weakness – be not driven from this earth, then with pity we shall nerve our resolve that never shall anything be lacking to support or comfort those who gave all for us and are so broken by their sacrifice.

As I write the sun is hot for the first time this year, and above the snow spring is in the air. Under Richmond Hill the river will be very bright, winding among the trees not yet green. And the helpless who are lying there already will be thinking: 'I shall never walk under trees again – nor by a riverside.'

If one dwells too much on the miseries this world contains, there must come a moment when one will say: 'Life's not worth living; I will end it!' But by some dispensation, few of us reach that point – too sanely selfish, or saved by the thought that we must work to reduce the sum of misery.

For these greatest of all sufferers – these helpless and incurable – can we do too much – ever reach the word: Enough?

To you, women of Great and Greater Britain, it has fallen to raise on Richmond Hill this refuge and home of our soldiers and sailors totally disabled. Where thirty-two are now lying, there will soon be two hundred more. Nearly all my life I have known the spot on which this home will stand – and, truly, no happier choice could have been made. If beauty consoles – and it can, a little – it is there in all the seasons; a benign English beauty of fields and trees and water spread below, under a wide sky.

One hundred thousand pounds you need to raise this monument of mercy in tribute to the brave. If it were five hundred thousand you would give it; for is not this monument to be the record and token of your gratitude, your love, and your pity? Each one of you, I think, however poor, must wish to lay one brick or stone of the house that is to prove your ministering.

If the misery through this war could be balanced in scales, I do not think men's suffering would pull down that of wives, and mothers, sisters, daughters; but this special suffering of incurable disablement – this has been spared you, who yet by nature are better at enduring than men. It has been spared you; and in return you have vowed this home for the helpless; a more sacred place than any church, for within it every hour of day and night, pain will be assuaged, despair be overcome, actual living tenderness be lavished.

When you have built this refuge for the prisoners of fate, when you have led them there to make out the rest of their lives as best they can – remember this: Men who are cut off in their youth from life and love will prize beyond all things women's sympathy, and the sight of women's beauty. Give, your money to build; your hands to lead them home; and, when they are there, take them your sympathy, take them your beauty!

3

For the maimed – now!

Galsworthy wrote this essay shortly after his visit to the Lord Roberts Memorial Workshops in London during the spring of 1916. It appeared originally in the *Morning Post* on 26 May and later – slightly abbreviated and retitled as 'Those whom the war has broken' – in the August 1916 issue of *Current History*, a monthly periodical published in the United States by the *New York Times*. The piece is notable for suggesting the restorative power of the very objects that were being produced by men disabled in the war, indeed Galsworthy's awareness of the essential role of *matériel* in 'after-care' regimes and the value of that role in promoting these regimes to the public. His observation about the toy products of the Lord Roberts Workshops was in tune with the message of publicity posters issued by the institution, which depicted a variety of its soldier-made, wooden-toy products for purchase.

I don't know how other people feel but when in the streets there passes some poor fellow who a few months ago was stronger and more active then one's self, had before him many more years of enjoyment and utility, almost a boy, perhaps, and who is now to be forever like a bird with a broken wing or a ship with a mast gone and half of its sails trailed down, there comes on one a sensation like no other that this war produces. Death, of course, by every form of violence, is snatching his millions, but we must all die some time; the waters close quickly – a little hole, a few bubbles, a sore heart or two, and the river flows on. All the other miseries, whipped on by that fell huntsman, War – starvation, destitution, imprisonment, anxiety, grief – if they do not kill you, they pass. Maiming abides. The armless, legless, the blinded, the paralysed – all live on into the green years when the wilderness will bloom again and flowers grow where this storm once withered the face of the earth; on into the calm years when men will look back and rub their eyes. It is this which comes down on the heart of him who sees the maimed men go by – this sensation of watching, from far on in the future when there shall not be another trace left of that hurricane, thousands upon thousands stricken out of full life into a half-existence, thousands upon thousands who, but for the merest chance, might be ourselves. Maimed for the duration of the war – that would be bearable, but maimed for the duration of life is the sacrifice that these have made and that we shall have to watch. And the grimness of it is that with each year which leaves the war further behind we shall watch and feel for them the less – a hard saying, but true – and they will feel the waste of their powers the more. And that is why now is the time to roll up every penny that we can, to put a sure foundation beneath these injured lives, so that however much we sag away from gratitude and justice in the future – and sag we shall, as sure as men are men – we shall have guaranteed our country against the crime of taking the best from her sons, for her reservation, and leaving them like hulks on the beach of fortune.

A national responsibility

This war is the nation's war as no war has yet ever been. Each man maimed in it has lost his limb, his sight, his power of movement, in the service of us all; and we shall be skunks to fail them. Yet, if I am not mistaken, such social conditions and feelings will follow this struggle throughout Europe – not at once, but within a few years – that everything which reminds people of it will come to be anathema; no hope then for the maimed of anything beyond what we have already secured for them! It is now that from ourselves, and from our Government, such money must be got, and such a comprehensive scheme laid out as to banish all fear of national shame. Pensions are all very well, but nothing is enough, short of our being able honestly to say that no man totally disabled in this war, however long it lasts, is left uncared for, and no man partially disabled left without such opportunity of suitable and dignified work as shall keep him in self-respect and a decent economic position. That is the minimum of justice, and less than the minimum of gratitude.

This is a deceptive moment. Labour is so scarce that the partially disabled easily find jobs, which peace will soon take from them. None of us would now admit that we shall ever forget the bravery and sacrifices of our soldiers and sailors, that we shall ever come to turn a cold shoulder on the maimed among them. The hot iron never thinks that it will cool; but cool it always does. Wait till danger is removed, till social troubles recommence, till we reap what the war is sowing! If full provision is not made while the war lasts it will never be made. We must put it out of our own power to betray our best instincts, under the chilly pressure of a troubled future. The funds raised and asked for up to now are as a drop in the jug of ultimate need.

The £100,000 so far asked for 'The Lord Roberts Memorial Workshops' Fund will provide for some three thousand partially disabled men. And there are already about twenty thousand. How many will there be before it is all over?

Thanks to the scarcity of labour and the gratitude of the public the needs of the moment are pretty well provided for: but what of the needs of a year hence, five years hence, when, in the pressure of unemployment, the maimed are pushed out of place all over the country? One dreads the thought that these crippled men who have deserved of the best may in the long run be left to a capricious charity. A scheme, elastic, coherent, practical, and covering the whole country, to ensure generous support for all who cannot work, to ensure well-paid, suitable, self-respecting work to all who can, is wanted at once. 'Too little and too late' need not always be our motto!

The danger of delay

The present moment, I repeat, is dangerous from the very fact that our hearts are warm with gratitude to these sufferers. We look round and see that for the time being they all are, or can be, provided for; the demand for the maimed exceeds, as one might say, the supply. But look forward! Ah! there's the rub – we are not good at looking forward! The British nose is short, and it would seem we seldom see beyond it. 'Tiens! Une montagne!' We are always riding up, and knocking our noses against, mountains that we never dreamed were there! It is a national habit that may help to foster a light-hearted tenacity in the able-bodied, but will hardly assure the well-being of those who have lost limbs, or sight, or the power of movement, for their country. They have a right to ask that we do not leave the dark mountain of their future unobserved until our noses crash into it.

Some say: 'All provision for sufferers by the war ought to be purely a State matter.' It is not so simple as all that. In the sense that the State must satisfy itself that the scheme of relief is coherent, large enough, practical, without waste or overlapping – yes! But, with that proviso, I for one would much rather see scope given to individual initiative and generosity than see it all fall under a deadening bureaucratic control. Personal sympathy, personal enthusiasm is the essence of a contract that has for its aim the support of men's spirits as well as – nay, more than – the support of what is left of their bodies. The State should lie behind, with its ultimate guarantee; but we individuals who have one and all benefited by these sacrifices would be eager to give such money and service as will keep this a work of love, not a mere institutional business, officially administered out of grudged rates and taxes.

The other day I was taken over 'The Lord Roberts Memorial Work-shops' in the Fulham Road. This is a queer world of ours – in those workshops men who have been through hell and left part of themselves behind are making toys, and the toys are remaking them. It seemed to me the most steadily busy place I was ever in, and I think the most hopeful.

Nothing keeps regret away like work. They work their fifty hours a week at the fair wages of the trade – no sweating, no undercutting; and in the first eight months they have made a net profit. The works has already been described much better and more exactly than I can do it; I only want to say that it struck me as the very thing wanted. We could not do better – it seems to me – than assist 'The Lord Roberts Memor-ial' Committee to carry out their scheme of establishing these workshops all over the country, with canteens and recreation rooms attached, on such a scale that, however many of the partially disabled the tides of this war cast up, not one hereafter, in the most bitter times of bad trade and unemployment, may be able to say with truth: 'I want a decent job, and can't get one.' But for this there would seem to be two essentials: The guarantee of enough Government contracts for no matter how many maimed men may be employed and sufficient money from the public to acquire and equip the necessary number of these workshops, which, once set on their feet, will pay their way. This means a great sum, and those of us who would be up and doing, to safeguard the well-being of our maimed, both now and in the far more difficult years to come, can give to 'The Lord Roberts Memorial Workshops' Fund, 122 Brompton Road, London, S.W., with, I think, perfect certainty that every penny brings aid and security to those who deserve more than we can ever do for them. 'Hope springs eternal,' they say, and so does pluck in British men. Give them but a chance, and they will make their lives as useful as they were before war scorched their wings. It is only natural to admire those who struggle on bravely against the odds. It is our privilege to help them.

4

Re-made or marred: a great national duty

Galsworthy wrote this essay in late September 1916, shortly after he donated his family home to the Red Cross for use as a hospital and shortly before he departed for France to serve as a volunteer at Hôpital Bénévole for rheumatic and neurasthenic soldiers. Appearing originally in *The Times* on 14 October and again in *A Sheaf*, this piece is notable for revealing Galsworthy's engagement in the contemporary debate about the Ministry of Pensions Act, which eventually established a single depart-ment – the Ministry of Pensions – to administer both military and naval war pensions. In 1917 an abbreviated version of this essay appeared in two local American newspapers, namely the *Adams County Union–Republican* of Corning, Iowa (on 24 and 31 January 1917 as well as on 14 February) and the *New Castle News* of New Castle, Pennsylvania (on 23 November 1917). These appearances point to Galsworthy's emerging international reputation as an advocate for the war wounded.

Time and the war go on and the thousands of our sick and wounded come flowing back to us to be re-made or – marred.

Does the nation realize that this great problem is still not being tack-led as a whole, is still hung up between diverse opinions? And does the nation understand that on what is decided within the next few weeks hangs the future civic usefulness and contentment of thousands on thousands of lives? Has it realized that under the system at present adopted the future civic utility of very many has already been jeopard-ized or lost? For the present system seems to be this: – Refit the man for the Army as quickly and as well as you can. If he can't be refitted for the Army, pension and discharge him at once.

But this is a national *not* merely an Army problem. If it remains simply an Army problem, our towns and countrysides, when the war is over, will be plastered for the next twenty and thirty years with well-nigh useless men, a burden to themselves, and to us all – men to whom we ought in gratitude to have given every chance and shall have given next to none. 'No good for a soldier any more; then dismiss him with so many shillings a week!' Is it what the country wants?

I take it the country wants two things. To rescue for each of these brave fellows as decent, self-respecting, happy a life as ever it can; and to secure for itself the civic and industrial usefulness of every possible citizen. To discharge disabled soldiers before all that is possible has been done for them, rescues nothing, either for the man or State. On the contrary, it fills a hero's cup, perhaps for ever, with incapacity, dejection and insecurity; it fills the cup of the State to overflowing with useless citizens. This waste of national material is a tragedy of the future, and in our country the future has frequently had to take care of itself.

Control of hospital patients

Let me not be misunderstood. Machinery exists, elaborate, careful, in many ways admirable, under the Statutory Committee appointed by the Government, for assisting disabled soldiers after their discharge – though, I believe, it is not yet actually at work. It will start, if I may say so, fatally handicapped. To retain control of the patient, so that his treatment may be coherent and sustained, seems to be of the very essence of what can be done for the future of most of these men. Such control, limited already by the simple fact that the State would never want to undertake unnecessary trouble and expense, will require, of course, careful safeguarding and delimitation; but without it the battle of rescue is as good as lost.

The practice of the French may, so far as I can discover, is be summed up thus: – 'Discharge from the Army is now habitually adjourned until all possible benefit from physiotherapy has been secured.' With us, wonderful things are being done by the State to restore men to the Army, to re-make them into soldiers; but nothing coherent is, up to now, being done by the State, before it parts with control, to restore men to civil life – useful and contented citizens. There are doubtless administrative difficulties. There is a question of money; but for what is vital to the State the State can pay. And vital it is that the most huge calamity of this war shall be divested of every consequence which foresight and ingenuity can strip away. Not all discharged men, of course, need refitting for civil life – there are some whom refitting cannot serve; but for the great majority it is essential. The disablement is so various; eighteen categories exist. Think what that means in the diversity of treatment required. This is no mere question of orthopaedics, of mending and restoring limbs. That is but one very wonderful and inspiring part of the problem. Neither is it a mere question of physical training, and what is called functional re-education, though there, too, miracles can be wrought. Nor, again, is it a mere question of what is called professional re-education. It is a question of all these being coherently, systematically, and for long enough applied. But beyond all it is a question of the man you put in charge of this whole regenerating process, of getting commandants and instructors – civil or military, no matter which, so long as they are the right sort – who can infuse hope and faith, as well as strength, into the disabled under their control. In short, the re-making of these victims for civil life is at least as much a question of spirit as of body. It takes time, wisdom, understanding and sustained effort. It cannot be effected piecemeal, by spasmodic doses. The moment has come for the State to take hold and to do a work which it alone can adequately accomplish. Every man who is discharged, without being first re-made so far a possible, goes back to civil life half beaten. The half-beaten man is soon done for altogether and becomes a ghost to haunt us all. Consider what it will mean to the thousands of these poor fellows – not at once, but a few years hence – pushed out everywhere, loafing on their pensions, driven into institutions – men to whom we now doff our hats and profess our gratitude, whom we praise and pet and assure that they will never be forgotten. Not such lip-service and promises, but a proper refitting in body before they go forth again into civil life, is their right.

The phase before discharge

Experience shows that wonders of retrieval can be wrought, physically, by the new discoveries of science; spiritually, by inspiration, encouragement and appeal. Our soldiers have shown that they possess inexhaustible reserves of fortitude in battle and the long endurance of hardship and wounds. The problem is to rouse again that fortitude – in very different circumstances, in cold blood, when glamour is dying – for the facing of their future. Handicapped they will be, anyway; we ought to make that handicap as light as possible. Monetary help alone is not enough.

STAR & GARTER HOME
for
TOTALLY DISABLED SOLDIERS AND SAILORS
PATRONS: H.M. THE QUEEN & H.M. QUEEN ALEXANDRA

Haven

You can never repay these utterly broken men. But you can show your gratitude by helping to build this Home,where they will be tenderly cared for during the rest of their lives.

LET EVERY WOMAN SEND WHAT SHE CAN TO-DAY to the Lady Cowdray, Hon. Treasurer, The British Women's Hospital Fund, 21 Old Bond Street, W

Special Reproductions of the Cartoon, 2|6 and 1|-, can be obtained at above address, or, Postage and Packing free, 2|10 and 1|2

Figure 39 Poster, 'Mr. Punch's appeal for the Star & Garter Fund' of the Star & Garter Home for Totally Disabled Soldiers and Sailors, which Galsworthy supported through his authorship of 'Re-made or marred: a great national duty'. (Library of Congress)

Looking ahead, one sees with horror the thousands 'on the beach'; the thousands most of whom we might have kept – may still keep – 'off the beach', if we do what we ought for them, and give them not only a pension, but strength, hope, and the chance of a fresh start. They may get jobs right now – jobs which they will have no chance of keeping when they have to meet the competition of millions returning to civil life. On what will they then fall back? Pension and complete freedom at once is a tremendous lure. The extra weeks or months of sustained treatment needed to give them what they will never else regain seem intolerable to those already weary of discipline and hospital. But how much more intolerable to them will be the years 'on the beach'! Few would refuse the chance if they could only realize what a vast difference a thorough refitting and a fair start must make to the rest of their lives.

But one thing is certain. Whether refitting be made compulsory or not, it is the duty and the interest of the State to offer it to all disabled soldiers before discharging them into civil life. There are two phases in this problem of rescue – the phase of re-making the man to the utmost before discharge; and the phase of securing after discharge the best national machinery to ensure that no honest man disabled or weakened by the war – no matter how hard times may become – and they will become very hard – shall be able to say with truth, 'I want a job, and can't get one.' Both are vital. But it is to the first phase – the phase before discharge – that the words here written draw attention.

Let not the shadow of a vast neglect dog our victory! Let it not be cynically said of us hereafter that we devoted all our science and good will to the task of making men, already wounded for us, fit to serve again and be perhaps re-wounded or killed for us; yet gave no science or good will to requite their sacrifice by restoring them what we could of life. Let not that be said!

5

The need for reality

Recalling Galsworthy's first-hand observations of French rehabilitation centres as he offered thoughts on voluntary versus compulsory retraining programmes, 'The need for reality' was published initially in an unillustrated format in the summer 1917 issue of the British *War Pensions Gazette* and it was reprinted shortly thereafter in the *American Journal of Care for Cripples*. In April 1918, it appeared in the Canadian journal *Reconstruction*, entitled 'Galsworthy sounds warning', with illustrations of occupational therapy and vocational training being undertaken in Canadian institutions. In August 1918 it appeared again in America – this time illustrated and retitled 'The need for reality: consider what will happen five or ten years from now' – in *Carry on: A Magazine on the Reconstruction of Disabled Soldiers and Sailors*, which was edited by the Office of the Surgeon General of the United States Army and published by the American Red Cross. Three photographs accompanied this version of the piece. The first depicted disabled American soldiers at Fort McHenry, Baltimore, Maryland, learning the 'profitable trade' of automotive mechanics; the second, disabled Canadian soldiers on a farm in Calgary, Alberta, learning how to operate a tractor; and the third, the Office of the Surgeon General of the US Army, Washington, DC. With their accompanying text by Galsworthy, these images helped to underscore his international reputation as an advocate for the war wounded.

In France, last winter and early spring, I saw several establishments for the professional re-education of the disabled French soldier, and put this question to their directors: 'Your system being voluntary, to what degree do you find men availing themselves of it?'

The gist of the answers was 'Not many came at first, but gradually more and more, till now perhaps we get one-half to two-thirds.' At La Maison Blanche, near Paris, which draws its men from a single hospital of 700, I found that – whereas when Sir Henry Norman paid his visit last autumn 270 were in process of training – 400 were in training when I paid my visit this March; 130 of the others did not need professional re-education, and the remaining 170 refused. The advance in the numbers training was obtained by continual propaganda at the hospital which fed the establishment.

Now if, in France, we estimate the proportion of those who, in the long run, for one reason or another, refuse to avail themselves of professional re-education, at even only one-fourth, the French are still going to have amongst them, in the future, a large number of men who will be almost dead weight industrially, and burdens to themselves into the bargain. True, the Frenchman is by nature an individualist as the Briton; moreover, he is quicker in the 'up-take', and more impressionable. Further, he is much less naturally improvident and careless of the morrow, and I think he has more pride.

Jobs easy to get now

What then is going to happen in England where our system is also voluntary? What proportion of disabled men will avail themselves of the chances offered? And what proportion will pass by this more promising scheme, and step out into the jobs that for the moment await almost anyone, in these days of scarce labour? There's the crux that may spill our effort. I should say that a good half will refuse their chances, and we shall find ourselves in the end with more dead weight even that the French, unless we can devise special means against this disaster.

We have to convince the disabled that to be re-educated not only physically but professionally is absolutely essential to them against a future which, fat enough for the moment, is going in a few years' time to be very lean and hard; and for men handicapped as they will be, simply impossible except for charity, which one imagines is the last thing they want.

It can't be said too often that the situation while the war lasts is utterly misleading. All civilians now feel grateful and want to pet and serve the wounded soldier. Labour is hard to find, so that anyone – even the handicapped – can get a job.

Ten years hence

All that will have gone by the time the war has been from five to ten years in its grave. Most of our disabled soldiers have thirty, forty, or fifty years before them. The man who slips his chance now, and trusts to luck and gratitude, will find himself on a beach where he will get more kicks than ha'pence ten years hence. It is absolutely natural that he who is sick of discipline and hospitals should want to get back to ordinary civil life without any intermediate period of hostels and attendance at training schools and so forth under a sort of discipline. I should myself, and so would any of us who write, wisely or foolishly, about these matters. I should hate to be hung-up another six or eight months, or maybe a year, learning a new job, when there are jobs that don't want learning waiting for me round the corner, especially if I had done my bit and felt that those who hadn't ought to keep me in comfort for the rest of my days. And if anyone came along and said to me: 'My man, how magnificent your patriotism has been in the war! I'm sure that you'll like to continue to be patriotic now that you are maimed, and serve your country nobly in the future as in the past, by making yourself efficient, instead of being lost to the industrial life of your native land!' Well – I should want to get up, and say 'Cant!' and smite him in the eye.

A natural attitude

When you have just lost a limb for the benefit of your country you cannot be expected to be precisely in the mood to appreciate talk about patriotism and all the rest of it, from those who haven't lost limbs. *No, if I were a maimed soldier, I could only be persuaded to get a special training by being shown convincingly that if I didn't, it was going to be the worse for me.*

We are all, soldiers included, inclined to forget in these roaring times of war the dour and dire struggle for existence that obtains in the so-called piping times of peace. Our pensions may be liberal, as pensions go, but they are not enough to live on – much less support a family, and the trouble is this: A few years hence, when people have begun to hate the memory of a war which will have made the struggle for existence harder, the universal feeling towards the maimed soldier will become: 'Well, he's got his pension, that ought to be enough. Besides, he had his opportunity to get training for special employment, and he didn't take it. Life's much too hard nowadays for sentiment – they much run their chances now with the rest of us, in fair competition.' We know what that means – the weakest go to the wall. A few years hence the maimed soldier will only be secure against an uncertain and perhaps miserable future, if he is not among the weakest.

Fogs the issue

I should say, speaking like a fool perhaps, that the only people capable of persuading the maimed soldier, for his own sake, to make his future position so strong as ever he can, are those who know what the life of labour is like in bad times, are not mealy-mouthed, and will put the thing bluntly in its naked grim reality. Just now we wrap things up with all sorts of natural and well-meant verbiage, about heroism and gratitude and never forgetting: this doesn't help – on the contrary, it fogs the issue, and endangers the future of those whom we want to make secure. The time has come for blunt speaking to the maimed soldier by people who know how hard life and human nature are, and how short our memories.

I can see this most promising scheme languishing into futility because the Briton will not look ahead, and must run his nose right up against a thing before he can realize it's there. I can see thousands of our maimed turning this scheme down with a shrug, and the words: 'Oh! that's all right! I'm not worrying. Some day, perhaps!' That 'some day' is not likely to come at all unless it comes at once, in hospital or as soon as a man leaves hospital.

6

Kitchener Houses: occupation and convalescence

The *Times* published this appeal by Galsworthy on 19 April 1917. A slightly abbreviated version – entitled 'Kitchener House for wounded sailors and soldiers' – appeared as the introduction to a publicity leaflet produced by Kitchener House in 1918. In his original draft, Galsworthy stated that 'The Red Cross will be ready, to some extent, with monetary help [to establish and maintain Kitchener House]'. However, unwillingness on the part of Red Cross officials to commit funds to the enterprise forced Galsworthy to remove this statement. The final version appears here. Significantly, Galsworthy did not give up on the effort to expand the Kitchener House scheme. As late as June 1917, he continued to press the Red Cross to support a Kitchener House for officers, and documents of the War Office – specifically its 1919, 1920 and 1921 editions of *Funds, Associations, and Societies, &c., for the Assistance of Officers and Men and their Dependants* – suggest that his efforts were successful, noting that a Kitchener House for convalescent officers could be found in 34 Grosvenor Place, London.

Kitchener House – credit for which is entirely due to its Honorary Secretary, that devoted American lady, Miss Heyneman – was an experiment. It has been running over a year, and, within its scope, may be acclaimed a success.

The object of Kitchener House, to put it crudely, if not rudely, was to fight what one may call the 'hospital look'. This look is not the fault of the hospitals, but everybody knows it on the faces of our men – a sort of apathy, the look of a mind inevitably divested of mental initiative by long spells of hospital life. To see it on face after face of the bravest and cheeriest souls on earth goes to the heart. Occupation, something to bite on, something more than the strolling in the streets, the outing to revue, play, or well-intentioned tea-party, is the only remedy for this lethargy, this mental fungus.

We are learning to spray our potatoes; we have not yet learned to spray the minds of our wounded soldiers. And we and they are going to regret it bitterly in the years to come. Kitchener House, which is under the auspices of the Red Cross, and follows to some extent the lines of California House, long run by Miss Heyneman for Belgian soldiers, is a club for wounded soldiers and sailors (not officers), with a recreation room where are papers to read, writing things, piano, gramophone, bagatelle board, &c.; a dining room where lunch and tea are served, and several rooms where classes are carried on. Every man is welcomed, and the utmost possible done to transport the seriously disabled to and from hospital.

At present the classes given are: – Commercial classes (accounts, short-hand, typewriting, bookkeeping, elements of business routine); arts and crafts department (picture-frame and screenmaking, including carpentry, gilding, etc.); languages (French; also Spanish, Italian and Dutch, by arrangement; music; inlaying wood-carving, and metal-work; book-binding; embroidery; and small crafts department (basket and soft bag making, fretsaw, knitting). Men who are in hospital long enough and can come often have here a serious chance to get into the swing of a new calling, or to learn a language; but the main object is just occupation for the mind during the long blank time in hospital.

We have not yet sufficiently realized that a man's body heals much faster when his mind and spirit are kept from rusting. True recuperation is mental just as much as it is bodily. The more one sees, the more one is convinced that these years of military life which practically the whole nation has now to undergo, followed in hundreds of thousands of cases by many months in hospital, are going to have a most disastrous effect on the mental activity of a people whose mental activity is not its strong point. Anything which can be done to mitigate the evil ought to be done. I know that many hospitals have valiant workers attached, who do their best to stimulate and interest the minds of the men; but I know, too, that most of them find hospital 'atmosphere' – the sense of arrested growth, of hopeless waiting – far too strong for them, and are breaking their hearts over the job. The stimulus must be applied outside hospital, not within. And I suggest that the best, perhaps the only, change is afforded by recreational and occupational clubs such as Kitchener House.

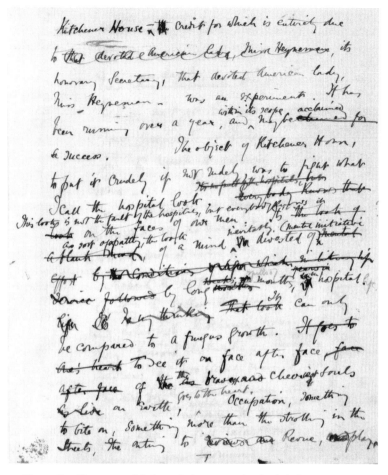

Figure 40 First page of Galsworthy's manuscript for 'Kitchener Houses: occupation and convalescence'. (Collection of Steve Forbes © all rights reserved. Image by Richard Holttum)

As chairman of its Executive Committee I urge people of good will all over the country to follow the lead of this experiment, and establish Kitchener Houses at once in their various districts – clubs to which soldiers in hospital may go, and find recreation, occupation, and stimulus for their minds, and often a new direction in civil life when it comes to them once more. It must be done now, or not all; for it is full late.

Arrangements are already being made for one at Bethnal Green. General Goodwin has promised that hospital authorities shall give all facilities their power. The Pensions Ministry welcome the effort. Printed suggestions for any who wish to start a Kitchener House can be obtained from the Hon. Secretary, Kitchener House, 8 Cambridge Gate, Regent's Park, London, N.W. 1.

The fungus spreads apace. Its growth can be checked. Why not try?

7

The sacred work

Galsworthy wrote 'The sacred work' during the spring of 1918 upon request of the Ministry of Pensions for the official proceedings of the second annual inter-allied conference and exhibition on the after-care of disabled men. Those proceedings appeared shortly after the event, 'The sacred work' serving as the foreword to the HMSO publication. This original version is reprinted here. During the final months of the war the essay appeared in America as 'So comes the sacred work' in the *American Journal of Care for Cripples*, and as 'The stricken' in *The Living Age*. After the war, Galsworthy included his original version of 'The sacred work' in *Another Sheaf*. On 20 June 1920 a substantially abbreviated version of the piece, including chiefly the first paragraph, appeared in America in the *Oakland Tribune* of Oakland, California, as 'a touchstone for highlighting the contemporary investigation by the education committee of the House of Representatives of the Federal Board for the Rehabilitation of Disabled Soldiers'. That body was accused of 'neglect, incompetency, [and] indifference' in executing its mission. Significantly, while the editors of the *Oakland Tribune* used this landmark composition to help their readers *remember* those who were disabled in the war, Galsworthy soon thereafter excluded this piece, among his many others related to disabled soldiers, from the Manaton Edition of his collected works, in his own effort to *forget* the conflict and the human damage it wrought.

The Angel of Peace, watching the slow folding back of this darkness, will look on an earth of cripples. The field of the world is strewn with half-living men. That loveliness which is the creation of the aesthetic

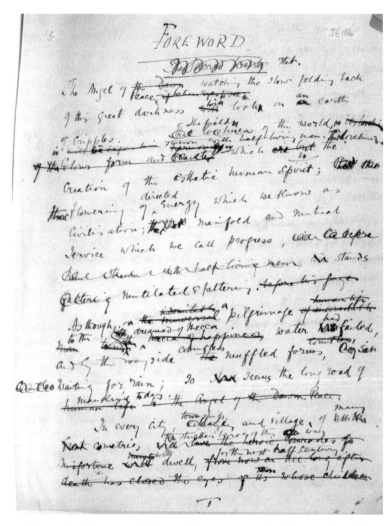

Figure 41 First page of Galsworthy's manuscript for 'The sacred work'.
(Collection of Steve Forbes © all rights reserved. Image by Richard Holttum)

human spirit; that flowering of directed energy which we know as civilisation; that manifold and mutual service which we call progress – all stand mutilated and faltering. As though, on a pilgrimage to the dreamed-of Mecca, water had failed, and by the wayside countless muffled forms sat waiting for rain; so will the long road of mankind look tomorrow.

In every township and village of our countries stricken heroes of the war will dwell for the next half-century. The figure of Youth must go one-footed, one-armed, blind of an eye, lesioned and stunned, in the home where it once danced. The half of a generation can never again step into the sunlight of full health and the priceless freedom of unharmed limbs.

So comes the sacred work

For what Youth has done, for what it will yet do before the long gale blows away over sea and sky, shall not Youth be praised for ever? Can there be limit to the effort of gratitude? Niggardliness and delay in restoring all of life that can be given back is sin against the human spirit, a smear on the face of honour.

Love of country, which, like some little secret lamp, glows in every heart, hardly to be seen of our eyes when the world is at peace – love of the old, close things, the sights, sounds, scents we have known from birth; loyalty to our fathers' deeds and our fathers' hopes; the clutch and kiss of Motherland – this love sent our soldiers and sailors forth to the long endurance, to the doing of such deeds, and the bearing of so great and evil a pain as can never be told. The countries for which they have dared and suffered have now to play their part.

I have seen those countries – nearly all – and something from each of special charm or wonder lingers yet in memory. Only the son of his country knows the hidden heart of her; but for the eager stranger other lands have faces and voices which tell him odd truths, show him grave beauties.

France! The country of the long romance! Who can see France and not love her – the land with the mysterious smile, with the clear thoughts and the gay, unconquerable, self-seeing spirit? France, the eternal type of Mother-country – she surely will not fail her sons who serve and suffer. Italy, whom the gods love, and chose, I think, for the land where Beauty should be embalmed for ever, so that man might look on it age after age and drink of inspiration – she will not forget again the lives of her wounded children with the hope of usefulness. And the Little

Country, trodden and ravished – none in the world had quite her teeming energy – she will be last of all to let the stricken go down their days of strength and interest.

And all our own far sister lands, having each her special flower of promise; having, all, the clear eyes and adventuring hearts of the young. To their pride of new race it will seem intolerable that their best and bravest should go starved of help and opportunity. Sooner would an Arab's hospitality fail than the free-masonry of the new worlds neglect their maimed heroes! And India, the wonder-land. She, too, will care for her children.

And this Britain of ours! Shall the work of restoration fail with us? Unthinkable! The draft will be honoured, the debt paid, so far as such a debt can be repaid.

America, too, I know, new as yet to this conflict and the wreckage thereof. Of that great, warm-hearted nation I prophesy deeds of restoration, most eager, most complete of all.

The conscience of to-day is burdened with a load well-nigh unbearable. Each hour of the sacred work unloads a little of this burden.

The Conference in Paris last year, and this Conference in London, were summoned that the countries who stand shoulder to shoulder in the fight may stand shoulder to shoulder also in the taste of remedy, profiting by each other's success, avoiding each other's failures; that the whole field of recovery may be surveyed; the holy purpose of this crusade of healing be fortified in the hearts of all who serve; and a sign made manifest to the peoples of each country that the debt due is remembered. To lift up the man who has been stricken on the battlefield, restore him to the utmost health and agility, give him an adequate pension, and re-equip him with an occupation suited to the forces left him – that is a process which does not cease till the sufferer fronts the future keen, hopeful and secure. And such restoration is at least as much a matter of spirit as of body. Consider what it means to fall suddenly out of full vigour into the dark certainty that you can never have full strength again, though you live on twenty, forty, sixty years. Though you have the soul of a hero, the flag of your courage may well be down half-mast! Apathy – that creeping nerve disease – is soon your bedfellow and the companion of your walks. A curtain has fallen before your vision; your eyes no longer range. The Russian 'Nichevo' – the 'what-does-it-matter?' mood – besets you. Fate seems to say to you: 'Take the line of least resistance, friend – you are done for!' But the sacred work says to Fate: 'Retro Satanas!'[1] This comrade of ours is not your puppet. He shall yet live as happy and as useful – if not active – a life as he ever lived before. Do your worst; you shall not crush him! We shall tend him from clearing station to his last hospital better than wounded soldier has ever yet been tended. In special hospitals, orthopaedic, paraplegic, neurasthenic, we shall give him back functional ability, solidity of nerve or lung. The flesh torn away, the lost sight, the broken ear-drum, the destroyed nerve, it is true, we cannot give back; but we shall so re-create and fortify the rest of him that he shall leave hospital ready for a new career. Then we shall teach him how to tread the road of it, so that he fits again into the national life, becomes once more a workman with pride in his work, a stake in the country, and the consciousness that, handicapped though he be, he runs the race level with his fellows, and is by that so much the better man than they. And beneath the feet of this new workman we shall put the firm plank of a pension. The sacred work fights the creeping dejections which lie in wait for each soul and body, for the moment stricken and thrown. It says to Fate: 'You shall not pass!'

And the greatest obstacle with which it meets is the very stoicism and nonchalance of the sufferer. To the Anglo-Saxon, especially, those precious qualities are dangerous. That horse, taken to the water, will too seldom drink. Indifference to the future has a certain lovability, but it is hardly a virtue when it makes of its owner a weary drone, eking out a pension with odd jobs. The sacred work is vitally concerned to defeat this hand-to-mouth philosophy. Side by side in man, and especially in Anglo-Saxon, there live two creatures. One of them lies on his back and smokes; the other runs a race; now one, now the other, seems to be the whole man. The sacred work has for its end to keep the runner on his feet; to proclaim the nobility of running. A man will do for Mankind or for his Country what he will not do for himself; but Mankind marches on, and Countries live and grow, and need our services in peace no less than in war. Drums do not beat, the flags hang furled, in time of peace; but a quiet music is ever raising its call to service. He who in war has flung himself, without thought of self, on the bayonet and braved a hail of bullets often does not hear that quiet music. It is the business of the sacred work to quicken his ear to it. Of little use to man or nation would be the mere patching-up of bodies, so that, like a row of old gossips against a sunlit wall, our disabled might sit and weary out their days. If that were all we could do for them, gratitude is proven fraudulent, device bankrupt; and the future of our countries must drag with a lame foot.

It seems, to one who has watched, rather from outside, that restoration worthy of that word will only come if the minds of all engaged in the sacred work are always fixed on this central truth: 'Body and spirit are inextricably conjoined; to heal the one without the other is impossible.' If a man's mind, courage and interest be enlisted in the cause of his own salvation, healing goes on apace, the sufferer is remade. If not, no mere surgical wonders, no careful nursing, will avail to make a man of him again. Therefore I would say: 'From the moment he enters hospital, look after his mind and his will; give them food; nourish them in subtle ways, increase that nourishment as his strength increases. Give him interest in his future; light a star for him to fix his eyes on. So that, when he steps out of hospital, you shall not have to begin to train one who for months, perhaps years, has been living, mindless and will-less, the life of a half-dead creature.'

That this is a hard task none who knows hospital life can doubt.

That it needs special qualities and special effort quite other than the average range of hospital devotion, is obvious. But it saves time in the end, and without success is more than doubtful. The crucial period is the time spent in hospital; use that period to re-create not only body, but mind and will-power, and all shall come out right; neglect to use it thus, and the heart of many a sufferer, and of many a would-be healer, will break from sheer discouragement.

The sacred work is not departmental; it is one long organic process from the moment when a man is picked up from the field of battle to the moment when he is restored to the ranks of full civil life. Our eyes must not be fixed merely on this stressful present, but on the world as it will be ten years hence. I see that world gazing back, like a repentant drunkard at his own debauch, with a sort of horrified amazement and disgust. I see it impatient of any reminiscence of this hurricane; hastening desperately to recover what it enjoyed before life was wrecked and pillaged by these blasts of death. Hearts, which now swell with pity and gratitude when our maimed soldiers pass the streets, will, from sheer familiarity, and through natural shrinking from reminder, be dried to a stony difference. 'Let the dead past bury its dead' is a saying terribly true, and perhaps essential to the preservation of mankind. The world of ten years hence will shrug its shoulders if it sees maimed and *useless* men crawling the streets of its day, like winter flies on a window pane.

It is for the sacred work to see that there shall be no winter flies. A niche of usefulness and self-respect exists for every man, however handicapped; but that niche must be found for him. To carry the process of restoration to a point short of this is to leave the cathedral without spire.

Of the men and women who have this work in hand I have seen enough – in France and in my own country, at least – to know their worth, and the selfless idealism which animates them. Their devotion, courage, tenacity, and technical ability are beyond question or praise. I would only fear that in the hard struggle they experience to carry each day's work to its end, to perfect their own particular jobs, all so important and so difficult, vision of the whole fabric they are helping to raise must often be obscured. And I would venture to say: 'Only by looking upon each separate disabled soldier as the complete fabric can you possibly keep that vision before your eyes. Only by revivifying in each separate disabled soldier the *will to live*, can you save him from the fate of merely continuing to exist.'

There are wounded men, many, whose spirit is such that they will march in front of any effort made for their recovery. I well remember one of these – a Frenchman – nearly paralysed in both legs. All day long he would work at his 'macramé,' and each morning, after treatment, would demand to try and stand. I can see his straining efforts now, his eyes like the eyes of a spirit; I can hear his daily words: '*Il me semble que j'ai un pen, plus de force dans mes jambes ce matin, Monsieur!*' though, I fear, he never had. Men of such indomitable initiative, though not rare, are but a fraction. The great majority have rather the happy-go-lucky soul. For them it is only too easy to postpone self-help till sheer necessity drives, or till someone in whom they believe inspires them. The work of re-equipping these with initiative, with a new interest in life, with work which they can do, is one of infinite difficulty and complexity. Nevertheless, it must be done.

The Great Publics of our Countries do not yet, I think, see that they too have their part in the sacred work. So far they only seem to feel: 'Here's a wounded hero; let's take him to the movies, and give him tea!' Instead of choking him with cheap kindness, each member of the public should seek to re-inspire the disabled man with the feeling that he is no more out of the main stream of life than they are themselves; and each, according to his or her private chances, should help him to find that special niche which he can best, most cheerfully, and most usefully fill in the long future.

The more we drown the disabled in tea and lip gratitude the more we unsteel his soul, and the harder we make it for him to win through when, in the years to come, the wells of our tea and gratitude have dried up. We can do a much more real and hopeful thing. I fear that there will soon be no one of us who has not some personal friend disabled. Let us regard that man as if he were ourselves; let us treat him as one who demands a full place in the ranks of working life, and try to find it for him.

In such ways alone will come a new freemasonry to rebuild this ruined temple of our day. The ground is rubbled with stones – fallen, and still falling. Each must be replaced; freshly shaped, cemented, and morticed in, that the whole may once more stand firm and fair. In good time, to a clearer sky than we are fortunate enough to look on, our Temple shall rise again. The birds shall not long build in its broken walls, nor lichens moss it. The winds shall not long play through these now jagged windows, nor will the rain drift in, nor moonlight fill it with ghosts and shadows. To the glory of man we will stanchion, and raise and roof it anew.

Each comrade who for his Motherland, for the moment, lost his future is a miniature of that shattered Temple.

To restore him, and with him the future of our countries, that is the sacred work.

Note

1 'Go back, Satan.'

8

The gist of the matter

'The gist of the matter', 'Looking ahead' and 'Spirit and letter' – appearing, respectively, here and in Chapters 9 and 10 – represent the complete body of non-fiction that Galsworthy contributed to *Reveille*, the Ministry of Pensions journal he edited and which succeeded *Recalled to Life*, edited by Lord Charnwood. 'The gist of the matter' appeared initially in the first issue of *Reveille*, dated August 1918. This original version is reproduced below complete with footnotes and a remarkable quantitative illustration of the text. An abbreviated version of this original text – including photographs of American disabled soldiers – was published in the January 1919 issue of *Carry on*. 'Looking ahead' appeared in the second issue of *Reveille*, dated November 1918. 'Spirit and letter' appeared in the third and final issue of *Reveille*, dated February 1919. The original versions of these essays, like 'The gist of the matter', appear here.

'Reveille' is the new name of the quarterly *Recalled to Life*, a review of all that is being done for the disabled sailor and soldier; and the hand writing these words that of its new editor. When Lord Charnwood, to whom we pay a grateful tribute for his unselfish efforts and courtesy, laid down his stewardship, it seemed that a phase had ended, the time come for a fresh departure. The field of information had, in a sense, been covered, for those directly concerned, in the three numbers of *Recalled to Life*; and the quarterly was beginning to fall between two stools. Its substance was too technical for the Public, and not perhaps technical enough for the experts. The faults of *Reveille* we shall discover in the due time. Its aims at being human, so there will be plenty.

The use of such a Review as this is to reveal what the work of restoration means, to those who are being restored, to those restoring them, but even more – to the nation at large. For only if the Public realizes the situation and the facts can we hope for success. Our object will be to animate all with comprehension of the full need of a work as sacred as ever taxed a great people; to stimulate effort, and not entirely to refrain from criticism.

We are very well aware that a certain practical and downright type of mind sees no use in any such attempt. 'Do the job, and don't bother to explain!' is his creed. With reverence for so business-like an attitude, we yet venture to think that there is some connection between motive and performance, demand and supply, and that before human endeavour will flower, the sap must run up the stem from a watered ground. You may have a lovely system carefully thought out; but, to make it work, the human material to which you would apply it must appreciate its necessity. And if the practical mean rejoins: 'But the Public isn't going to read *Reveille*; it won't have the smallest influence either on the mind of the disabled man or his friends, who only read the most popular journals,' we answer that there are ways of elevating a cat besides hanging him; nor is it ever safe to dogmatize about the formation of that most subtle creature, Public Opinion. Even if *Reveille* cannot hope to reach the million, it can at least knock at the doors of ardent spirits, each of whom forms the centre of an ever-widening circle of knowledge and goodwill. At all events, like the practical man we speak of, we can but do our job and trust to a Providence which recognizes that jobs are many and diverse, and concerned with the spirit no less than with the body.

The new title *Reveille* was chosen because, though we look as if our eyes are open, we are not awake; and because while Death still blows his bugle in those fields, we would blow a call against him. No need to remind a nation in arms that we pronounce and perhaps should now spell the word: Revelly.

And if the passionate or the gentler reader comes, in the pages of *Reveille*, on renowned names and items of mere Art and Literature, and, rubbing his eyes: 'What has this and that to do with the disabled soldier?' let him not thereby be discouraged and turn away in disgust; let him pardon a poor editor who never edited before, and thought perhaps they might amuse. And let him doggedly read on.

One thing more we would like known. Contributors to this Review profit not a penny thereby. They are rewarded only by the thought of giving for those whose lives have been risked and whose future is compromised for them.

While we write, the earth is at Spring – for the reader will remember that this is a quarterly, and aeons pass between brandishing the pen and reading the strokes thereof – that moment of Spring so beautiful, when the lilac is out and the fruit blossom not yet ready to fall. Every tree is dowered with young beauty, and no two the same. Last evening they stood against the sunset, magical and delicate, with pale-gold light between the curling quiet leaves; far away on the sky-line some elms had their topsails set; the birds had lost their senses, singing. In such moments this green Land of ours has incomparable beauty, seeming to promise happiness which can satisfy even the human heart. The thought of wounds, of disfigurement and blindness, of lost limbs, twisted limbs, the thousand and one bodily disasters which this war has brought, becomes unbearable unless we keep the hope and the will to give back to the wounded something of this Spring and of the Summer which Spring leads to. We do not hold that hope to be forlorn, nor that will for a waste of heat and purpose. All paths lead to Rome, they say. The roads along which a man, however handicapped, can trudge to happiness are as varied as the swallow-tracks on the sunlight over a buttercup field. For each man disabled in this war there is a way to usefulness, a happy niche to be discovered; for this is the first war since the world began which has seriously disturbed the conscience of mankind and set it working on the duties of active remorse and active gratitude.

What men think and believe attainable, is to be attained. A brave man, now blind, said to us the other day: 'The world's attitude to the blind, and the blind man's attitude to himself, has hitherto been formed by the whine of the blind beggar, which by the way meant so many more pennies in the blind man's cap. We know better nowadays. The blind man can be useful – and happy.' If *he* can be, so can the rest of the disabled.

Facile optimism and easy-going pessimism are alike roads to ruin. The man who says: 'It'll be all right on the night!' and he who remarks: 'Wot's the good of anyfink – why, nuffink!' are a light-hearted couple who will be found on the rocks together. Balance between vision and reality alone makes endeavour fruitful. And if – not being fools or children – we wish to give back to our disabled the utmost of health, utility, and joy, we must all see what we and they are up against, as well as scheme and dream of what they may become.

From the Sunday hush, as we write, it is borne in on us that man is still made for the Sabbath; and – quite candidly – there is always the

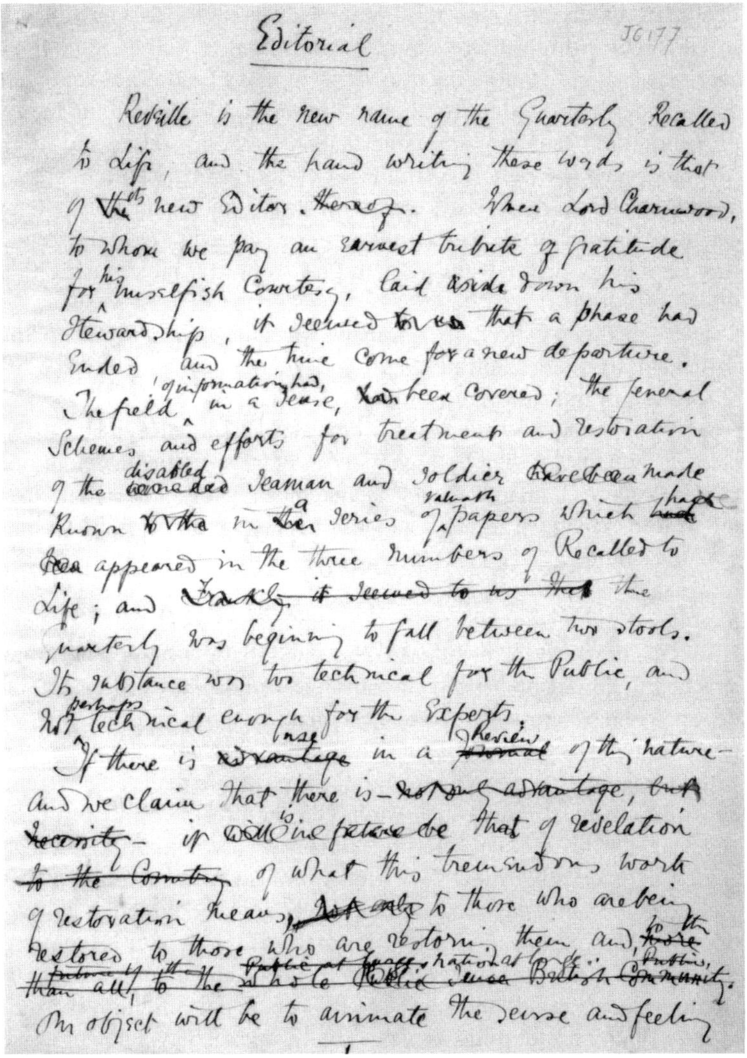

Editorial

JG177

Reveille is the new name of the Quarterly Recalled to Life, and the hand writing these words is that of ~~the~~ its new Editor ~~thereof~~. Since Lord Charnwood, to whom we pay an earnest tribute of gratitude for his unselfish courtesy, laid aside down his stewardship, it seemed ~~to us~~ that a phase had ended and the time come for a new departure. The field, of information had, in a sense, ~~has~~ been covered; the general schemes and efforts for treatment and restoration of the disabled ~~wounded~~ seaman and soldier ~~have been~~ made known ~~to the~~ in a ~~the~~ series of valuable papers which have ~~been~~ appeared in the three numbers of Recalled to Life; and ~~frankly it seemed to us that~~ the Quarterly was beginning to fall between two stools. Its substance was too technical for the Public, and perhaps not technical enough for the Experts.

If there is ~~advantage~~ use in a ~~Journal~~ Review of this nature – and we claim that there is – ~~not only advantage, but necessity~~ – it ~~will in the future be~~ is that of revelation ~~to the Country~~ of what this tremendous work of restoration means, ~~not only~~ to those who are being restored to those who are restoring them and, to the ~~Public at large~~ nation at large, ~~than all, to the whole Public sense British Community.~~

Our object will be to animate the sense and feeling

Figure 42 First page of Galsworthy manuscript for 'The gist of the matter'. (Collection of Steve Forbes © all rights reserved. Image by Richard Holttum) danger of the disabled man existing for the sake of the System which is to cure him. Administrators, aware of this danger, will endeavour by every means not to enfold the disabled man till he becomes as some lost soul wandering from door to door within the vast barrack of the House of Restoration. It is for him alone that the building exists, and in all his wanderings through its corridors on his journey back to civil life, he should be able to read, writ clear on the walls, the meaning and use of each step in the journey. He should never be allowed to have the feeling that he is being driven from pillar to post without, as it seems to him, design or purpose.

The early stages, from the moment when he is picked up on the battlefield, or the deck of his ship, to the moment when he finds himself in one of our homeland Military Hospitals, are clear enough. The trouble for him and for the System starts at the point when he begins to recover. Systems are wont to think in terms of facts and figures; wounded men in terms of human feeling. The System exists for a double purpose; the wounded man wishes it existed for one – to cure him, and – let him go. He is either: (1) Obviously returnable to the Army; (2) doubtfully returnable; (3) clearly returnable. For the first of these classes the System provides a most complete process of physical restoration in Military Hospitals, of which the orthopaedic hospitals[1] have curative workshops attached; followed by periods in convalescent hospitals and command depots. We have one general remark to make anent the process. By how much we remember that each man, though a soldier, and soon to be back with his regiment, is gifted with a mind which requires constant exercise and stimulus by so much shall we hasten the process of his recovery, and heighten his morale. The professional soldier, except in the high grades, is practically extinct. 'We are all civilians now,' a young officer said to us the other day. That should surely never be forgotten by anyone who takes part in the work of restoration. The System is bound to return to the Army or Navy every man it reasonably can, but it ought to attend to men's minds and spirits, so far as material conditions permit.

Cure is a matter of mind as well as body, and anxiety a potent cause of slow recovery. In all cases of men *doubtfully returnable* there would seem to be one golden rule: Cast the issue on the knees of the gods, and do the best you can for the *man*, lavishing on him every possible care, physical and mental, and remembering always this: Many a man would recover in his home surroundings, if freed at least temporarily from thought of return to the Army, who will never recover in hospital. In such borderland cases, both for the good of the Army and of the men, we think there might well be instituted some measure of discharge subject to periodic revision. We have known instances where the System's natural eagerness to return men to the Army has ended in utter frustration of that possibility.

But all men returnable are ultimately either returned to the Army or discharged. And it is the *definitely disabled* man – discharged or about to be discharged – who is the chief concern of this Review.

Editors, with any sense of humour, must always look on themselves askance, conscious that a professional omniscience is very wearisome. That is why we take you with a fleeting pen over facts perhaps familiar to you already. The disabled man falls into nineteen categories. (Figure 43).[2] While still awaiting discharge he continues to be treated in Military Hospitals, of many sorts, under the Director-General, General Goodwin, C.M.G. But on discharge he becomes subject to the Pensions Ministry for any further physical treatment, or training for civil life, which he consents to undergo; and, of course, to their control in all matters relating to his pension.[3] The further physical *treatment* of discharged men is carried on in special hospitals, institutions, colonies, or in annexes to the Military Orthopaedic hospitals, under the general control of Sir John Collie, M.D., C.M.G.[4] The *training* or re-education for civil life (under the Ministry of Pensions, co-operating with the Ministry of Labour) is in the hands of Local Committees, established by the Ministry of Pensions, under the general direction of Major Robert Mitchell, C.B.E.[5]

Such, in blunt outline, is the general scheme, which has reached a bold, and we believe a final shape, subject to improvement in detail. It is a colossal work, and each department has a Herculean task before it. To this scheme, for better or worse, the Country is committed and with a clear call, all hands and hearts are summoned to make it live. For there is an enormous lot yet to be done.

Up to May 31 last, 358,160 officers and men had been pensioned for disability; up to June 5, 38,480 were receiving or have received continued physical treatment, and only some 15,000 have taken or are taking retraining for civil life. It is not, of course, suggested that anything like all the discharged require either treatment or training, or both. But it is certain that a great proportion of them do. And none of us, least of all those responsible for the scheme, are satisfied with results, so far. A vast number of men were discharged before the present plans for continued physical treatment came into operation, but they have become merged in industry, and are most difficult to get hold of. Again, great numbers

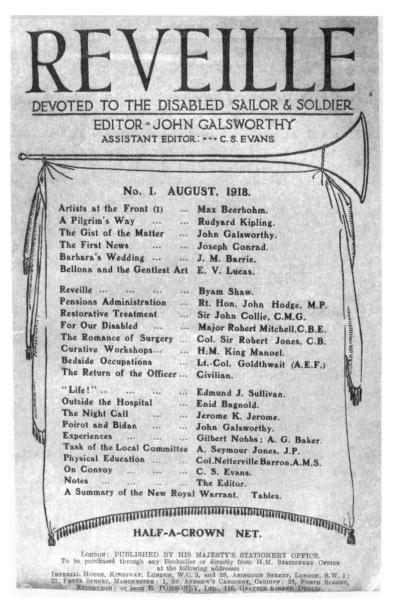

Figure 43   Reveille No. 1 (August 1918), edited by Galsworthy, in which his essay 'The gist of the matter' originally appeared. Only three issues of this popular and path-breaking journal appeared by the time Galsworthy resigned his editorship of the project. (Private collection. Image by the author)

of discharged men slipped away into the first jobs which came along, before the present retraining schemes for civil life were started, and of those who are now being discharged, only a small proportion are as yet coming forward to be taught special occupations in which they can be sure of keeping a foothold when the full tide of industrial competition runs in once more. Why?

Let the reader imagine that for one, two, or three years he has been cut off from his home folk and all those occupations, interests and amusement which made up for him the sum of life; that from morning to night he has done what he was told; that for long months together, perhaps, he has been confronted with the fires of hell; that for longer months he has lain in bed staring at a hole in the opposite wall, or trailed hospital and street, still under discipline, still without power or initiative to decide anything, still a number – haled here, haled there, fed like a child, amused like a child; suffering from paternalism and patronage; sitting in the parks with his eyes on nothing; blank of all definite expectation; provided with all material comforts and sunk in a sort of Capuan dream; or eating his heart out under a cheery, or at worst, an expressionless mask – let him imagine all this, and consider what he would do when his discharge comes. In his long-idle and cruelly-tried soul there would be no other impulse but to shake the dust of discipline off his feet, and make a bee-line for home. Whatever his state, bitterly in want perhaps of continued treatment and training for a new start in life, utterly incapable of making good in the future without this help, yet he cannot – you cannot expect him to – to stay and take it at once. A good long draught of home and freedom is his imperative demand; and when that is over, and he begins to own his soul again, he takes too often the line of least resistance.

Our friends, the Italians, have an invaluable specific against this. They make the man's discharge provisional on his returning to a training school for a month or six weeks, that he may be shown the process, and tempted to take the necessary training to secure his future. At the end of that time he may depart if he likes, but as a general rule he stays. Seeing the shape that our system has taken, there are now perhaps insurmountable difficulties in embodying this specific. But it seems a very great pity. For there is no blinking the fact that, at present, owing to lack of moral pressure on them at the right moment, our men are only coming forward for retraining in minimum numbers. Hospital life is an ideal foster-mother of lethargy, mental and physical. With few exceptions, the wounded man in hospital is rusting mentally; he is, automatically, encouraged thereto by every condition of his life – the lassitude left by severe strain, hardwork, and pain; the helplessness of his body; the monotony of the routine; the very care with which he is tended; his eagerness to have finished with it and get out, which would destroy him if it did not soon turn to stoic apathy; anxiety about his future, presently reduced perforce to a don't-care mood; aimless walks and amusements in his hours of leave; lack of any say in his own fate. All these conditions soon dry up his mental energy. He becomes what is called 'hospitalized,' and goes back home on discharge, almost incapable of initiative; indisposed to a wide and resolute view over his jeopardized future. On top of this mood comes the present fatal facility with which he can get work. For him and for the Public the present scarcity of labour grievously blurs the real nature of his position, cruelly deceives him about his future chances. Often, he is able to take up his old job; if he is really as efficient as he was nothing can be better. As a rule, he is not; but he finds his former employer sympathetic, and short-handed – head and heart for once agree. Neither of them stops to consider how long he can keep that old job. The disabled man does not pause to remember that he is only, say, twenty-five or thirty years old, and has thirty to forty working years before him; the benevolent employer does not pause to recollect that he used to find it necessary, before the war, to get the most efficient labour, or go under to his rivals; that his maxim was and will be again: 'No square pegs in round holes.' While the war lasts the square pegs are welcome, and all's well. But when the war is over, the cruel forces of industrial competition will come into fuller play than ever before. What rude awakening is coming for them both! It seems hard to counsel an employer to consider whether he is really serving the interests of a disabled man by taking him back under these present highly exceptional conditions, instead of saying: 'My friend, I can easily take you back now, but in your own best interests I won't. Go and get trained for a job *which you will be able to keep*, no matter what is the future state of trade and industrial competition. We must both look ahead. There are hard times coming, and you are young.' That is, however, exactly what we do counsel employers to think and say, unless the disabled man is worth 100 per cent, or at least 90 per cent, in comparison with able workmen.

Even those who do not go back to their old jobs find little difficulty just now in getting work of a sort near their old homes, and, helped by their pensions, think themselves all right. We cannot repeat too often or with too great emphasis our conviction that they are living in a fools' paradise. There *is* a square hole to be found for all these square pegs, a

*Figure 44   Carry On: A Magazine on the Reconstruction of Disabled Soldiers
and Sailors* 1: 5 (January 1919), in which an abbreviated version of 'The gist
of the matter' was reprinted – with uniquely American images – for an
American audience. (US National Library of Medicine, National Institutes
of Health. Image by the author)

proper niche for every disabled man, often a better position than that which he held before; but if he will not fit himself for it, and if the Public will not help him, nay, force him to find it, we are in for the most horrible tragedy and disgrace a few years hence.

There is yet another hindrance to the working of the scheme – the British character. The Briton is an incurable amateur, sometimes of genius, generally of merit, but always an amateur. This amateurism is our strength and our weakness; it brings sportsmanship, elasticity and gusto; but it hampers us with fecklessness, extravagance and muddle. The Briton is also – we speak in the large – a practical person with short views; the greatest and most generous spendthrift under the sun; very combative and competitive deep down, yet very lazy till he is roused. And, of all men, he loves to paddle his own canoe. These qualities make him fascinating to the observer, and would break the heart of any administrator who was not himself a Briton.

The Briton disabled by this war belongs, of course, chiefly to what are called the working classes; add to his British character the working man's philosophy always to make the best of to-day without considering too much what to-morrow may bring forth, and we have perfect conditions for a hand-to-mouth treatment of his endangered future. His whole instinct and habit is to say: 'I'm not worrying; something will turn up.' Micawber was very British. 'Time enough to bother' – we seem to hear him say – 'when we see the rocks.' The attitude of his leaders is sometimes not dissimilar.

According to some, the present indifference of the disabled man to the schemes provided for his rehabilitation is of little consequence. 'There is the machinery of training,' they say, 'not only for now, but for whenever he likes to avail himself of it. When the war is over and he gets pushed out of work, he will be glad enough to come and get trained for the jobs which he can do.' We by no means share this cheery view. It is based on a misconception of human nature, especially of the British nature. We think that when a man has been back in civil life some time, and is beginning to forget the jolt and jar of the war, he will rather stay even on the rocks, living on his pension, on charity, and odd jobs, than put himself to school again. Further, we think that the energy of Local Committees, and of people generally interested now in this great problem, will rapidly evaporate when the war is over and we are no longer in danger, and moreover have become troubled by a new crop of economic difficulties. Human memory is very short, and human gratitude not too long. We are not all angels – like soldiers in time of war, editors when writing their screeds, poets before, and mayors after, dinner. Finally, we think that those special permanent niches which could now be secured by disabled men, if they would train for them, will be usurped by the flood of returning labour, and that what is at present a real opportunity will rapidly become invisible. We are convinced that if the Government's scheme for special treatment and special training is not made proper use of within the next two or three years, it never will be.

We pass now from the four broad reasons – human nature, hospital lethargy, easily-found, well-paid, impermanent work, and the British character – which stand in the way of success, to certain points in the working out of the scheme, which are recognized as capable of improvement.

First, we believe that if at all possible – as aforesaid – it would be excellent to insist on all men who cannot take up their old work as efficiently as before, attending for just a month's experimental course at a training school, after a spell of home leave, before they receive their discharge from the Army.

Next, we feel that the success depends on breaking up the hospitalized state of mind, of enlivening a man's intellect and interest while he is still in hospital, and fostering in him the inclination to come to grips with his future. The orthopaedic hospitals have their excellent curative workshops,[6] but too few other hospitals, for lack of space and other reasons, have any form of instruction. Somehow or other, a man must be given more occupation, either in hospital, or *better*, outside during his leave hours, to take him out of himself, sharpen his faculties, hearten his will-power, and incline him to some new and suitable life-job. Most, if not all, hospitals have, of course, visitors, who give much unselfish devotion to the men; but, in our conviction, every hospital from which men are discharged needs some civilian, definitely appointed and equipped with a bureau, who will give his or her whole heart and *whole time* to the wounded man's affairs, his past, home circumstances, future hopes and wants; act as a liaison officer between him and his Local Committee, and keep before him constantly the necessity of making the utmost of the chances for after-treatment and training offered. Devoted, tactful, practical, whole-time persons are hard to find, but to find and attach them to such hospitals seems to us a *sine qua non* of success. This suggestion has been made before, but not adopted, so far as we are aware, up to the time of writing.

We think it is vital too, that all Local War Pension Committees should also have at least one carefully selected person giving their *whole time* to the work, and always accessible to the applicants.[7] For some of these posts, both in hospitals and on Local Committees, disabled officers, cunningly chosen, and adequately paid, might perhaps be found, with sufficient knowledge, interest and tact. All such appointments are subject to the caveat: 'Better none than the wrong,' but that is hardly a reason for not trying to find the right. We hope that the search for them may be general before these words are read.

Speaking with the diffidence which becomes laymen, we believe that all the departments which administer this vast work fully appreciate the great importance of co-operation. They are all concerned with the one business of restoring the wounded to the utmost, whether it is for return to the Army or to civil life. And just as it has been found vital to fuse the Allied Forces in France and Flanders, so it is vital here to fuse the efforts of the Red Cross, War Office, Pensions Ministry, and Labour Ministry. Weakness or leakage at points of juncture can detract dismally from the force of a general effort. The motto of all may well run: 'Be not trustees of your own departments first, and servers of the general purpose second; keep the restoration of the wounded man in the forefront of your minds, and sacrifice everything else – even your own dignities – to that. Restoration of the man, and nothing else, matters!'

The proportions of this war are so vast, the numbers so huge, the future so gravely menaced, that there is really no time for dispersion, overlapping or red tape. This, after troubled experience, has become the common-sense view of all who have the matter at heart. Fearful complexities have had to be faced, vast machinery has had to be evolved. The plan is at last complete, and on a generous scale; devotion and ability are behind it, in abundance; enormous obstacles and a jungle of difficulties still lie in front. It cannot be too zealously fused and speeded up. But in all there is a real faith that the thing can and must be done; the debt of gratitude weighing on the nation's conscience wiped out, within the limits of human effort; and a great cause, which honours human nature, brought to fruition.

With words to the Public we would close this screed.

Our eyes look on a Britain daily more and more peopled by sufferers of this war. In every street, on every road and village-green we meet them – crippled, half crippled, or showing little outward trace, though none the less secretly deprived of health. Yet there are but few who cannot be fitted again into our national structure, and restored to the happiness of a useful, self-respecting life. Many openings are available, many occupations suitable. A huge jig-saw puzzle confronts us, and there is not one among us all who cannot take a hand in solving it. To

think that it is none of our business is to be woefully in error. The
Public – and by the Public we mean every man and woman in these
islands – can do more than the System. What the Public thinks and
wishes, the disabled man will come to think and wish. If we, who know
or watch the sufferer, are foolish or indifferent about his future, he
too will be foolish and indifferent. If a man's friends and people acqui-
esce in his drifting into the first job, however unsuitable, which comes
along, he will surely drift; if they are content that he should drone away
a future of twenty to fifty years on a pension and makeshift earnings,
he will do so in a vast number of cases. We must make him feel that this
can only end miserably for him; impress on him that by a little effort and
a little gumption he can be fitted with a secure and profitable job; persuade and urge him till he makes the necessary effort. Then only will he
rally to recovery of full working powers, full self-respect and happiness.

Those of us who, by easy-going indulgence or indifference, now encourage the disabled man to drift, are guilty of ingratitude to him, and
will be the first to show impatience and heartlessness when, five or ten
years hence, we see him cumbering the ground, hopeless and embittered, often out of work, and always an eyesore to a nation which will
wish to forget there ever was this war.

Each of us has a duty to these men, and an immense debt to pay; not
by mere 'treating' and washy promise, but by doing something for him,
by strengthening his will to 'make good' again, by urging him and helping
him to find the job best suited to him. If we let him take a short-sighted
view of his case we speed him down the hill. We all know personally
some disabled man; let us set to, and persuade him that he is capable of
much more in the future than he thinks he is, more perhaps than he was
before the war. Many a disabled man can earn better money at more
interesting work than he ever before had the chance to. If he looks on
himself as done for, he *is* done for. We must prevent that; and above all,
make him understand that present conditions are hopelessly misleading.
A few years hence he will often be no more able to keep the job which
easily comes to his hand now than the lame, the halt, the poor in health
were able to keep their jobs in those old peace times, so much easier
than peace times will be henceforth. Now is the time to say to him:
'Pluck up your spirit; better you position in life. Take the permanent
and special chances given you while they are still open. Don't hesitate.
Don't drift. It's fatal!'

Patriotism and gratitude demand this of every wife, father, mother
and friend of each disabled man; demand it for his sake who gave so

much for them; and for the sake of our Country, whose wings are clipped by the devastation of this war.

What sort of Land will it be if, five and ten years hence, tens of thousands injured in this long tragedy are drifting unhappy amongst us, without the anchorage of permanent, well-paid, self-respecting work? We have not realised yet. If we do not realise soon, and make the disabled realise, it will be too late. We are entering on the fifth year of the war; we do not know when it will finish. The economic aftermath may not come on us at once, but when it comes it will be unexampled for severity. The disabled, unprovided for by special work, will, by the laws of Nature and of human nature, be the first to suffer. At present, possibly not one in three of our discharged soldiers who needed further physical treatment has taken it; and perhaps not one in ten who really require to be re-educated to special work is being trained for it. The System is helpless without a great awakening of the Public, and through the Public of the disabled man.

Notes

1 Under Colonel Sir Robert Jones, C.B., an article ['The romance of surgery'] from whose pen appears in this number [of *Reveille*; not reproduced here].

2 See Table A ['Return of officers and men pensioned for disability from outbreak of war to May 31, 1918', here Figure 43 but originally] at the end of this Review.

3 See the article by the Right Hon. John Hodge, M.P. ['Pensions administration'] at the end of the Review [not reproduced here]; and a Summary of 'The New Royal Warrant,' at the end of the Review [not reproduced here].

4 See his article ['Restorative treatment', not reproduced here]; and Appendix attached.

5 See his article ['For our disabled', not reproduced here]; and Tables B ['Of occupations, and the disabilities to which they are suited, with maximum periods of training: compiled from a record of men who have finished their courses'] and C ['Courses of training under the ministry of pensions'], at the end of the Review [not reproduced here].

6 An account of which is given by King Manoel, to whose initiative we owe them.

7 See an article by Mr A. Seymour Jones, on the 'Task of the Local War Pensions Committee.'

TABLE A.

RETURN OF OFFICERS AND MEN PENSIONED FOR DISABILITY
FROM OUTBREAK OF WAR TO MAY 31, 1918.

	OFFICERS		WARRANT OFFICERS, PETTY OFFICERS, NON-COMMISSIONED OFFICERS AND MEN		Total
	Army	Navy	Army	Navy	
Eyesight cases	97	46	8,911	1,141	10,195
Wounds and injuries to leg (necessitating amputation)	101	4	9,120	223	9,448
Wounds and injuries to arms (necessitating amputation)	46	1	4,880	116	5,043
Wounds and injuries to leg (not necessitating amputation)	374	16	41,992	444	42,826
Wounds and injuries to arms (not necessitating amputation)	145	1	30,961	382	31,489
Wounds and injuries to hands (not necessitating amputation)	31	4	15,382	300	15,717
Wounds and injuries to head	178	7	13,447	558	14,190
Hernia	35	5	2,740	149	2,929
Miscellaneous wounds and injuries	392	6	19,007	581	19,986
Chest complaints	311	58 }	37,494	2,985	41,155
Tuberculosis	251	56 }			
Rheumatism	248	38	22,265	1,017	23,568
Heart disease	429	57	34,408	1,675	36,569
Epilepsy	57	6	3,403	231	3,667
Nervous diseases—					
Shell-shock	170	3 }	18,468	1,432	21,283
Neurasthenia	706	116 }			
Miscellaneous	308	80 }			
Insanity	107	26	2,107	576	2,816
Deafness	57	15	6,549	426	7,047
Frost-bite (including cases of amputation of feet or legs)	4	—	3,139	—	3,143
Miscellaneous disabilities—					
Bright's disease	101	20 }	62,959	2,245	66,351
Debility	201	6 }			
Ulcer of stomach	69	14 }			
Varicocele	41	3 }			
Enteric and malaria	217	22 }			
Spinal	29	13 }			
Appendicitis	55	4 }			
Other disabilities	283	69 }			
Not classified (awards made by War Office and Admiralty which have lapsed or not come up for renewal by Ministry of Pensions)	693	15	—	—	708
	5,736	711	337,232	14,481	358,160

From this table, *which only comprises men and officers finally discharged and pensioned,*
some conception of the size of the task before us may be gained.—EDITOR.

Figure 45 From *Reveille* No. 1 (August 1918): table A, 'Return of officers and men pensioned for disability from outbreak of war to May 31, 1918', referenced by Galsworthy in 'The gist of the matter' to reveal 'some conception of the size of the task before us'. (Private collection. Image by the author)

9

Looking ahead

The more the problem of our disabled is considered the more certain it seems that we are still hanging over the edge of an abyss.

There were, to start with, two possible ways of dealing with this great question. The first was simple, centralized, and autocratic. The Government might have retained disabled soldiers in the Army till everything possible had been done for them physically and by way of retraining for work to which they were suited in civil life. Two objections – our national belief in Liberty, and the logical need of justifying such a drastic method by guaranteeing to every man so restored permanent work on his discharge – were apparently fatal; and the idea softly and silently vanished away.

The second was the decentralized and democratic way, which has been adopted. The disabled are discharged, as soon as reasonably possible, to their own homes; and their continued treatment and training are left to Local War Pensions Committees to arrange so far as may be, in local hospitals and local institutes and workshops. Very well! The scheme is more organic, better in accord with our British instincts, and though modifications are in the wind, we appear to be at this time of day irrevocably committed to the main lines of it. But it is inevitably slower than a drastic highly centralized method. Take the most recent figures. Fresh pension claims of disabled soldiers dealt with between April 1 and September 17 number 134,013; men admitted to training in that period, about 6,200. The percentage of discharged men back in their old employment is estimated at about 50. Making that and other allowances, men are still being discharged *into the open labour market* at a much greater rate than that at which they are being specially refitted for civil life. We have not only to equalize those rates, but great arrears to make up, and shall have ultimately to deal with many men, now back in old jobs, who, later on, will be shouldered out of them by competition – in fact, a balance of disability which will not be disclosed till industrial conditions are normal again.

In a democratic country supply is apt to wait on demand; and demand takes a long time to make itself felt in its true proportions. The conditions in this case are such that it cannot make itself felt in full until too late – until the Army is demobilized, industrialism reshuffled, competition in fierce blast, and thousands of our more or less disabled elbowed out of places they are now able to fill. The extent of the demand may very well not be really visible till five years after the war.

We confess to being haunted by a fear more solid than ever was ghost. From the time these words are read we may have but a year and a half at most to make our peace with the Honour of our Country. To speak quite frankly, we fear disgrace and disaster. Do people realize what a dreadful thing it will be, if all the butter of fair words about 'our heroes' melts into one vast disfiguring grease spot; and instead of men honoured and contented we have an army of broken wanderers with such curses on their lips? The beginnings of it are here already. There had better be no illusions. Every such broken cursing man will be in the right and we in the wrong of it. And the strife and disruption they will breed will be deserved. Nor will it be much use to blame the Government, which is our favourite way out of all difficulties that the happy-go-lucky British temperament brings on itself. Those who blame the Government are often they who would have been the first to mete out blame if a swifter autocratic scheme had been adopted. The Government, in deference to our national susceptibilities, has inaugurated a democratic scheme which can only to a limited extent be run from the centre; its real go and vitality depend on public interest and local effort. If these are lacking the scheme fails. Even if the Ministry were to drop all the red tape they have left, and the Treasury were to widen indefinitely the mouth of its purse, even then the success of a voluntary scheme could only come from the goodwill and effort of the Public and of the disabled man himself. The employer must come forward with his interest and his promise of employment, with his experience, his personal touch, and his foresight; the craftsman who can teach must be ready to teach; the trades union leader – he who knows how hard and bitter times can be for the working-man – must use all his influence and persuasive powers on the mind of the disabled; and all of us who know individual disabled men must join in the effort to secure for them a safe and worthy future. Above all must the disabled soldier in his own interest look ahead. We plead for unity, for co-operation in this work.

An old clergyman came into our study the other day and most unexpectedly demonstrated that the be-all and end-all of the Universe was Love. He had been round this earth three times. We, who have not yet been even once round the stellar plan, are not so certain; we think the Creative Principle less simple. But of this we are sure: There are moments in the course of each human enterprise when the principle of love, or co-operation as we may soberly call it, is more important than the principle of strife or disruption. The process of restoring our disabled has come on such a moment. Sometimes criticism and destruction really aid construction. This is not one of them, if we are to rebuild a very shattered house. Whatever the demerits of the official schemes – and they probably fall as far short of perfection as human plans generally do – it is too late to go back on them; remedy or supplement for their deficiencies can best be supplied by supporting them with all our hearts. Helpful criticism is still needed; but the sands are running out – there is no longer time for destructive criticism. We want enthusiasm, goodwill, give and take, and, above all, the right men and women in the right places.

We say all this without even the shadow of a political axe to grind; without any bias whatever in favour of this or any other Government. Only an ignoramus will reproach us with having political ends in view, or any intention of camouflaging the work of the Ministry who has these matters in hand. We say it because we are convinced that there is no longer time for tearing things to pieces; we have had four years to do that in, and the scheme which has survived the process (supplemented, as we shall hope to show must be) is our only chance. The moment the grip of national danger is relaxed, selfishness will at once begin to scramble, a thousand new problems and difficulties will absorb our energies, the chance will pass, and the weakest go to the wall. What would be the use of a perfect scheme, when this time for getting it to work is overpast? The chance of the disabled is *while the war is on*; and the moving force of the scheme-in-being will only come when people see the facts – the waste here, the wreckage there – and the danger scrolled across our sky. Let all out enthusiastic frondeurs concentrate their energies on making people see that danger; on persuading the discharged soldier of his needs, rather than of his grievances, heavy and bitter though they sometimes be, lest in the future they become ten times more bitter. Let them open the eyes of his friends and relations to the ominous future which awaits us and him unless he can fit himself to meet it. Let them devote themselves to rousing employers to a sense of their duty to employ; and the trades to a feeling of shame that obstacles should be put in the way of men before whom we ought to bow.

Even if everybody's goodwill were engaged, there would still be great difficulty in making up the leeway. There is a shortage of doctors, of labour and building material for hospitals and workshops, and of instructors. There are countless prejudices and jealousies to overcome; vested interests to fight; and a huge newly-formed machinery to get into running order. It would be a miracle if there were not as yet too many checks and departments, so that there is not enough co-ordination and speed at the heart of the machine, and too little is left to individual initiative at the extremities. Above all, there is the size of the problem. Over 400,000 already discharged, disabled, and as many more, perhaps to come. Not claimed by the Ministry as unnaturally perfect, the existing official schemes ought now to be helped by every person of good will, so that they may be brought to the greatest possible fruition.

But supposing, for a moment, that they are so helped, will they, in and of themselves, be sufficient to deal with the host of our disabled? No. We are absolutely convinced that when everything possible under the Government's present scheme has been done to retrain men for civil life, find them suitable employment, or set them up in business through the King's or other funds, there will still be many thousands of disabled men, for one reason or another, on the rocks – a great number, whose injury definitely disqualifies them for business and for anything but light work, of which there is only a limited supply of a skilled nature; a great many whose disability makes them intermittent workers, men whose nervous system has been irremediably affected; and many by nature slack, now made hopelessly slack. (And there will be the consumptives, of whom 41,000 odd have been discharged up to September; but that is a separate problem, to which attention is drawn in another article.)

It is time we took this prospect for a certainty, and began to consider the possible ways by which disaster may be avoided. Some scheme there will have to be, some ultimate guarantee against seething discontent, the country's dishonour, and our brave men's wretchedness. We are content now to indicate three such schemes, pointing out shortly their qualities and defects, without even attempting to make up our mind or to suggest that they are better than other schemes which might be devised.

The Rothband scheme is well known both to the Ministry and to most of us who have interested ourselves in this question. It is suggested that the King should invite all considerable employers to sign their names on a Roll of Honour, and promise that they and their successors will employ one or more men disabled in this war. It is claimed that by this means every disabled man would be absorbed into normal industry for so long as disabled men remained; that all employers would thereby be penalized (or complimented, as we should prefer to call it) equally; that honourable sentiment and gratitude would be funded now, while it is still alive and general, for the long hard future. It is claimed that it could be easily and inexpensively inaugurated, and would in no way interfere with the existing official plans for training, indeed that it would further them, because, as its promoters quite truly say, retraining of itself is of no use unless permanent employment is provided for the retrained. This Rothband scheme is a serious proposition, has wide support, and there is a good deal to be said for it. As we see things, there are three really grave objections. First, that it would probably *not* absorb all the disabled; and that many employers would join the Roll, get the kudos, and shirk the obligations, by taking one or two disabled men where they should be taking ten or twenty. Secondly, that employers (who, though no worse than any other class, are not all benevolent, painstaking, and wise) would in many cases be inclined, as gratitude waned and public opinion grew less vigilant, to put even those disabled, who were capable of better work, into blind-alley jobs – making them liftmen, timekeepers, watchmen, and so forth; in other words, to give them non-creative employment, which would waste productive power, and keep the men's energies and will-power rusting all the rest of their lives; for it must never be forgotten that the disabled are mostly young. Thirdly, that if the disabled soldier knew now for certain that there was a light, protected job of some sort always open to him for the asking, he would in very many cases refuse retraining for special pursuits in which he could well make good entirely on his own, and would thereby stand in the way of his own fuller future, and greater happiness – for we are, nationally, all to prone to take the line of least resistance.

The second plan, already more than hinted at by the Minister of Pensions, is practically the Rothband scheme made compulsory. *All* employers forced by the Act of Parliament to take soldiers disabled in this war *in due proportion* to the number of hands they employ. This scheme would be free of the first objection to the Rothband scheme; it probably *would* absorb all the disabled, not otherwise accounted for, but would be subject to the two other objections, and it remains, of course, to be seen whether employers will stand compulsion, or public opinion permit the attempt.

In a few words towards the end of the last number of *Reveille* we pointed out a third plan, which might have to be adopted: A system of Government workshops for townsmen, and of rural colonies for countrymen, employing only the disabled, at standard wages, and refusing no disabled man who at any time presented himself. Not disciplinary institutions, in any way, just ordinary industries – the men living or lodging with their families, outside, in the usual way. Such workshops and colonies would, of course, need formation and support on the most elastic scale, suited to good times and bad. They might well in some years be almost empty, in others fill to overflowing. But if they existed we should all know that the right to work and a decent life has been permanently secured to every disabled man. They would probably be self-supporting, and would automatically form training schools for men who wished to pass on to work again in open competition, as the Lord Roberts Workshops do now on a small scale. Against this scheme there is the housing difficulty for a fluctuating number of workers; and the grave objection that such Government workshops and rural colonies would be aggregations, though not segregations, of disabled men. There is no need to labour the disadvantages of that. In all other respects they might be places of normal industry, neither institutions nor homes of charity, and they would not be open to the particular objections which haunt the other two schemes.

We do not know of any other plans which would cover the whole ground, and clear the country's conscience. Possibly a combination of the first or second with the third may be necessary. But we invite the Government, the Public, and the Disabled to a private view of the state of this country five or ten years hence, if, by the time the war ends, some comprehensive plan, securing justice and contentment to the great unabsorbed residue of the injured, be not set on foot, and placed behind to supplement and round off the present arrangements for treatment and training: Men in workhouses, men at street corners, men on tubs, men miserably idle on pensions which barely keep the life in them; bitter men and justly bitter; young men with long years of disillusionment and resentfulness before them, the centres of little swirls of discontent and revolution. And all these men, with the black horrors they went through for their country's sake burnt into their brains, hating us

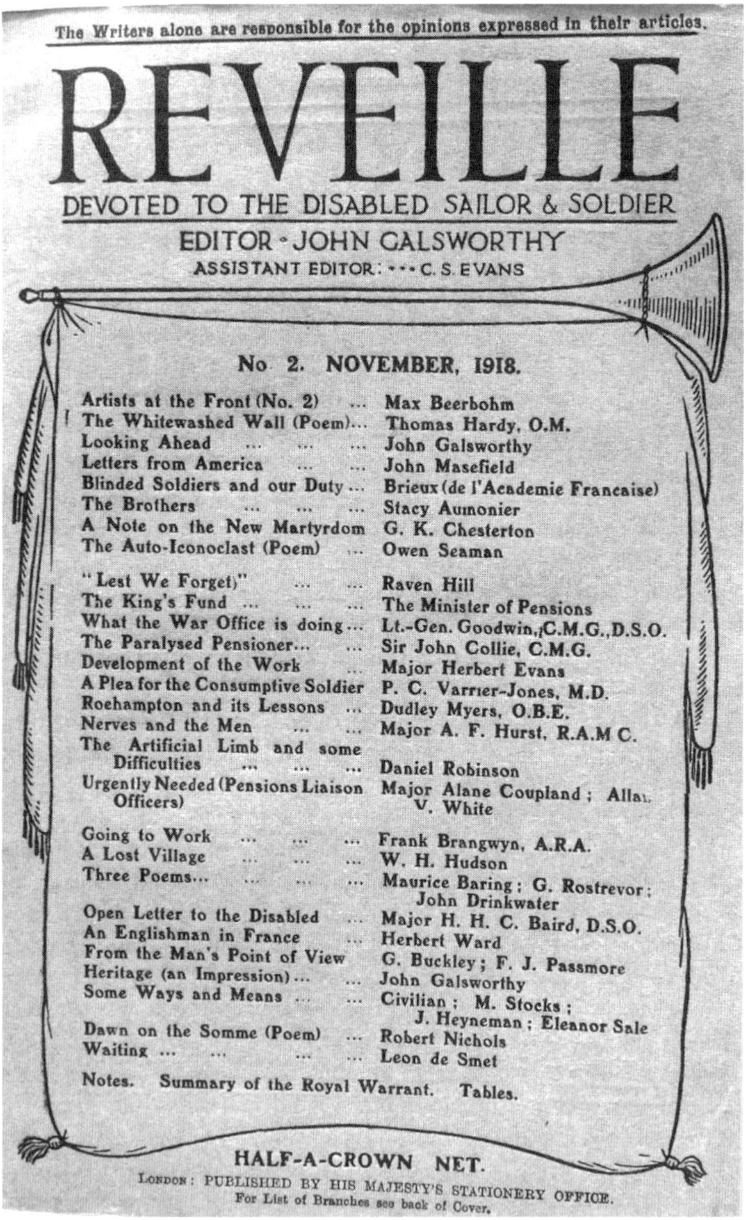

The Writers alone are responsible for the opinions expressed in their articles.

REVEILLE

DEVOTED TO THE DISABLED SAILOR & SOLDIER

EDITOR - JOHN GALSWORTHY

ASSISTANT EDITOR: --- C. S. EVANS

No. 2. NOVEMBER, 1918.

Artists at the Front (No. 2) ...	Max Beerbohm
The Whitewashed Wall (Poem)...	Thomas Hardy, O.M.
Looking Ahead	John Galsworthy
Letters from America	John Masefield
Blinded Soldiers and our Duty ...	Brieux (de l'Academie Francaise)
The Brothers	Stacy Aumonier
A Note on the New Martyrdom	G. K. Chesterton
The Auto-Iconoclast (Poem) ...	Owen Seaman
"Lest We Forget)"	Raven Hill
The King's Fund	The Minister of Pensions
What the War Office is doing ...	Lt.-Gen. Goodwin, C.M.G., D.S.O.
The Paralysed Pensioner... ...	Sir John Collie, C.M.G.
Development of the Work ...	Major Herbert Evans
A Plea for the Consumptive Soldier	P. C. Varrier-Jones, M.D.
Roehampton and its Lessons ...	Dudley Myers, O.B.E.
Nerves and the Men	Major A. F. Hurst, R.A.M.C.
The Artificial Limb and some Difficulties	Daniel Robinson
Urgently Needed (Pensions Liaison Officers)	Major Alane Coupland; Allan V. White
Going to Work	Frank Brangwyn, A.R.A.
A Lost Village	W. H. Hudson
Three Poems...	Maurice Baring; G. Rostrevor; John Drinkwater
Open Letter to the Disabled ...	Major H. H. C. Baird, D.S.O.
An Englishman in France ...	Herbert Ward
From the Man's Point of View	G. Buckley; F. J. Passmore
Heritage (an Impression)... ...	John Galsworthy
Some Ways and Means	Civilian; M. Stocks; J. Heyneman; Eleanor Sale
Dawn on the Somme (Poem) ...	Robert Nichols
Waiting	Leon de Smet

Notes. Summary of the Royal Warrant. Tables.

HALF-A-CROWN NET.

LONDON: PUBLISHED BY HIS MAJESTY'S STATIONERY OFFICE.
For List of Branches see back of Cover.

Figure 46 *Reveille* No. 2 (November 1918), edited by Galsworthy, in which 'Looking ahead' appeared. (Private collection. Image by the author)

who did not go through those horrors but could talk about what we would do for them – and then not do it!

Pensions and monetary aids are all very well, but they will never stop the brooding and the bitterness of those who gave up their best energy for ever in the prime of their youth – you can't cure that ache with money! Occupation and the sense of usefulness alone will do it. To assure everyone the chance of that is the very least we can do for men who did so much for us. The situation demands not only all our energy and co-operation now, but *far sight into the future*. It demands that we should for once falsify our British happy-go-luckiness, our ingrained habit of waiting till we're forced; for once go ahead of disgrace and trouble, which otherwise will come so surely as these words are put on paper.

10

Spirit and letter

How difficult it is to keep the breath of life in any large work of public utility. How fatally easy to become bureaucratic and treat creatures of flesh and blood as if they were autonomous. To change from keen folk only too ready to help, into formal persons carrying on from a sense of duty, is an unconscious process only too rapidly accomplished.

Slow petrifaction of eager humanity by the drip thereon of forms is minor tragedy being played all the time on thousands of tiny stages. Nor is that drip the only petrifying agency. Those of us who have dabbled in philanthropy know well what paralysis can come over sympathy out of mere damnéd iteration. In truth man is not constituted to deal out sympathy and living helpfulness wholesale; at least, he very rarely is. He loves helping Tom, he likes helping Dick, he wonders if he likes helping Harry, and is sure he dislikes helping Bartholomew. Fortunately, this fatal decrescendo is retarded in the matter of our disabled by consciousness of a debt owed and a genuine desire to pay it; but it is not wholly overcome, it cannot be, while man remains what he is, a being who needs novelty to keep eagerness alive within him. And the worst of it is, no disabled man who comes for help and sympathy is petrified. No, indeed! His case is as new to himself as a bud just opened; his feelings as real and poignant as departmental sympathy is liable to become blunt and weary.

Just think what lies behind every letter written by a disabled man to the Ministry of Pensions or to his Local Committee, and of what has gone on in the soul of him before he forces his body to enter precincts where his future shall be wrapped into filled-up forms and bandied from one to another. We never realize how passionately we prize our

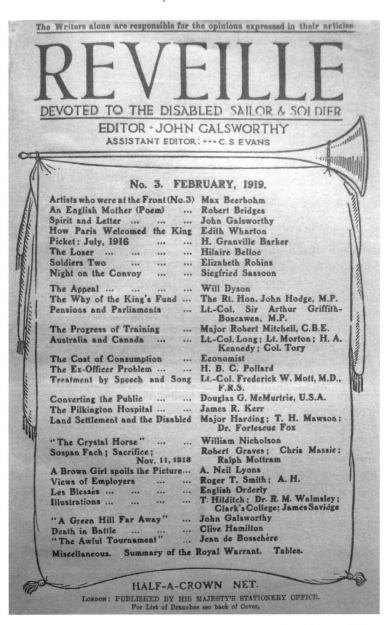

The Writers alone are responsible for the opinions expressed in their articles

REVEILLE

DEVOTED TO THE DISABLED SAILOR & SOLDIER

EDITOR · JOHN GALSWORTHY
ASSISTANT EDITOR : ··· C. S. EVANS

No. 3. FEBRUARY, 1919.

Artists who were at the Front (No.3)	Max Beerbohm
An English Mother (Poem) ...	Robert Bridges
Spirit and Letter	John Galsworthy
How Paris Welcomed the King	Edith Wharton
Picket : July, 1916	H. Granville Barker
The Loser	Hilaire Belloc
Soldiers Two	Elizabeth Robins
Night on the Convoy	Siegfried Sassoon
The Appeal	Will Dyson
The Why of the King's Fund ...	The Rt. Hon. John Hodge, M.P.
Pensions and Parliaments ...	Lt.-Col. Sir Arthur Griffith-Boscawen, M.P.
The Progress of Training ...	Major Robert Mitchell, C.B.E.
Australia and Canada	Lt.-Col. Long ; Lt. Morton ; H. A. Kennedy ; Col. Tory
The Cost of Consumption ...	Economist
The Ex-Officer Problem	H. B. C. Pollard
Treatment by Speech and Song	Lt.-Col. Frederick W. Mott, M.D., F.R.S.
Converting the Public	Douglas G. McMurtrie, U.S.A.
The Pilkington Hospital	James R. Kerr
Land Settlement and the Disabled	Major Harding ; T. H. Mawson ; Dr. Fortescue Fox
"The Crystal Horse"	William Nicholson
Sospan Fach ; Sacrifice ; Nov. 11, 1918	Robert Graves ; Chris Massie ; Ralph Mottram
A Brown Girl spoils the Picture...	A. Neil Lyons
Views of Employers	Roger T. Smith ; A. H.
Les Blessés	English Orderly
Illustrations	T. Hilditch ; Dr. R. M. Walmsley ; Clark's College ; James Savidge
"A Green Hill Far Away" ...	John Galsworthy
Death in Battle	Clive Hamilton
"The Awful Tournament" ...	Jean de Bosschère
Miscellaneous. Summary of the Royal Warrant. Tables.	

HALF-A-CROWN NET.

LONDON : PUBLISHED BY HIS MAJESTY'S STATIONERY OFFICE.
For List of Branches see back of Cover.

Figure 47 Reveille No. 3 (February 1919), edited by Galsworthy, in which 'Spirit and letter' appeared. (Private collection. Image by the author)

independence and how deeply interesting we find our own futures until we have to submit them to be delved into, docketed and doled out. And to have to submit them at the end of four years of risk and hardship and pain which have saved the country must indeed seem like insult added unto injuries.

Departments are no less sensitive than individuals, and we intend no unkindness by these remarks – far from it, being very conscious that we should not be able to keep as soft beneath the drip of forms or remain as sympathetic under iteration as do most of our officials. Departments are as human nature makes them, and human nature must always be taken with a prayer. Many devoted men and women are working departmentally for the disabled: they deserve nothing but sympathy and respect, and certainly receive them in full measure from ourselves. They are serving their country, often by a patient, featureless labour which should earn them crosses of merit.

But the fact remains that in departments generally 'forms' tend to bury human sympathy, as falling leaves to bury babes; they mean delays, and delays are dangerous. If, then, we may venture, we urge departments ever to keep before their eyes and minds the intense reality, the agonizing importance that each 'case; which comes before them has *for the man who is that case*. We English are not good at wearing our hearts on our sleeves nor adepts [*sic*] at showing our feelings. Of the disabled who come – nervous, stolid, stoical, surly – all could a tale unfold of issues so moving to themselves that each formality and delay must seem to them almost ridiculous; and many no doubt could sit down and cry at what seems to them the slow inadequacy of things, if crying were permitted to a Briton.

Without 'forms' confusion would, of course, be worse confounded, but between that confusion and delays which produce in the minds of countless sufferers from the war a rankling sense that justice is being grudged them, there is a mean which, if not golden, is at all events far better than either of those extremes. It is worth while to take many risks to save sending men away with the feeling that they were owed bread and have been given stones. Now that we have the measure of this great problem at last, we hope it may be possible to open the money bags wider, and to bring forth their contents quicker. We hope the time has come, too, to see whether 'forms' can be reduced in number, simplified in phrase, and issued faster. A sense of injustice among silver-badge men is ill-balanced by a few millions saved to the pockets of us taxpayers.

To put it on the lowest ground, the unrest which a sense of injustice will cause in this country for the next generation will cost taxpayers fivefold those few millions in the long run. Better be recklessly liberal than even more recklessly thrifty.

In our conviction the really successful man in the affairs of this life is not, as most suppose, the hard-headed bargainer, but he who of his own accord ever offers rather more than his neighbour, or opponent, would naturally expect to get, provided, always, that he offers out of a good heart. In this particular matter of our disabled we would all, including the Treasury (no less composed of human beings than other departments), prefer to be generous; but we all seem to be afraid for each others' pockets. Under the weight of this vicarious caution, the breath of life is in danger of being squeezed out of what should be a work of broad and human gratitude. We have spent money like water to win the war; dare we grudge money to put on their feet again those whom we have used in the winning?

The great trouble, of course, has been the alarming rise in the cost of living. Pensions and allowances which seemed generous, became skimpy. The price of food, fuel, lighting, and perhaps clothing will come down rather quickly now; if not, there are very hard times in front of British Industry. We hope wages will remain comparatively high, but unless they are lowered to some extent, industry, even on a profit-sharing basis, will never pay its way under Peace conditions. The first need of Peace, therefore, is the employment of released energy in producing food, coal, and better and more abundant transport, for unless the prime costs of living are lowered wages cannot be.

Many of the other costs of living, however, such as taxes, rates, rents, furniture, and amusements are likely to remain high, much longer than food or coal. In any case the assessment of increase to pensions and allowances is extraordinarily difficult. The costs and conditions of life will be shifting for some time to come. And in future the average cost of living, carefully calculated, should surely be made known, monthly at least, in order that the public may be acquainted at all times with the exact proportion which wages, pensions, allowances, &c., bear to that cost. One of the chief reasons of social bitterness and suspicion in the past has been such general ignorance on this important point that public opinion has never been able to judge the merits of discontent for itself. Pensions and allowances have recently been increased by a twenty per cent. bonus; but even that generous addition hardly makes up as yet for the rise in the cost of living. Men still hesitate to take training;

for human nature is very fond of the bird in the hand. The counter-attractions of war-work wages are of course diminishing already, but the change is slow, and it is *now* that disabled men who cannot take up their old work must be trained if they are to hold their own when demobilization is in full blast.

If the breath of life is to be kept in this work of restoration, *elastic* financial help is a vital consideration. We should like, for instance, to see swifter discretionary powers given to the local committees to tide men over tight places; a momentary want of money is a very usual block on the line of a man's new departure. We should like to see (though this by no means affects disabled men alone) all officers and men whom the country trains for agriculture supplied with capital really sufficient to start them in their new calling. To put men on the land, without a fair chance of making good there, would be a flagrant instance of fulfilling the letter of restoration and neglecting its spirit. The two essentials of settlement on the land, whether of able or disabled soldiers, are, first, most careful selection of the candidate, and, second, adequate financial backing. In every direction we should prefer to see the State going a little in advance of disabled men's demands, instead of lagging a little or far behind them, out of too tender regard for the taxpayer's pocket. What sort of sanctity would that pocket now be enjoying if it had not been for these disabled men? It goes without saying that we want neither folly nor extravagance, but we do want very great liberality.

There are those debatable cases, too, where the sufferer's private sense of justice turns away lacerated by refusal based on the letter of the law. Take the much-vexed question of whether illness – say tuberculosis – for which a man is discharged was caused or aggravated by military service. Such a man, if his medical board decides that it was not so caused or aggravated, receives free sanatorium treatment and separation allowances while he is there, but no pension. He cannot be kept indefinitely in a sanatorium; he will not be permanently cured when he is discharged, he will only have learned under what conditions he can keep the disease arrested; but he will have no pension to help him to those conditions. He naturally says to himself: 'They passed me fit when I went into the Army: they were glad enough to get me. I did my bit. In doing it I developed this which was not developed when they passed me in, or they would not or *should not* have done so. / I ought to have a pension.' Logically he may not be right; his military life may have been holding the disease down rather than exciting it. But our point is this: The letter of the Law forbids the pension. The spirit ought to welcome the chance of giving it. Such cases may be few, but tuberculosis is only one of the many diseases for which men are discharged, and many a mickle makes a muckle. Far better to take a little more liberty with taxpayers' pockets, than to risk the lives, or the future earning power, of men who have so well served their country, and send them away fasting, but full of indignation. The State, like the humblest citizen, cannot have it both ways. If it talks – as talk it does, with the mouth of every public man who speaks on this subject – of heroes, and of doing all it can for them, then it must not cheese-pare as well, for that makes it ridiculous. Britain has climbed the high moral horse – as usual – over the great question of our disabled; she cannot stay in that saddle if she rides like a slippery lawyer. In all cases of doubt, then, let us err on the side of generosity.

So much for spirit and letter on the economic side. On the human side the need for breadth and living sympathy is even more important. If we were a hard-driven official buried up to the eyes in work, we should be exasperated if we were urged by some irresponsible pen to be broader and more sympathetic; but if we were a disabled soldier making an attempt to get on terms with life again we should be still more exasperated if we were met with a lack of breadth and sym-pathy. The gods have been good to us who, by accident, have stayed at home, and very evil to these our brothers who went out to fight. Whether we be officials, employers, or merely people in the street, anything we can do for them can at least be done patiently, ungrudgingly, with a real desire to forestall their wants; for otherwise we are weighed in the balance and found to be base metal. In all this work, changes in the Warrant, altera-tion in machinery, renewals of personality, must be for ever going on. The one thing which need not change is the spirit in which we try to serve those who have truly served us. It is lugubrious indeed to think that in the hearts of many men injured in this war there burns, some-times fiercely, a feeling that the country they have served is grudging them a fair recovery and a decent living. The country is *not* grudging it to them, but, because there is so much 'letter' to the work of restoration, with all that this means of delay, of hope deferred, and sick hearts, it must often seem so. 'Letter,' we well know, is necessary, only it should be watched and kept in bounds as much as possible, even though our officials are hard-worked, often over-driven. To a man who is hungry the knowledge that a benevolent person has a full meal waiting for him in a room with a padlocked door is of little use. Men judge intention by very simple things. Little obstacles seem to them as big as mountains. When their wives and children want this necessary or that and they themselves the other, and those necessaries are not quickly forthcoming, the State may proclaim its good intentions all day to ears which have no power of hearing. The disabled soldier is often no doubt an impatient and restive man – what should we be if we had lived his life these last four years? So much the more need for patience and sympathy in those who want to help him. Understanding is what he wants, more even than he wants larger pensions and better allowances. He wants to feel that those whose duty and pleasure it is to deal with his hard case can realize the nature of that case in terms of human emotion, that they can really understand how such and such extra amount means that he won't have to watch a woman or a child he loves growing bleak and pinched in the face, or feel himself always a little below par from want of proper food, or air, or leisure; that to get a training in what he really fancies, instead of in what others fancy for him, may mean all the difference between an interesting future and blank drudgery; that to go back under a doctor who has begun his cure and gained his confidence, would be half the battle of recovery.

We repeat our admiration of the devoted work so many men and women are doing; we record our conviction that in the Minister who is now laying down office we have had a leader who has always encouraged to the full of his powers the human side of this great question; and we think that the Ministry of Pensions, considering all its difficulties, has done better than could ever have been expected. But in a world where machines rule, and we strike more and more the statistical attitude, we need all the broad humanism we can get, so that when an applicant comes into office or institution he may always feel friendliness around him, and know that he will be treated not in accordance with the letter, but with the spirit of the law.

PART II

Select Fiction by John Galsworthy

At home in England

$\widetilde{11}$

The recruit

Written for *The Blinded Soldiers and Sailors Gift Book in Aid of St Dunstan's Hostel*, this short story appeared in the collection along-side contributions by H. G. Wells, G. K. Chesterton and Anthony Hope Hawkins, among others. Galsworthy subsequently reprinted it in *Tatterdemalion*, in the Manaton Edition of his collected works and in *Caravan*. While the narrative of this story did not involve St Dunstan's *per se*, the composition deserves attention for being of a piece – via *The Blinded Soldiers and Sailors Gift Book* itself – with other material means by which authorities of St Dunstan's shaped the public image of their institution and its men, indeed much like their counterparts did at Roehampton through that institution's own gift book, to which Galsworthy contributed the foreword reprinted here in chapter one.

Several times since that fateful Fourth of August he had said: 'I sh'll 'ave to go.'

And the farmer and his wife would look at him, he with a sort of amusement, she with a queer compassion in her heart, and one or the other would reply, smiling: 'That's all right, Tom, there's plenty Germans yet. Yu wait a bit.'

His mother, too, who came daily from the lonely cottage in the little combe on the very edge of the big hill to work in the kitchen and farm dairy, would turn her dark taciturn head, with still plentiful black hair, towards his face, which, for all its tan, was so weirdly reminiscent of a withered baby, pinkish and light-lashed, with forelock and fair hair thin and rumpled, and small blue eyes, and she would mutter:

'Don't yu never fret, boy. They'll come for 'ee fast enough when they want 'ee.' No one, least of all perhaps his mother, could take quite seriously that little square short-footed man, born when she was just seventeen. Sure of work because he was first-rate with every kind of beast, he was yet not looked on as being quite 'all there'. He could neither read nor write, had scarcely ever been outside the parish, and then only in a shandrydan on a Unionist Club treat, and he knew no more of the world than the native of a small South Sea Island. His life from childhood on had been passed year in, year out, from dawn till dark, with cattle and their calves, the sheep, the horses and the wild moor-ponies; except when hay or corn harvest or any exceptionally exacting festival absorbed him for the moment. From shyness he never went into the pub., and so had missed the greater part of village education. He could of course enjoy no papers, a map was to him but a mystic mass of marks and colours; he had never seen the sea, never a ship; no water broader then the parish streams; until the war had never met anything more like a soldier than the constable of the neighbouring village. But he had seen a sailor in his uniform. What sort of creatures these Germans were to him – who knows? They were cruel – he had grasped that. Something noxious, perhaps, like the adders whose backs he broke with his stick; something dangerous like the chained dog at Shaptor farm, or the big bull at Vannacombe. When the war first broke out, and they had called the young blacksmith (a reservist and noted village marksman) back to his regiment, the little cowman had smiled and said: 'Wait till regiment gets to front, Jim'll soon shoot 'em up.'

But weeks and months went by, and it was always the Germans, the Germans; Jim had clearly not yet shot them up; and now one and now another went off from the village, and two from the farm itself; and the great Jim returned; slightly injured, for a few weeks' rest; full of whisky from morning till night, he made the village ring, and finally went off again in a mood of manifest reluctance. All this weighed dumbly on the mind of the little cowman, the more heavily that because of his inarticulate shyness he could never talk that weight away, nor could anyone by talk relieve him, no premises of knowledge or vision being there. From sheer physical contagion he felt the grizzly menace in the air, and a sense of being left behind when others were going to meet that menace with their fists, as it might be. There was something proud and sturdy in the little man, even in the look of him, for all the he was 'poor old Tom', who brought a smile on the mouths of all. He was passionate, too, if rubbed up the wrong way; but it needed the malevolence and ingenuity

of human beings to annoy him – with his beasts he never lost his tem-
per, so that they had perfect confidence in him. He resembled, indeed,
herdsmen of the Alps, whom one may see in dumb communion with
their creatures up on those high solitudes; for he, too, dwelt in a high
solitude cut off from real fellowship with men and women by lack of
knowledge and by the supercilious pity in them. Living in such a remote
world, his talk – when he did say something – had ever the surprising
quality attaching to the thoughts of those to whom the normal proportions of things are quite unknown. His short, square figure, hatless and
rarely coated in any weather, dotting from foot to foot, a bit of stick in
one hand, and often a straw in the mouth – he did not smoke – was
familiar in the yard, where he turned the handle of the separator, in the
fields and cowsheds, from daybreak to dusk, save for the hours of dinner and tea, which he ate in the farm kitchen, making sparse and
surprising comments. To his peculiar whistles and calls the cattle and
calves, for all their rumination and stubborn shyness, were amazingly
responsive. It was a pretty sight to seem them pushing against each
other round him – after all, he was as much the source of their subsist-
ence, especially through the scanty winter months, as a mother starling
to her unfledged young.

When the Government issued their request to house-holders to return the names of those of military age ready to serve if called on, he
heard of it, and stopped munching to say in his abrupt fashion: 'I'll go
fight the Germans.' The farmer did not put him down, but said to his
wife:

''Twidden be 'ardly fair – they'd be makin' game of 'im.'

And his wife, her eyes shining with motherliness, answered: 'Poor lad,
he's not fit-like.'

The months went on – winter passing to spring; and the slow decking
of the trees and fields began with leaves and flowers, with butterflies and
the songs of birds. How far the little cowman would notice such a thing
as that no one could ever have said, devoid as he was of the vocabulary
of beauty, but like all the world his heart must have felt warmer and
lighter under his old waistcoat, and perhaps more than most hearts, for
he could often be seen standing stock-still in the fields, his browning
face turned to the sun.

Less and less he heard talk of Germans – dogged acceptance of the
state of war having settled on that far countryside – the beggars were not
beaten and killed off yet, but they would be in good time. It was un-
pleasant to think of them more than could be helped. Once in a way a

youth went off and "listed', but the parish had given more perhaps than the average, a good few of military age still clinging to life as they had known it. Then some bright spirit conceived the notion that the county regiment should march through the remoter districts to rouse them up.

The cuckoo had been singing now five days; the lanes and fields, the woods and the village-green were as Joseph's coat, so varied and so bright the foliage, from the golden oak buds to the brilliant little lime-tree leaves, the feathery green shoots of larches, and the already darkening bunches of the sycamores. The earth was dry – no rain for a fortnight. The cars containing the brown-clad men and a recruiting band drew up before the inn. Here were clustered the farmers, the innkeeper, the grey-haired postman; by the church gate and before the school-yard were knots of girls and children, schoolmistresses, schoolmaster, parson; down on the lower green stood a group of likely youths, an old labourer or two; and apart from human beings, as was his wont, the little cowman in brown corduroys tied below the knee, an old waistcoat, the sleeves of a blue shirt dotted with pink rolled up to the elbows of his brown arms, and his brown neck and shaven-looking head quite bare. So he stood, with his bit of stick wedged between his waist and the ground, star-ing with his light-lashed, water-blue eyes from under the thatch of his forelock.

The speeches rolled forth glib; the khaki-clad men drank their second fill that morning of coffee and cider; the little cowman stood straight and still, his head drawn back. Two figures – officers, men who had been at the front – detached themselves and came towards the group of unlikely youths. These wavered a little, were silent, sniggered, stood their ground – the khaki-clad figures passed among them. Hackneyed words, jests, the touch of flattery, changing swiftly to chaff – all the customary performance, hollow and pathetic; and then the two re-emerged; their hands clenched, their eyes shifting here and there, their lips drawn back in fixed smiles. They had failed, and were trying to hide it. They must not show contempt – the young slackers might yet come in, when the band played.

The cars were filled again, the band struck up 'It's a long, long way to Tipperary'.

And at the edge of the green, within two yards of the car's dusty passage, the little cowman stood apart and stared. His face was red. Behind him they were cheering – the parson and farmers, schoolchil-dren, girls, and even the group of youths. He alone did not cheer, but his face grew redder. When the dust above the road and the distant blare of Tipperary had dispensed and died, he walked back to the farm, dotting from one to other of his short feet. All that afternoon and evening he spoke no word; but that flush seemed to have settled in his face for good and all. He milked some cows, but forgot to bring the pails up. Two of his precious cows he left unmilked till their distressful lowing caused the farmer's wife to go down and see. There he was, standing against a gate, moving his brown neck from side to side like an animal in pain, oblivious seemingly of everything. She spoke to him:

'What's matter, Tam?'

All he could answer was: 'I'se goin', I'se goin'.'

She milked the cows herself.

For the next three days he could settle to nothing, leaving his jobs half done, speaking to on one save to say: 'I'se goin', I'se got to go.' Even the beasts looked at him surprised.

One Saturday the farmer, having consulted his wife, said quietly:

'Well, Tam, don't yu never get excited, ef yu want to go yu shall. I'll drive 'ee down Monday. Us won't du nothin' to keep yu back.'

The little cowman nodded. But he was restless as ever all through that Sunday, eating nothing.

On Monday morning, arrayed in his best clothes, he got into the dog-cart. There, without good-bye to anyone, not even to his beasts, he sat staring straight before him, square, and jolting up and down beside the farmer, who turned on him now and then a dubious, almost anxious, eye.

So they drove the eleven miles to the recruiting station. He got down and entered, the farmer with him.

'Well, my lad,' they asked him, 'what d'you want to join?'

'Royal Marines.'

It was a shock. The farmer took him by the arm.

'Why, yu'm an Exmoor man, Tam; better take county regiment. An't they gude enough for yu?'

Shaking his head, he answered: 'Royal Marines.'

Was it the glamour of the words, or what, that moved him to wish to join that outlandish corps? There was the wish immovable; they took him to the recruiting station for the Royal Marines.

Stretching up his short, square body and blowing out his cheeks to increase his height, he was put before the reading board. His eyes were splendid; little that passed in the hedgerows, the heavens, on the hill-sides, could escape them. They asked him to read the print.

'L.'

'No, my lad, you're guessing.'

'L.'

The farmer plucked at the recruiting officer's sleeve, his face twitched, and he whispered hoarsely:

''E don' know 'is alphabet.'

The officer turned and contemplated that figure with the browned face so reminiscent of a withered baby, and the little blue eyes staring out from under the dusty forelock. He grunted kindly; then going up and laying a hand on his shoulder, said:

'*Your* heart's all right, my lad, but you can't pass.'

Without a word the little cowman turned, and went out. An hour later he sat again beside the farmer on the way home, staring before him and jolting up and down, by no sign or word intimating what – if anything – he felt. But that evening he ate his tea.

Next day he had settled down again among his beasts.

12

Heritage: an impression

Written shortly after his visit to the Chailey Heritage School, East Sussex, 'Heritage' appeared in the second issue of *Reveille* and, after the war, Galsworthy reprinted it in *Tatterdemalion*. While this piece focused on the intangible elements of the institution, the tangible – indeed, material – aspects of the environment were nonetheless apparent to Galsworthy much in the same way they had been following his visit to the Lord Roberts Workshops in London. Beyond this aspect of the composition, Galsworthy offered no answers in response to his question about the future of Chailey's soldier-patients. Rather, he issued a condemnation that spoke directly to past abuses and suggested the new ones which had emerged with the return of so many men broken in battle. Juxtaposed to official images of the institution, such condemnation appeared ironic, since the very 'industrialism' of Chailey's 'clean bright workshops' was the very hope – indeed, the focus of treatment – for children broken by the Victorian Age and for soldiers broken by the 'war to end all wars'. More remarkable here, however, was Galsworthy's prophetic vision. As he had done in his previous writings about the war disabled he looked to the future even while he was aware of the exigencies of the present.

From that garden seat one could see the old low house of pinkish brick, with a path of queer-shaped flagstones running its length, and the tall grey chapel from which came the humming and chanting and organ drone of the Confirmation service. But for that, and the voices of two gardeners working below us among the fruits and flowers, the July hush was complete. And suddenly one became aware of being watched.

That thin white windmill on the hill!

Away past the house, perhaps six hundred yards, it stood, ghostly, with a face like that of a dark-eyed white owl, made by the crossing of its narrow sails. With a black companion – a yew-tree cut to pyramid form, on the central point of Sussex – it was watching us, for though one must presume it built of old time by man, it looked, up there against the sky, with its owl's face and its cross, like a Christo-Pagan presence.

What exactly Paganism was we shall never know; what exactly Christianism is, we are as little likely to discover; but here and there the two principles seem to dwell together in amity. For Paganism believed in the healthy and joyful body; and Christianism in the soul superior thereto. And, where we were sitting that summer day was the home of the bodies wrecked yet learning to be joyful, and of souls not above the process.

We moved from the grey-wood seat, and came on tiptoe to where house and chapel formed a courtyard. The doors were open, and we stood unseen, listening. From the centre of a square stone fountain a little bubble of water came up, and niched along one high wall a number of white pigeons were preening their feathers, silent, and almost mo- tionless, as though attending to the Service.

The sheer emotion of church sounds will now and then steal away reason from the unbeliever, and take him drugged and dreaming. 'De- fend, O Lord, this Thy child! . . .' So it came out to us in the dream and drowse of summer, which the little bubble of water cooled.

In his robes – cardinal, and white, and violet – the good Bishop stood in full sunlight, speaking to the crippled and the aid-raid children in their drilled rows under the shade of the doves' wall; and one felt far from this age, as if one had strayed back into that time when the build- ers of the old house laid slow brick on brick, wetting their whistles on mead, and knowing not tobacco.

And then, out by the chapel porch moved three forms in blue, with red neckties, and we were again in this new age, watching the faces of those listening children. The good Bishop was making them feel that he was happy in their presence, and that made them happy in his. For the great thing about life is the going-out of friendliness from being to being. And if a place be beautiful, and friendliness ever on the peace- path there, what more can we desire? And yet – how ironical this place of healing, thus beautiful 'Heritage!' Verily a heritage of our modern civilisation which makes all this healing necessary! If life were the off- spring of friendliness and beauty's long companionship, there would be no crippled children, no air-raid children, none of those good fellows in blue with red ties and maimed limbs; and the colony to which the Bishop spoke, standing grey-headed in the sun, would be dissolved. Friendliness seems so natural, beauty so appropriate to this earth! But in this torn world they are as fugitives who nest together here and there. Yet stumbling by chance upon their dove-cotes and fluttering happiness, one makes a little golden note, which does not fade off the tablet.

How entrancing it is to look at a number of faces never seen before – and how exasperating! – stamped coins of lives quite separate, quite different from every other; masks pallid, sunburned, smooth, or crumpled, to peep behind which one longs, as a lover looking for his lady at a carnival, or a man aching at summer beauty which he cannot quite fathom and possess. If one had a thousand lives, and time to know and sympathy to understand the heart of every creature met with, one would want – a million! May life make us all intuitive, strip away self-consciousness, and give us sunshine and unknown faces!

What were they all feeling and thinking – those little cripples doing their drill on crutches; those air-raid waifs swelling their Cockney chests, rising on their toes, puffing their cheeks out in anxiety to do their best; those soldiers in their blue 'slops,' with a hand gone there and a leg gone here, and this and that grievous disability, all carrying on so cheerfully?

Values are queer in this world. We are accustomed to exalt those who can say 'bo' to a goose; but that gift of expression which twines a halo round a lofty brow is no guarantee of goodness in the wearer. The really good are those plucky folk who plod their silent, often suffering, generally exploited ways, from birth to death, out of reach of the music of man's praise.

The first thing each child cripple makes here is a little symbolic ladder. In making it he climbs a rung on the way to his sky of self-support; and when at last he leaves this home, he steps off the top of it into the blue, and – so they say – walks there upright and undismayed, as if he had never suffered at Fate's hands. But what do he and she – for many are of the pleasant sex – think of the sky when they get there; that dusty and smoke-laden sky of industrialism which begat them? How can they breathe in it, coming from this place of flowers and fresh air, of clean bright workshops and elegant huts, which they on crutches built for themselves?

Masters of British industry, and leaders of the men and women who slave to make its wheels go round, make a pilgrimage to this spot, and learn what a foul disfigurement you have brought on the land of England these last five generations! The natural loveliness in this Heritage is no greater that the loveliness that used to be in a thousand places which you have blotted out of the book of beauty, with your smuts and wheels, your wires and welter. And to what end? To manufacture crippled children, and pale peaky little Cockneys whose nerves are gone; (and, to be sure, the railways and motor cars which will bring you here seem to them coming to life once more in sane and natural surroundings!) Blind and deaf and dumb industrialism is the accursed thing in this land and in all others.

If only we could send all our crippled soldiers to relearn life, in places such as this; if, instead of some forty or fifty, forty or fifty thousand could begin again, under the gaze of that white windmill! If they could slough off here not only those last horrors, but the dinge and drang of their upbringing in towns, where wheels go round, lights flare, streets reek, and no larks sing, save some little blinded victim in a cage. Poor William Blake:

> I will not cease from fighting, nor shall my sword sleep in my hand,
> Till we have built Jerusalem in England's green and pleasant land!

A long vigil his sword is keeping, while the clock strikes every hour of the twenty-four. We have not yet even laid Jerusalem's foundation stone. Ask one of those maimed soldier boys. 'I Like it here. Oh, yes, it's very pleasant for a change.' But he hastens to tell you that he goes in to Brighton every day to his training school, as if that saved the situation; almost surprised he seems that beauty and peace and good air are not intolerable to his town-bred soul. The towns have got us – nearly all. Not until we let beauty and the quiet voice of the fields, and the scent of clover creep again into our nerves, shall we begin to build Jerusalem and learn peacefulness once more. The countryman hates strife; it breaks his dream. And life should have its covering of dream – bird's flight, bird's song, wind in the ash-trees and the corn, tall lilies glistening, the evening shadows slanting out, the night murmuring of waters. There is no other genuine dream; without it to sweeten all, life is harsh and shrill and the east-wind dry, and evil overruns her more quickly than blight be-gums the rose-tree or frost blackens fern of a cold June night. We elders are past re-making England, but our children, even these crippled children here, may yet take a hand . . .

We left the tinies to the last – Montessorians, and some of the little cripples, too, but with cheeks so red that they looked as if the colour must come off. They lived in a house past the white mill, across the common; and they led us by the hand down spotless corridors into white dormitories. The smile of prettiest little maid of them all was the last thing one saw, leaving that 'Heritage' of print frocks and children's faces, of flowers and nightingales, under the lee of a group of pines, the only dark beauty in the long sunlight.

13

Addresses some soldiers on their future

This is the full text of chapter 13 of Galsworthy's novel *The Burning Spear*, which he published in 1919 under the pseudonym 'A.R.P.–M.' and again – this time with attribution – in 1923. The novel appeared during the following year as part of the Manaton edition of Galsworthy's collected works. It was not republished again until 1969–1970 when Heron Books of London included it in a reprint series of Galsworthy's 'collected works'. That series also included *Beyond: A Modern Comedy, Caravan: The Assembled Tales, The Country House, The Dark Flower, The Forsyte Saga, Fraternity, The Freelands, The Inn of Tranquillity, The Island Pharisees, A Modern Comedy, One More River, The Patrician* and *Saint's Progress*. Now in the public domain alongside much of Galsworthy's canon – including *A Sheaf, Another Sheaf, Caravan* and *Tatterdemalion* – *The Burning Spear* is widely available in various print-on-demand editions. However, none of these situates the novel, let alone this revealing chapter of the work, in the historical contexts offered by the preceding historical analysis.

On pleasant afternoons Mr Lavender would often take his seat on one of the benches which adorned the Spaniard's Road to enjoy the beams of the sun and the towers of the City confused in smoky distance. And strolling forth with Blink on the afternoon of the day on which the doctor had come to see him he sat down to read a periodical, which enjoined on everyone the necessity of taking the utmost interest in soldiers disabled by the war. 'Yes,' he thought, 'it is indeed our duty to force them, no matter what their disablements, to continue and surpass the heroism they displayed out there, and become superior to what they once were.' And it seemed to him a distinct dispensation of Providence when the rest of his bench was suddenly occupied by three soldiers in the blue garments and red ties of hospital life. They had been sitting there for some minutes, divided by the iron bars necessary to the morals of the neighbourhood, while Mr Lavender cudgelled his brains for an easy and natural method of approach, before Blink supplied the necessary avenue by taking her stand before a soldier and looking up into his eye.

'Lord!' said the one thus accosted, 'what a fyce! Look at her moustache! Well, cocky, 'oo are you starin' at?'

'My dog,' said Mr Lavender, perceiving his chance, 'has an eye for the strange and beautiful.'

'Wow,' said the soldier, whose face was bandaged, 'she'll get it 'ere, won't she?'

Encouraged by the smiles of the soldier and his comrades, Mr Lavender went on in the most natural voice he could assume.

'I'm sure you appreciate, my friends, the enormous importance of your own futures?'

The three soldiers, whose faces were all bandaged, looked as surprised as they could between them, and did not answer. Mr Lavender went on, dropping unconsciously into the diction of the article he had been reading: 'We are now at the turning-point of the ways, and not a moment is to be lost in impressing on the disabled man the paramount necessity of becoming again the captain of his soul. He who was a hero in the field must again lead us in those qualities of enterprise and endurance which have made him the admiration of the world.'

The three soldiers had turned what was visible of their faces towards Mr Lavender, and, seeing that he had riveted their attention, he proceeded: 'The apathy which hospital produces, together with the present scarcity of labour, is largely responsible for the dangerous position in which the disabled man now finds himself. Only we who have not to face his future can appreciate what that future is likely to be if he does not make the most strenuous efforts to overcome it. Boys,' he added earnestly, remembering suddenly that this was the word which those who had the personal touch ever employed, 'are you making those efforts? Are you equipping your minds? Are you taking advantage of your enforced leisure to place yourselves upon some path of life in which you can largely hold your own against all comers?'

He paused for a reply.

The soldiers, silent for a moment, in what seemed to Mr Lavender to be sheer astonishment, began to fidget; then the one next him turned to his neighbour, and said:

'Are we, Alf? Are we doin' what the gentleman says?'

'I can answer that for you,' returned Mr Lavender brightly; 'for I can tell by your hospitalized faces that you are living in the present; a habit which, according to our best writers, is peculiar to the British. I assure you,' he went on with a winning look, 'there is no future in that. If you do not at once begin to carve fresh niches for yourselves in the temple of industrialism you will be engulfed by the returning flood, and left high and dry upon the beach of fortune.'

During these last few words the half of an irritated look on the faces of the soldiers changed to fragments of an indulgent and protective expression.

'Right you are, guv'nor,' said the one in the middle. 'Don't you worry, we'll see you home all right.'

'It is you,' said Mr Lavender, 'that I must see home. For that is largely the duty of us who have not had the great privilege of fighting for our country.'

These words, which completed the soldiers' conviction that Mr Lavender was not quite all there, caused them to rise.

'Come on, then,' said one; 'we'll see each other home. We've got to be in by five. You don't have a string to your dog, I see.'

'Oh no!' said Mr Lavender, puzzled. 'I am not blind.'

'Barmy,' said the soldier soothingly. 'Come on, sir, an' we can talk abaht it on the way.'

Mr Lavender, delighted at the impression he had made, rose and walked beside them, taking insensibly the direction for home.

'What do you advise us to do, then, guv'nor?' said one of the soldiers.

'Throw away all thought of the present,' returned Mr Lavender, with intense earnestness; 'forget the past entirely, wrap yourselves wholly in the future. Do nothing which will give you immediate satisfaction. Do not consider your families, or any of those transient considerations such as pleasure, your homes, your condition of health, or your economic position; but place yourselves unreservedly in the hands of those who by hard thinking on this subject are alone in the condition to appreciate the individual circumstances of each of you. For only by becoming a flock of sheep can you be conducted into those new pastures where the grass of your future will be sweet and plentiful. Above all, continue to be the heroes which you were under the spur of your country's call, for you must remember that your country is still calling you.'

'That's right,' said the soldier on Mr Lavender's left. 'Puss, puss!' 'Does your dog swot cats?'

At so irrelevant a remark Mr Lavender looked suspiciously from left to right, but what there was of the soldiers' faces told him nothing.

'Which is your hospital?' he asked.

'Down the 'ill, on the right,' returned the soldier. 'Which is yours?'

'Alas! it is not in a hospital that I –'

'I know,' said the soldier delicately, 'don't give it a name; no need. We're all friends 'ere. Do you get out much?'

'I always take an afternoon stroll,' said Mr Lavender, 'when my public life permits. If you think your comrades would like me to come and lecture to them on their future I should be only too happy.'

'D'you 'ear, Alf?' said the soldier. 'D'you think they would?'

The soldier addressed put a finger to the sound side of his mouth and uttered a catcall.

'I might effect a radical change in their views,' continued Mr Lavender, a little puzzled. 'Let me leave you this periodical. Read it, and you will see how extremely vital all that I have been saying is. And then, perhaps, if you would send me a round robin, such as is usual in a democratic country, I could pop over almost any day after five. I sometimes feel' – and here Mr Lavender stopped in the middle of the road, overcome by sudden emotion – 'that I have really no right to be alive when I see what you have suffered for me.'

'That's all right, old bean,', said the soldier on his left; 'you'd 'a done the same for us but for your disabilities. We don't grudge it you.'

'Boys,' said Mr Lavender, 'you are men. I cannot tell you how much I admire and love you.'

'Well, give it a rest, then; t'ain't good for yer. And, look 'ere! Any time they don't treat you fair in there, tip us the wink, and we'll come over and do in your 'ousekeeper.'

Mr Lavender smiled.

'My poor housekeeper!' he said. 'I thank you all the same for your charming goodwill. This is where I live,' he added, stopping at the gate of the little house smothered in lilac and laburnum. 'Can I offer you some tea?'

The three soldiers looked at each other, and Mr Lavender, noticing their surprise, attributed it to the word tea.

'I regret exceedingly that I am a total abstainer,' he said. The remark, completing the soldiers' judgement of his case, increased their surprise at the nature of his residence; it remained unanswered, save by a shuffling of the feet.

Mr Lavender took off his hat.

'I consider it a great privilege,' he said, 'to have been allowed to converse with you. Goodbye, and God bless you!'

So saying, he opened the gate and entered his little garden, carrying his hat in his hand, and followed by Blink.

The soldiers watched him disappear within, then continued on their way down the hill in silence.

'Blimey,' said one suddenly. 'Some of these old civilians 'ave come it barmy on the crumpet since the war began. Give me the trenches!'

At Hôpital Bénévole in France

14

Flotsam and Jetsam: a reminiscence

This composition, with 'Cafard' and 'Poirot and Bidan', represents three
of the four pieces of fiction written by Galsworthy between March and
July 1917, during the weeks and months following his volunteer service
in Hôpital Bénévole. The fourth piece, entitled 'Impressions of France,
1916–1917', is not included here due to its chief focus being on the
wartime 'French character', not specifically the disabled soldiers with
whom Galsworthy interacted at Hôpital Bénévole. 'Flotsam and Jetsam:
a reminiscence' appeared originally in the December 1917 issue of
Scribner's Magazine, accompanied by pen-and-ink sketches by the artist
and illustrator Reginald Birch. Galsworthy subsequently reprinted it in
Tatterdemalion and in the Manaton Edition of his collected works.

The tides of the war were washing up millions of wrecked lives on all the
shores; what mattered the flotsam of a conscripted deep-sea Breton
fisherman, slowly pining away for lack of all he was accustomed to; or
the jetsam of a tall glassblower from the 'invaded countries', drifted into
the hospital – no one quite knew why – prisoner for twenty months
with the Boches, released at last because of his half-paralysed tongue –
What mattered they? What mattered anything, or anyone, in days like
those?
　Corporal Mignan, wrinkling a thin, parchmenty face, full of suffering
and kindly cynicism, used to call them '*mes deux phénomènes*'. Riddled
to the soul by gastritis, he must have found them trying roommates,
with the tricks and manners of sick and naughty children towards a
long-suffering nurse. To understand all is to forgive all, they say; but,
though he had suffered enough to understand much, Mignan was

tempted at times to deliver judgement – for example, when Roche, the Breton fisherman, rose from his bed more than ten times in the night, and wandered out into the little courtyard of the hospital to look at the stars, because he could not keep still within four walls – so unreasonable of the '*type*'. Or when Gray, the tall glassblower – his grandfather had been English – refused with all the tenacity of a British workman to wear an undervest, with the thermometer below zero centigrade.

They inhabited the same room, Flotsam and Jetsam, but never spoke to one another. And yet in all that hospital of French soldiers they were the only two who, in a manner of speaking, had come from England. Fourteen hundred years have passed since the Briton ancestors of Roche crossed in their shallow boats. Yet he was as hopelessly un-French as a Welshman of the hills is to this day un-English. His dark face, shy as a wild animal's, his peat-brown eyes, and the rare, strangely sweet smile which once in a way strayed up into them; his creased brown hands always trying to tie an imaginary cord; the tobacco pouched in his brown cheek; his improperly buttoned blue trousers; his silence eternal as the stars themselves; his habit of climbing trees – all marked him out as no true Frenchman. Indeed, that habit of climbing trees caused every soul who saw him to wonder if he ought to be at large: monkeys alone pursue this pastime. And yet, – surely one might understand that trees were for Roche the masts of his far-off fishing barque, each hand-grip on the branch of plane or pine-tree solace to his overmastering hunger for the sea. Up there he would cling, or stand with hands in pockets, and look out, far over the valley and the yellowish grey-pink of the pantiled town-roofs, a mile away, far into the mountains where snow melted not, far over this foreign land of '*midi trois quarts*', to an imagined Breton coast and the seas that roll from there to Cape Breton where the cod are. Since he never spoke unless spoken to – no, not once – it was impossible for his landsmen comrades to realise why he got up those trees, and they would summon each other to observe this '*phénomène*,' this human ourang-outang, who had not their habit of keeping firm earth beneath their feet. They understood his other eccentricities better. For instance, he could not stay still even at his meals, but must get up and slip out, because he chewed tobacco, and, since the hospital regulations forbade his spitting on the floor, he must naturally go and spit outside. For '*ces types-là*' to chew and drink was – life! To the presence of tobacco in the cheek and the absence of drink from the stomach they attributed all his un-French ways, save just that one mysterious one of climbing trees.

And Gray – though only one-fourth English – how utterly British was that 'arrogant civilian', as the '*poilus*' called him. Even his clothes, some-how, were British – no one knew who had given them to him; his short grey workman's jacket, brown dingy trousers, muffler and checked cap; his long, idle walk, his absolute *sans-gêne*, regardless of anyone but himself; his tall, loose figure, with a sort of grace lurking somewhere in its slow, wandering movements, and long, thin fingers. That wambling, independent form might surely be seen any day outside a thousand British public-houses, in time of peace. His face, with its dust-coloured hair, projecting ears, grey eyes with something of the child in them, and something of the mule, and something of a soul trying to wander out of the forest of misfortune; his little, tip-tilted nose that never grew on pure-blooded Frenchmen; under a scant moustache his thick lips, dis-figured by infirmity of speech, whence passed so continually a dribble of saliva – sick British workman was stamped on him. Yet he was pas-sionately fond of washing himself: his teeth, his head, his clothes. Into the frigid winter he would go, and stand at the '*Source*' half an hour at a time, washing and washing. It was a cause of constant irritation to Mignan that his '*phénomène*' would never come to time, on account of this disastrous habit; the hospital corridors resounded almost daily with the importuning of those shapeless lips for something clean – a shirt, a pair of drawers, a bath, a handkerchief. He had a fixity of purpose; not too much purpose, but so fixed. – Yes, he was English!

For '*les deux phénomènes*' the soldiers, the servants, and the 'Powers' of the hospital – all were sorry; yet they could not understand to the point of quite forgiving their vagaries. The twain were outcast, wander-ing each in a dumb world of his own, each in the endless circle of one or two hopeless notions. It was irony – or the French system – which had ordered the Breton Roche to get well in a place whence he could see nothing flatter than a mountain, smell no sea, eat no fish. And God knows what had sent Gray there. His story was too vaguely understood, for his stumbling speech simply could not make it plain. '*Les Boches – ils vont en payer cher – les Boches*,' muttered fifty times a day, was the burden of his song. Those Boches had come into his village early in the war, torn him from his wife and his '*petite fille*'. Since then he had 'had fear', been hungry, been cold, eaten grass; eyeing some fat little dog, he would leer and mutter: '*J'ai mangé cela, c'est bon!*' and with fierce triumph add: '*Ils ont faim, les Boches!*' The 'arrogant civilian' had never done his military service, for his infirmity, it seemed, had begun before the war.

Dumb, each in his own way, and differing in every mortal thing except the reality of their misfortunes, never were two beings more lonely. Their quasi-nurse, Corporal Mignan, was no doubt right in his estimate of their characters. For him, so patient in the wintry days, with his '*deux phénomènes*', they were divested of all that halo which misfortune sets round the heads of the afflicted. He had too much to do with them, and saw them as they would have been if undogged by Fate. Of Roche he would say: '*Il n'est pas mon rêve. Je n'aime pas ces types taciturnes; quand même, il n'est pas mauvais. Il est marin – les marins – !*' and he would shrug his shoulders, as who should say: 'Those poor devils – what can you expect?' '*Mais ce Gray*' – it was one bitter day when Gray had refused absolutely to wear his great-coat during a motor drive – '*c'est un mauvais type! Il est malin – il sait très bien ce qu'il veut. C'est un egoiste!*' An egoist! Poor Gray! No doubt he was, instinctively conscious that if he did not make the most of what little personality was left within his wandering form, it would slip and he would be no more. Even a winter fly is mysteriously anxious not to become dead. That he was '*malin*' – cunning – became the accepted view about Gray; not so '*malin*' that he could 'cut three paws off a duck', as the old grey Territorial, Grandpère Poirot, would put it, but '*malin*' enough to know very well what he wanted, and how, by sticking to his demand, to get it. Mignan, typically French, did not allow enough for the essential Englishman in Gray. Besides, one must be *malin* if one has only the power to say about one-tenth of what one wants, and then not be understood once in twenty times. Gray did not like his great-coat – a fine old French-blue military thing with brass buttons – the arrogant civilian would have none of it! It was easier to shift the Boches on the western front than to shift an idea, once in his head. In the poor soil of his soul the following plants of thought alone now flourished: Hatred of the Boches; love of English tobacco – '*Il est bon – il est bon!*' he would say, tapping his Virginian cigarette; the wish to see again his 'petite fille'; to wash himself; to drink a '*café natur*' and bottled beer every day after the midday meal, and to go to Lyons to see his uncle and work for his living. And who shall say that any of these fixed ideas were evil in him?

But back to Flotsam, whose fixed idea was Brittany! Nostalgia is a long word, and a malady from which the English do not suffer, for they carry their country on their backs, walk the wide world in a cloud of their own atmosphere, making that world England. The French have eyes to see, and, when not surrounded by houses that have flatness, shutters, and subtle colouring – yellowish, French-grey, French-green

– by cafés, by plane-trees, by Frenchwomen, by scents of wood-smoke and coffee roasted in the streets; by the wines, and infusions of the herbs of France; by the churches of France and the beautiful silly chiming of their bells – when not surrounded by all these, they know it, feel it, suffer. But even they do not suffer so dumbly and instinctively, so like a wild animal caged, as that Breton fisherman, caged up in a world of hill and valley – not the world as he had known it. They called his case 'shell-shock' – for the French system would not send a man to convalescence for anything so essentially civilian as home-sickness, even when it had taken a claustrophobic turn. A system recognises only causes which you can see; holes in the head, hamstrung legs, frostbitten feet, with other of the legitimate consequences of war. But it was not shell-shock. Roche was really possessed by the feeling that he would never get out, never get home, smell fish and the sea, watch the bottle-green breakers roll in on his native shore, the sun gleaming through wave-crests lifted and flying back in spray, never know the accustomed heave and roll under his feet, or carouse in a seaport cabaret, or see his old mother – *la veuve* Roche. And, after all, there was a certain foundation for his fear. It was not as if this war could be expected to stop some day. There they were, in the trenches, they and the enemy set over against each other, 'like china dogs,' in the words of Grandée Poirot; and there they would be, so far as Roche's ungeared nerves could grasp, for ever. And, while like china dogs they sat, he knew that he would not be released, not allowed to go back to the sea and the smells and the sounds thereof; for he had still all his limbs, and no bullet-hole to show under his thick dark hair. No wonder he got up the trees and looked out for sight of the waves, and fluttered the weak nerves of the hospital 'Powers,' till they saw themselves burying him with a broken spine, at the expense of the subscribers. Nothing to be done for the poor fellow, except to take him motor-drives, and to insist that he stayed in the dining-room long enough to eat some food.

Then, one bright day, a 'Power,' watching his hands, conceived the idea of giving him two balls of string, one blue, the other buff, and all that afternoon he stayed up a single tree, and came down with one of his rare sweet smiles and a little net, half blue, half buff, with a handle covered with a twist of Turkey-red twill – such a thing as one scoops up shrimps with. He was paid for it, and his eyes sparkled. You see, he had no money – the '*poilu*' seldom has; and money meant drink, and tobacco in his cheek. They gave him more string, and for the next few days it rained little nets, beautifully if simply made. They thought that his salvation was in sight. It takes an eye to tell salvation from damnation, sometimes. . . . In any case, he no longer roamed from tree to tree, but sat across a single branch, netting. The 'Powers' began to speak of him as 'rather a dear', for it is characteristic of human nature to take interest only in that which by some sign of progress makes you feel that you are doing good.

Next Sunday a distinguished doctor came, and, when he had been fed, some one conceived the notion of interesting him, too, in Flotsam. A learned, kindly, influential man – well-fed – something might come of it, even that '*réforme*', that sending home, which all agreed was what poor Roche needed, to restore his brain. He was brought in, therefore, amongst the chattering party, and stood, dark, shy, his head down, like the man in Millet's 'Angelus', his hands folded on his cap, in front of his unspeakably buttoned blue baggy trousers, as though in attitude of prayer to the doctor, who, uniformed and grey-bearded, like an old somnolent goat, beamed on him through spectacles with a sort of shrewd benevolence. The catechism began. So he had something to ask, had he? A swift, shy lift of the eyes: 'Yes.' 'What then?' 'To go home.' 'To go home? What for? To get married?' A swift, shy smile. 'Fair or dark?' No answer, only a shift of hands on his cap. 'What!' Was there no one – no ladies at home? '*Ce n' est pas ça qui manque!*' At the laughter greeting that dim flicker of wit the uplifted face was cast down again. That lonely, lost figure must suddenly have struck the doctor, for his catechism became a long, embarrassed scrutiny; and with an: '*Eh bien! mon vieux, nous verrons!*' ended. Nothing came of it, of course. '*Cas de réforme?*' Oh, certainly, if it had depended on the learned, kindly doctor. But the system – and all its doors to be unlocked! Why, by the time the last door was prepared to open, the first would be closed again! So the 'Powers' gave Roche more string – so good, you know, to see him interested in something! . . . It does take an eye to tell salvation from damnation! For he began to go down now of an afternoon into the little old town – not smelless, but most quaint – all yellowish-grey, with rosy-tiled roofs. Once it had been Roman, once a walled city of the Middle Ages; never would it be modern. The dogs ran muzzled; from a first floor a goat, munching green fodder, hung his devilish black beard above your head; and through the main street the peasant farmers, above military age, looking old as sun-dried roots, in their dark *pèlerines*, drove their wives and produce in little slow carts. Parched oleanders in pots one would pass, and old balconies with wilting flowers hanging down over the stone, and perhaps an umbrella with a little silver handle, set out to dry.

Roche would go in by the back way, where the old town gossips sat on a bench in the winter sunshine, facing the lonely cross shining gold on the high hill-top opposite, placed there in days when there was some meaning in such things; past the little '*Place*' with the old fountain and the brown plane-trees in front of the Mairie; past the church, so ancient that it had fortunately been forgotten, and remained unfinished and beautiful. Did Roche, Breton that he was – half the love-ladies in Paris, they say – falsely, no doubt – are Bretonnes – ever enter the church in passing? Some rascal had tried to burn down its beautiful old door from the inside, and the flames had left on all that high western wall smears like the fingermarks of hell, or the background of a Velasquez Crucifixion. Did he ever enter and stand, knotting his knot which never got knotted, in the dark loveliness of that grave building, where in the deep silence a dusty-gold little angel blew on his horn from the top of the canopied pulpit, and a dim carved Christ of touching beauty looked down on His fellow-men from above some dry chrysanthemums; and a tall candle burned quiet and lonely here and there, and the flags of France hung above the altar, that men might know how God – though resting – was with them and their country? Perhaps! But, more likely, he passed it, with its great bell riding high and open among scrolls of ironwork, and – Breton that he was – entered the nearest cabaret, kept by the woman who would tell you that her soldier husband had passed 'within two fingers' of death. One cannot spend one's earnings in a church, nor appease there the inextinguishable longings of a sailor.

And lo! – on Christmas day Roche came back so drunk that his nurse Mignan took him to his bedroom and turned the key of the door on him. But you must not do this to a Breton fisherman full of drink and claustrophobia. It was one of those errors even Frenchmen may make, to the after sorrow of their victims. One of the female 'Powers,' standing outside, heard a roar, the crash of a foot against the panel of a door, and saw Roche, 'like a great cat' come slithering through the hole. He flung his arm out, brushed the 'Power' back against the wall, cried out fiercely: '*La boîte – je ne veux pas la boîte!*' and rushed for the stairs. Here were other female 'Powers'; he dashed them aside and passed down. But in the bureau at the foot was a young Corporal of the '*Légion Etrangère*' – a Spaniard who had volunteered for France – great France; he ran out, took Roche gently by the arm, and offered to drink with him. And so they sat, those two, in the little bureau, drinking black coffee, while the young Corporal talked like an angel and Roche like a wild man – about his mother, about his dead brother who had been sitting on his bed, as he said, about '*la boîte,*' and the turning of that key. And slowly he became himself – or so they thought – and all went in to supper. Ten minutes later one of the 'Powers,' looking for the twentieth time to make sure he was eating, saw an empty place: he had slipped out like a shadow and was gone again. A big cavalryman and the Corporal retrieved him that night from a *café* near the station; they had to use force at times to bring him in. Two days later he was transferred to a town hospital, where discipline would not allow him to get drunk or climb trees. For the 'Powers' had reasoned thus: To climb trees is bad; to get drunk is bad; but to do both puts on us too much responsibility; he must go! They had, in fact, been scared. And so he passed away to a room under the roof of a hospital in the big town miles away – *la boîte* indeed! – where for liberty he must use a courtyard without trees, and but little tobacco came to his cheek; and there he eats his heart out to this day, perhaps. But some say he had no heart – only the love of drink, and climbing. Yet, on that last evening, to one who was paying him for a little net, he blurted out: 'Some day I will tell you something – not now – in a year's time. *Vous êtes le seul* – !' What did he mean by that, if he had no heart to eat? . . . The night after he had gone, a little black dog strayed up, and among the trees barked and barked at some portent or phantom. 'Ah! the camel! Ah! the pig! I had him on my back all night!' Grandpère Poirot said next morning. That was the very last of Flotsam. . . .

And now to Jetsam! It was on the day but one after Roche left that Gray was reported missing. For some time past he had been getting stronger, clearer in speech. They began to say of him: 'It's wonderful – the improvement since he came – wonderful!' His salvation also seemed in sight. But from the words 'He's rather a dear!' all recoiled, for as he grew stronger he became more stubborn and more irritable – 'cunning egoist' that he was! According to the men, he was beginning to show himself in his true colours. He had threatened to knife anyone who played a joke on him – the arrogant civilian! On the day that he was missing it appears that after the midday meal he had asked for a 'café natur' and for some reason had been refused. Before his absence was noted it was night already, clear and dark; all day something as of Spring had stirred in the air. The Corporal and a 'Power' set forth down the wooded hill into the town, to scour the *cafés* and hang over the swift, shallow river, to see if by any chance Gray had been overtaken by another paralytic stroke and was down there on the dark sand. The sleepy gendarmes too were warned and given his description. But the only news next morning was that he had been seen walking on the main road up the valley. Two days later he was found, twenty miles away, wandering towards Italy. '*Perdu*' was his only explanation, but it was not believed, for now began that continual demand: '*Je voudrais aller à Lyon, voir mon oncle – travailler!*' As the big cavalryman put it: 'He is bored here!' It was considered unreasonable, by soldiers who found themselves better off than in other hospitals; even the 'Powers' considered it ungrateful, almost. See what he had been like when he came – a mere trembling bag of bones, only too fearful of being sent away. And yet, who would not be bored, crouching all day long about the stoves, staunching his poor dribbling mouth, rolling his inevitable cigarette, or wandering down, lonely, to hang over the bridge parapet, having thoughts in his head and for ever unable to express them. His state was worse than dumbness, for the dumb have resigned hope of conversation. Gray would have liked to talk if it had not taken about five minutes to understand each thing he said – except the refrain which all knew by heart: '*Les Boches – ils vont en payer cher – les Boches!*' The idea that he could work and earn his living was fantastic to those who watched him dressing himself, or sweeping the courtyard, pausing every few seconds to contemplate some invisible difficulty, or do over again what he had just not done. But with that new access of strength, or perhaps the open weather – as if Spring had come before its time – his fixed idea governed him completely; he began to threaten to kill himself if he could not go to work and see his uncle at Lyons; and every five days or so he had to be brought back from far up some hill road. The situation had become so ridiculous that the 'Powers' said in despair: 'Very well, my friend! Your uncle says he can't have you, and you can't earn your own living yet; but you shall go and see for yourself!' And go he did, a little solemn now that it had come to this point – in specially bought yellow boots – he refused black – and a specially bought overcoat with sleeves – he would have none of a *pèlerine*, the arrogant civilian, no more than of a military *capote*. For a week the hospital knew him not. Deep winter set in two days before he went, and the whole land was wrapped in snow. The huge, disconsolate crows seemed all the life left in the valley, and poplar-trees against the rare blue sky were dowered with miraculous snow-blossoms, beautiful as any blossom of Spring. And still in the winter sun the town gossips sat on the bench under the wall, and the cross gleamed out, and the church bell, riding high in its whitened ironwork, tolled almost every day for the passing of some wintered soul, and long processions, very black in the white street, followed it, followed it – home. Then came a telegram from Gray's uncle: 'Impossible to keep Aristide (the name of the arrogant civilian), takes the evening train to-morrow. Albert Gray.' So Jetsam was coming back! What would he be like now that his fixed idea had failed him? Well! He came at midday; thinner, more clay-coloured in the face, with a bad cold; but he ate as heartily as ever, and at once asked to go to bed. At four o'clock a 'Power', going up to see, found him sleeping like a child. He slept for twenty hours on end. No one liked to question him about his time away; all that he said – and bitterly – was: 'They wouldn't let me work!' But the second evening after his return there came a knock on the door of the little room where the 'Powers' were sitting after supper, and there stood Gray, long and shadowy, holding on to the screen, smoothing his jaw-bone with the other hand, turning eyes like a child's from face to face, while his helpless lips smiled. One of the 'Powers' said: 'What do you want, my friend?'

'*Je voudrais aller à Paris, voir ma petite fille.*'

'Yes, yes; after the war. Your *petite fille* is not in Paris, you know.'

'*Non?*' The smile was gone; it was seen too plainly that Gray was not as he had been. The access of vigour, stirring of new strength, 'improvement' had departed, but the beat of it, while there, must have broken him, as the beat of some too-strong engine shatters a frail frame. His 'improvement' had driven him to his own undoing. With the failure of his pilgrimage he had lost all hope, all 'egoism.' . . . It takes an eye, indeed, to tell salvation from damnation! He was truly Jetsam now – terribly thin and ill and sad; and coughing. Yet he kept the independence of his spirit. In that bitter cold, nothing could prevent him stripping to the waist to wash, nothing could keep him lying in bed, or kill his sense of the proprieties. He would not wear his overcoat – it was invalidish; he would not wear his new yellow boots and keep his feet dry, except on Sundays: '*Ils sont bons!*' he would say. And before he would profane their goodness, his old worn-out shoes had to be reft from him. He would not admit that he was ill, that he was cold, that he was – anything. But at night, a 'Power' would be awakened by groans and, hurrying to his room, find him huddled nose to knees, moaning. And now, every evening, as though craving escape from his own company, he would come to the little sitting-room, and stand with that deprecating smile, smoothing his jawbone, until someone said: 'Sit down, my friend, and have some coffee.' '*Merci, ma soeur – il est bon, il est bon!*' and down he would sit, and roll a cigarette with his long fingers, tapering as any artist's, while his eyes fixed themselves intently on anything that moved. But soon they would stray off to another world, and he would say thickly, sullenly, fiercely: '*Les Boches – ils vont en payer cher*

– *les Boches!*' On the walls were some trophies from the war of 'seventy'. His eyes would gloat over them, and he would get up and finger a long pistol, or an old *papier-maché* helmet. Never was a man who so lacked *gêne* – at home in any company; it inspired reverence, that independence of his, which had survived twenty months of imprisonment with those who, it is said, make their victims salute them – to such a depth has their civilisation reached. One night he tried to tell about the fright he had been given. The Boches – it seemed – had put him and two others against a wall, and shot those other two. Holding up two tapering fingers, he mumbled: '*Assassins – assassins! Ils vont en payer cher-les Boches!*' But sometimes there was something almost beautiful in his face, as if his soul had rushed from behind his eyes, to answer some little kindness done to him, or greet some memory of the days before he was 'done for' – *foutu*, as he called it.

One day he admitted a pain about his heart; and time, too, for at moments he would look like death itself. His nurse, Corporal Mignan, had long left his '*deux phénomènes!*', having drifted away on the tides of the system, till he should break down again and drag through the hospitals once more. Gray had a room to himself now; the arrogant civilian's groaning at night disturbed the others. Yet, if you asked him in the morning if he had slept well, he answered invariably, '*Oui – oui – toujours, toujours!*' For, according to him, you see, he was still strong; and he would double his arm and tap his very little muscle, to show that he could work. But he did not believe it now, for one day a 'Power,' dusting the men's writing-room, saw a letter on the blotter, and with an ashamed eye read these words: –

Cher Oncle,

J'ai eu la rage contre toi, mais c'est passé maintenant. Je veux seulement me reposer. Je ne peux pas me battre pour la France – j'ai voulu travailler pour elle; mais on ne m'a pas permi.

Votre neveu, qui t'embrasse de loin.

Seulement me reposer – only to rest! Rest he will, soon, if eyes can speak. Pass, and leave for ever that ravished France for whom he wished to work – pass, without having seen again his *petite fille*. No more in the corridor above the stove, no more in the little dining-room or the avenue of pines will be seen his long, noiseless, lonely figure, or be heard his thick stumbling cry:

'*Les Boches – ils vont en payer cher – les Boches!*'

~15~

'Cafard'

'Cafard' appeared originally in the January 1918 issue of *Scribner's Magazine* and subsequently in the November 1919 issue of *Current Opinion* and in *Tatterdemalion*. Galsworthy also included 'Cafard' in the Manaton Edition of his collected works and in *Caravan*. The story appeared once more before Galsworthy's death when George R. MacMinn and Harvey Eagleson included it in their *College Readings in the Modern Short Story* (Boston, MA: Ginn & Co., 1931). Nearly forty years later, the novelist and critic Anthony West included 'Cafard' in *The Galsworthy Reader* (New York: Scribner's, 1968). The original *Scribner's* version of Cafard appears here.

The soldier Jean Liotard lay, face to the earth, by the bank of the river Drôme. He lay where the grass and trees ended, and between him and the shrunken greenish current was much sandy foreshore; for summer was at height, and the snows had long finished melting and passing down. The burning sun had sucked up all moisture, the earth was parched, but to-day a cool breeze blew. Willow and aspen leaves were fluttering and hissing as if millions of tiny kisses were being given up there; and a few swathes of white cloud were – it seemed – drawn, not driven along the blue. The soldier Jean Liotard had fixed his eyes on the ground, where was nothing to see but the dried grasses. He had '*cafard*', for he was due to leave the hospital to-morrow and go up before the military authorities, for 'prolongation.' There he would answer perfunctory questions, and be told at once: '*Au dépôt*'; or have to lie naked before them that some '*major*' might prod his ribs to find out whether his heart, displaced by shell-shock, had gone back sufficiently to normal

197

position. He had received one 'prolongation,' and so, wherever his heart might be now, he felt sure he would not get another. '*Au dépôt*' was the fate before him, fixed as that river flowing down to its death in the sea. He had '*cafard*' – the little black beetle in the brain, which gnaws and eats and destroys all hope and heaven in a man. It had been working at him all last week, and now he was at a monstrous depth of evil and despair. To begin again the cursed barrack-round, the driven life, until in a month perhaps, packed like bleating sheep in the troop-train, he made that journey once more to the fighting line – '*A la hachette – à la hachette!*'

He had stripped off his red flannel jacket, and lay with shirt opened to the waist, to get the breeze against his heart. In his brown good-looking face the hazel eyes, which in these three God-deserted years had acquired a sort of startled gloom, stared out like a dog's, rather prominent, seeing only the thoughts within him – thoughts and images swirling round and round in a dark whirlpool, drawing his whole being deeper and deeper. He was unconscious of the summer hum and rustle, the cooing of the dove up in that willow-tree, the winged enamelled fairies floating past, the chirr of the *cicadas*, that little brown lizard among the pebbles, almost within reach, seeming to listen to the beating of summer's heart, so motionless it lay; unconscious, as though in verity he were again deep in some stifling trench, with German shells whining over him, and the smell of muck and death making fetid the air. He was in the mood to curse God and die; for he was devout – a Catholic, and still went to Mass. And God, it seemed, had betrayed the earth, and Jean Liotard. All the enormities he had seen in his two years at the Front – the mouthless, mangled faces, the human ribs whence rats would steal; the frenzied, tortured horses, with leg or quarter rent away, still living; the rotted farms, the dazed and hopeless peasants; his innumerable suffering comrades; the desert of no-man's-land; and all the thunder and moaning of war; and the reek and the freezing of war; and the driving – the callous, perpetual driving – by some great Force which shovelled warm human hearts and bodies, warm human hopes and loves by the million into the furnace; and over all, dark sky without a break, without a gleam of blue, or lift, anywhere – all this enclosed him, lying in the golden heat, so that not a glimmer of life or hope could get at him. Back into it all again! Back into it, he who had been through forty times the hell that the 'majors' ever endured, five hundred times the hell ever glimpsed at by those journalists, safe on their chairs with their ink-pots full of eloquence – Ah! he was sick of them! Let them allow the soldiers, whose lives were spent like water – poor devils who bled, and froze, and starved, and sweated – let them suffer those to talk for once! The black blood mounted in his brain. Ah! if only he could see the *sacré* politicians and journalists hanging in rows in every country; the mouth-fighters, the pen-fighters, the fighters with other men's blood! Those comfortable citizens would never rest till there was not a young man with whole limbs left in France! Had he not killed Boches enough that they might leave him and his tired heart in peace? He thought of his first charge; of how queer and soft that Boche body felt when his bayonet went through; and another, and another. Ah! he had *joliment* done his duty that day! And something wrenched at his ribs. Only Boches – but their wives and children, their mothers, faces questioning, faces pleading for them – pleading with whom? Not with him! Who was he that had taken those lives, and others since, but a poor devil without a life himself, without the right to breathe or move except to the orders of a Force that had no mind, that had no heart, that had nothing but a blind will to go on. If only he survived – it was not possible – but if only he survived, and with his millions of comrades could come back and hold the reckoning? Some scare-the-crows then would waggle in the wind! The butterflies would perch on a few mouths empty at last; the flies enjoy a few silent tongues! Then slowly his maddened, unreasoning rancour vanished into a mere awful pity for himself. Was a fellow never again to look at the sky, and the good soil, the fruit, the corn, without this dreadful black cloud above him; never again make love among the trees, or saunter down a lighted boulevard, or sit before a *café*? Never again attend Mass without this black dog of disgust and dread sitting on his shoulders, riding him to death? Angels of pity! Was there never to be an end? One was going mad under it – yes, mad! And the face of his mother came before him, as he had seen her last, just three years ago, when he left his home in the now invaded country to join his regiment – his mother who, with all his family, was in the power of the Boche. He had gone gaily, and she had stood like stone, her hand held over her eyes, in the sunlight, watching him while the train ran out. Usually the thought of the cursed Boches holding in their heavy hands all that was dear to him was enough to sweep his soul to a clear and definite hate, which made all this nightmare of war seem natural and made him ready to fight again; but now it was not enough – he had 'cafard.'

He turned on his back. The sky above the mountains might have been black for all the joy its blue gave him. The butterflies, those drifting flakes of joy, passed unseen. He was thinking: No rest, no end, except by walking over bodies, dead, mangled bodies of poor devils like himself, poor hunted devils, who wanted nothing but never to lift a hand in combat again so long as they lived, who wanted – as he wanted – nothing but laughter and love and rest! *Quelle vie!* A carnival of leaping demonry! A dream – unutterably bad! 'And when I go back to it all,' he thought, 'I shall go all shaven and smart, and wave my hand as if I were going to a wedding, as we all do. *Vive la France!* Ah! Can't a poor devil have a dreamless sleep!' He closed his eyes, but the sun struck hot on them through the lids, and he turned over on his face again, and looked longingly at the river; they said it was deep in mid-stream; it still ran fast there! But what was that down by the water? Had he really gone mad? And he uttered a queer laugh. There was his black dog – the black dog off his shoulders, the black dog which rode him, yes, that had become his very self, just going to wade in! And he called out:

'*Hé! Le copain!*' It could not be his own nightmare dog, for it stopped drinking, tucked its tail in, and cowered at the sound of his voice. Then it came from the water and sat down on its base among the stones and looked at him. A real dog. But what a guy! What a thin wretch of a little black dog! It sat and stared – a mongrel who might once have been pretty. It stared at Jean Liotard with the pathetic gaze of a dog so thin and hungry that it earnestly desires to go to men and get fed once more, but has been so kicked and beaten that it dare not. It seemed held in suspense by the equal overmastering impulses, fear and hunger. And Jean Liotard stared back. The lost, as it were despairing, look of the dog began to penetrate his brain. He held out his hand, and said: '*Viens!*' At the sound the little dog only squirmed away a few paces, then sat down again and resumed its stare. Again Jean Liotard uttered his queer laugh. If the good God were to hold out His hand and say to him, '*Viens!*' he would do exactly as that little beast; he would not come, not he! What was he, too, but a starved and beaten dog – a driven wretch, kicked to hell! And again, as if experimenting with himself, he held out his hand and said: '*Viens!*' and again the beast squirmed a little further away, and again sat down and stared. Jean Liotard lost patience. His head drooped till his forehead touched the ground. He smelt the parched herbs, and a faint sensation of comfort stole through his nerves. He lay unmoving, trying to fancy himself dead and out of it all. The hum of summer, the scent of grasses, the caress of the breeze going over! He pressed the palms of his outstretched hands on the warm soil, as one might on a woman's breast. If only it were really death – how much better than life in this butcher's shop! But death – *his* death – was waiting for him away over there, under the moaning shells, under the whining bullets, at the end of a steel prong – a mangled, fetid death. Death – *his* death – had no sweet scent, and no caress, save the kisses of rats and crows. Life and Death, what were they? Nothing but the preying of creatures the one on the other – nothing but that; and Love, nothing but the blind instinct which made these birds and beasts of prey. *Bon sang de bon sang!* The Christ hid his head finely nowadays! That cross up there on the mountain top, with the sun gleaming on it – they had been right to put it up where no man lived, and not even a dog roamed, to be pitied! 'Fairy tales! Fairy tales!' he thought; 'those who drive and those who are driven, those who eat and those who are eaten – we are all poor devils together. There is no pity, no God!' And the flies drummed their wings above him.

The sun, boring into his spine through his thin shirt, made him reach for his jacket. There was the little dog, still sitting on its base twenty yards away. It cowered and drooped its ears when he moved, and he thought: 'Poor beast! Some one has been doing the devil's work on you, not badly!' There were some biscuits in the pocket of his jacket, and he held one out. The dog shivered, and its pink tongue lolled, panting with desire and fear. Jean Liotard tossed the biscuit gently about half-way. The dog cowered back a step or two, crept forward three, and again squatted. Then very gradually it crept up to the biscuit, bolted it, and regained its distance. The soldier took out another. This time he threw it five paces only in front of him. Again the little beast cowered, slunk forward, seized the biscuit, devoured it; but this time it only recoiled a pace or two, and seemed, with panting mouth and faint wagging of the tail, to beg for more. Jean Liotard held a third biscuit as far out in front of him as he could, and waited. The creature crept forward and squatted just out of reach. There it sat, with saliva dripping from its mouth; seemingly it could not make up its mind to that awful venture. The soldier sat motionless; his outstretched hand began to tire, but he did not budge – he meant to conquer its fear. At last it snatched the biscuit. Jean Liotard instantly held out a fourth. That too was snatched, but at the fifth he was able to touch the dog. It cowered almost into the ground at touch of his fingers, and then lay, still trembling violently, while the soldier continued to stroke its head and ears. And suddenly his heart gave a twitter; the creature had licked his hand. He took out his last biscuit, broke it up, and fed the dog slowly with the bits, talking all the time; when the last crumb was gone he continued to murmur and crumple its ears softly. He had become aware of something happening within the dog – something in the nature of conversion, as if it were saying: 'My master, my new master – I worship, I love you!' The creature came gradually closer, quite close; then put up its sharp black nose and began to lick his face. Its little hot, rough tongue licked and licked, and with each lick the soldier's heart relaxed, just as if the licks were being given there and something licked away. He put his arms round the thin body and hugged it, and still the creature went on feverishly licking at his face, and neck, and chest, as if trying to creep inside him. The sun poured down, and lizards rustled and whisked among the pebbles; the kissing never ceased up there among the willows and aspen leaves and every kind of flying thing went past drumming its wings. There was no change in the summer afternoon. God might not be there, but Pity had come back; Jean Liotard no longer had '*cafard*.' He put the little dog gently off his lap, got up, and stretched himself.

'*Voyons, mon brave, faut aller voir les copains! Tu es à moi.*' The little dog stood up on its hind legs, scratching with its fore paws at the soldier's thigh, as if trying to get at his face again; as if begging not to be left; and its tail waved feverishly, half in petition, half in rapture. The soldier caught the paws, set them down, and turned his face for home, making the noises that a man makes to his dog; and the little dog followed, close as he could get to those moving ankles, lifting his snout, and panting with anxiety and love.

~16~

Poirot and Bidan: a recollection

'Poirot and Bidan: a recollection' appeared initially in the first issue of *Reveille* (August 1918) and subsequently in *Tatterdemalion*.

Coming one dark December evening out of the hospital courtyard into the corridor which led to my little workroom, I was conscious of two new arrivals. There were several men round the stove, but these two were sitting apart on a bench close to my door. We used to get men in all stages of decrepitude, but I had never seen two who looked so completely under the weather. They were the extremes – in age, in colouring, in figure, in everything; and they sat there, not speaking, with every appearance of apathy and exhaustion. The one was a boy, perhaps nineteen, with a sunken, hairless, grey-white face under his peaked cap – never surely was a face so grey! He sat with his long grey-blue overcoat open at the knees, and his long emaciated hands nervously rubbing each other between them. Intensely forlorn he looked, and I remember thinking: 'That boy's dying!' This was Bidan.

The other's face, in just the glimpse I had of it, was as if carved out of wood, except for that something you see behind the masks of driven bullocks, deeply resentful. His cap was off, and one saw he was grey-haired; his cheeks, stretched over cheekbones solid as door-handles, were a purplish red, his grey moustache was damp, his light blue eyes stared like a codfish's. He reminded me queerly of those Parisian *cochers* one still sees under their shining hats, wearing an expression of being your enemy. His short stocky figure was dumped stolidly as if he meant never to move again; on his thick legs and feet he wore mufflings of cloth boot, into which his patched and stained grey-blue trousers were tucked.

One of his gloved hands was stretched out stiff on his knee. This was Poirot.

Two more dissimilar creatures were never blown together into our haven. So far as I remember, they had both been in hospital about six months, and their ailments were, roughly speaking, Youth and Age. Bidan had not finished his training when his weak constitution gave way under it; Poirot was a Territorial who had dug behind the Front till rheumatism claimed him for its own. Bidan, who had fair hair and rather beautiful brown eyes over which the lids could hardly keep up, came from Aix-en-Provence, in the very south; Poirot from Nancy, in the north-east. I made their acquaintance the next morning.

The cleaning of old Poirot took, literally speaking, days to accomplish. Such an encrusted case we had never seen; nor was it possible to go, otherwise than slowly, against his prejudices. One who, unless taken exactly the right way, considered everyone leagued with nature to get the better of him, he had reached that state when the soul sticks its toes in and refuses to budge. A coachman – in civil life – a socialist, a freethinker, a wit, he was the apex of – shall we say? – determination. His moral being was encrusted with perversity, as his poor hands and feet with dirt. Oil was the only thing for him, and I, for one, used oil on him morally and physically, for months. He was a 'character'! His left hand – which was never tired of saying the '*majors*' had ruined ('*Ah! Les cochons!*') by leaving it alone – was stiff in all is joints, so that the fingers would not bend; and the little finger of the right hand, '*le petit*', '*le coquin*, '*l'empereur*', as he would severally call it, was embellished by chalky excrescences. The old fellow had that peculiar artfulness which comes from life-long dealing with horses, and he knew exactly how far and how quickly it was advisable for him to mend in health. About the third day he made up his mind that he wished to remain with us at least until the warm weather came. For that it would be necessary – he concluded – to make a cheering amount of progress, but not too much. And this he set himself to do. He was convinced, one could see, that after Peace had been declared and compensation assured him, he would recover the use of his hand, even if '*l'empereur*' remained stiff and chalky. As a matter of fact, I think he was mistaken, and will never have a supple left hand again. But his arms were so brawny, his constitution so vigorous, and his legs improved so rapidly under the necessity of taking him down into the little town for his glass, of an afternoon, that one felt he might possibly be digging again sooner than he intended.

'*Ah, les cochons!*' he would say; 'while one finger does not move, they shall pay me!' He was very bitter against all '*majors*' save one, who it seemed had actually sympathised with him, and all *députés*, who for him constituted the powers of darkness, drawing their salaries, and sitting in their chairs. ('*Ah! Les chameaux!*')

Though he was several years younger than oneself, one always thought of him as 'Old Poirot'; indeed, he was soon called '*le grand-père*', though no more confirmed bachelor ever inhabited the world. He was a regular 'Miller of Dee', caring for nobody; and yet he was likable, that humorous old stoic, who suffered from gall-stones, and bore horrible bouts of pain like a hero. In spite of all his disabilities his health and appearance soon become robust in our easy-going hospital, where no one was harried, the food excellent, and the air good. He would tell you that his father lived to eighty, and his grandfather to a hundred, both 'strong men' though not so strong as his old master, the squire, of whose feats in the hunting-field he would give the most staggering accounts in an argot which could only be followed by instinct. A great narrator, he would describe at length life in the town of Nancy, where, when the War broke out, he was driving a market cart, and distributing vegetables, which had made him an authority on municipal reform. Though an incorrigible joker, his stockfish countenance would remain perfectly grave, except for an occasional hoarse chuckle. You would have thought he had no more power of compassion than a cat, no more sensibility than a Chinese idol; but this was not so. In his wooden, shrewd, distrustful way he responded to sympathy, and was even sorry for others. I used to like very much his attitude to the young 'stable-companion' who had arrived with him; he had no contempt, such as he might easily have felt for so weakly a creature, but rather a real indulgence towards his feebleness. 'Ah!' he would say at first; 'he won't make old bones – that one!' But he seemed extremely pleased when, in a fortnight or so, he had to modify that view, for Bidan (Prosper) prospered more rapidly even than himself. That grey look was out of the boy's face within three weeks. It was so wonderful to watch him come back to life, till at last he could say, with his dreadful Provençal twang, that he felt '*très biang*'. A most amiable youth, he had been a cook, and his chief ambition was to travel till he had attained the summit of mortal hopes, and was cooking at the Ritz in London. When he came to us his limbs seemed almost to have lost their joints, they wambled so. He had no muscle at all. Utter anaemia had hold of all his body, and all but a corner of his French spirit. Round that unquenchable gleam of gaiety the rest of him slowly rallied. With proper food and air and freedom, he began to have a final faint pink flush in his china-white cheeks; his lids no longer drooped, his limbs seemed to regain their joints, his hands ceased to swell. He complained less and less of the pains about his heart. When, of a morning, he was finished with, and '*le grand-père*' was having his hands done, they would engage in lively repartee – oblivious of one's presence. We began to feel that this grey ghost of a youth had been well named, after all, when they called him Prosper, so lyrical would he wax over the constitution and cooking of '*bouillabaisse*', over the South, and the buildings of his native Aix-en-Provence. In all France you could not have found a greater contrast than those two who had come to us so under the weather; nor in all France two better instances of the way men can regain health of body and spirit in the right surroundings.

We had a tremendous fall of snow that winter, and had to dig ourselves out of it. Poirot and Bidan were of those who dug. It was amusing to watch them. Bidan dug easily, without afterthought. '*Le grand-père*' dug with half an eye at least on his future; in spite of those stiff fingers he shifted a lot of snow, but he rested on his shovel whenever he thought you could see him – for he was full of human nature.

To see him and Bidan set off for town together! Bidan pale, and wambling a little still, but gay, with a kind of birdlike detachment; '*le grand-père*' stocky, wooden, planting his huge feet rather wide apart and regarding his companion, the frosted trees, and the whole wide world, with his humorous stare.

Once, I regret to say, when spring was beginning to come Bidan-Prosper returned on '*le grand-père's*' arm with the utmost difficulty, owing to the presence within him of a liquid called Clairette de Die, no amount of which could subdue '*le grand-père's*' power of planting one foot before the other. Bidan-Prosper arrived hilarious, revealing to the world unsuspected passions; he awoke next morning sad, pale, penitent. Poirot, *au contraire*, was morose the whole evening, and awoke next morning exactly the same as usual. In such different ways does the gift of the gods affect us.

They had their habits, so diverse, their constitutions, and their dreams – alas! Not yet realized. I know not where they may be now; Bidan-Prosper cannot yet be cooking at the Ritz in London town; but *grand-père* Poirot may perchance be distributing again his vegetables in the streets of Nancy, driving his two good little horses – *des galliards* – with the reins hooked round '*l'empereur*'. Good friends – good luck.

Select chronology, 1914–33

In developing this select chronology I am indebted to Geoffrey Harvey's own 'Chronology of John Galsworthy' which appears in his edition of *The Forsyte Saga* (Oxford: Oxford University Press, 1995), pp. xxiv–xxvii, to Marrot, *A Bibliography*, Marrot, *Life and Letters* and to Ian Westwell, *World War I: Day by Day* (St Paul, MN: MBI Publishing Co., 1999).

1914

28 June. Archduke Franz Ferdinand, heir to the throne of Austro-Hungarian empire, assassinated in Sarajevo, Bosnia.

28 July. Austria-Hungary declares war on Serbia.

29 July. Galsworthy reflects in his diary that 'These war-clouds are monstrous. If Europe is involved in an Austro-Servian [*sic*] quarrel one will cease to believe in anything.'

1 August. Germany declares war on Russia. Galsworthy observes events of the day as 'Blacker and blacker!' with 'little or no chance now'.

2 August. 'Too ghastly for words,' Galsworthy observes of the emerging conflict. 'The European war has come true. The nightmare of it. We rode [horses] to distract the thought. I wish to Heaven I could work.'

3 August. Germany declares war on France. Galsworthy experiences 'a miserably anxious day, ourselves hovering on the verge of war . . . If Germany will not respect [Belgium's neutrality], we shall be in. I hate and abhor war of all kinds; I despise and loathe it. And the thought of the million daily acts of its violence and hateful brutishness keeps riving my soul . . .'

4 August. Germany invades neutral Belgium; Britain declares war on Germany.

7–13 August. Galsworthy has incessant 'thoughts on the war', which eventually cause a 'strain' that 'simply wears away a little the capacity for feeling . . . [E]very now and then the horror of it sweeps one.'

14 August. Battle of the Frontiers begins.

17–19 August. Russia invades East Prussia.

28 August. James B. Pinker, Galsworthy's literary agent, writes to Charles Scribner, Galsworthy's American publisher, that 'Since the War broke out [Galsworthy] has not, he tells me, written anything creative, but he is trying again now, and in a week or two he will know whether he can get on or not . . .'

Early September. Galsworthy joins War Propaganda Bureau (WPB) following a 2 September 'meeting . . . of chief literary men at Wellington House to concert measures of putting forward principles for which England is fighting'.

17–18 September. The *Times* publishes 'Britain's destiny and duty: declaration by authors, a righteous war', signed by Galsworthy and fifty-two other British luminaries, including J. M. Barrie, Arnold Bennett, Arthur Conan Doyle and Rudyard Kipling. The *New York Times* reprints the declaration for American audiences.

1915

29 May. Galsworthy composes 'The recruit' for *The Blinded Soldiers and Sailors' Gift Book*, in aid of St Dunstan's Hostel for Blinded Sailors and Soldiers, London.

October. Galsworthy visits Queen Mary's Auxiliary Convalescent Hospital at Roehampton.

1916

Late February. Galsworthy composes 'Appeal for the totally disabled', which is published soon thereafter as 'Totally disabled' in the 19 March issue of the *Observer.*

Circa 29 April–1 May. Galsworthy composes 'Appeal for the maimed', which is published soon thereafter as 'For the maimed – now!' in the 26 May issue of the *Morning Post* and later as 'Those whom the war has broken' in the August 1916 issue of *Current History.* Galsworthy's authorship of these works coincides with his recent visit to the Lord Roberts Memorial Workshops, London.

7 May. Galsworthy begins arrangement of 'a book of published humanitarian and other writings to be called *A Sheaf of Wild Oats*', later shortened to *A Sheaf.*

10 July. Galsworthy hosts seventy wounded soldiers for tea at his home in Manaton, Devon.

8 September. Galsworthy offers his family home at 8 Cambridge Gate, London, to the British Red Cross for a Wounded Soldiers' Club, and 'up to the extent of £400 . . . to fit it up'.

11 September. Galsworthy arranges with Dorothy Allhusen to volunteer at Hôpital Bénévole in France, Allhusen's convalescent hospital for rheumatic and neurasthenic French soldiers at Martouret, Die, Drôme, 'I as a bathman and masseur . . . [My wife] Ada as a linen superintendent . . .'

26 September. Galsworthy visits Shepherd's Bush Military Orthopaedic Hospital, London.

Circa 28 September. Galsworthy composes 'Re-made or Marred', which is published as 'Re-made or marred: a great national duty' in the 14 October issue of *The Times*, and later included in *A Sheaf*.

30 September. A Sheaf published in America by Charles Scribner's Sons.

12 October. A Sheaf published in Britain by William Heinemann.

13 November. Galsworthy departs England, with Ada, for Allhusen's Hôpital Bénévole.

18 November. Arrives at Hôpital Bénévole.

1917

3 March. Galsworthy departs Hôpital Bénévole, with Ada, for Cassis-sur-Mer, via Marseille, Valence and Arles.

Circa 6–15 March. Galsworthy composes 'Flotsam and Jetsam', based on his experiences at Hôpital Bénévole.

16 March. In Lyon, Galsworthy visits École Joffre and 'the establishment at Tourville'.

20–26 March. In Paris, Galsworthy visits the Saint-Maurice institutions for disabled French soldiers.

28 March. Galsworthy returns to England.

April. Second edition of A *Sheaf* published.

8–12 May. First inter-allied conference on the after-care of disabled men, held in Paris.

July. Galsworthy composes 'Cafard' and likely also 'Poirot and Bidan', based on his experiences at Hôpital Bénévole.

4 November. Galsworthy dines 'with Sir Robert Jones and other doctors' at the Automobile Club, London.

14 December. Galsworthy lunches with Jones and Major Osgood at the Reform Club and discusses the sluggishness of the Pensions Committee. 'I made the suggestion of permanent persuaders to be attached to Military Orthopaedic Hospitals.'

19 December. Galsworthy visits Sir Matthew Nathan of the Pensions Committee 'with a suggestion [again] that they should have permanent persuaders attached to Military Orthopaedic Hospitals'.

20 December. Galsworthy meets with Lord Charnwood 'about . . . joining him over *Recalled to Life*'; agrees to 'co-edit the reports of the [second] International Conference on the Disabled [*sic*] in London in May next, and to help him with the Journal [*sic*] *Recalled to Life*'.

1918

6 February. Kitchener House for Wounded Soldiers formally opened in Galsworthy's family home, 8 Cambridge Gate.

15 February. Galsworthy assumes chairmanship of the executive committee of Kitchener House.

16 April. British government passes manpower Bill, conscripting men aged eighteen to fifty-six; Galsworthy, now aged fifty, qualifies for National Service Medical Board.

17 April. Galsworthy assumes editorship of *Reveille.*

14 May. Galsworthy receives from the Ministry of Pensions his own admission ticket to the upcoming inter-allied conference and exhibition on the after-care of disabled men.

20 May. Galsworthy records in his diary 'Days very full; run here and there about *Reveille*, etc., etc. Attending Training Conference of the Interallied [*sic*] Conference on the Disabled every morning.'

20–26 May. Second inter-allied conference and exhibition, the proceedings of which Galsworthy edits and introduces with his essay 'The sacred work'.

May. Galsworthy writes '100 pages of a new novel: *The Burning Spear*', eventually subtitled *Being the Experiences of Mr John Lavender in Time of War*, and which he would call a 'comedic satire'.

13 July. Galsworthy visits Summerdown Convalescent Camp and The Old Heritage, Chailey, east Sussex.

22 July. Galsworthy examined by Exeter National Service Medical Board; 'totally rejected . . . This day, the turning point of the war, was the day I came nearest to taking fighting part in it.'

10 August. Reveille issue number one published.

Circa 1 September. Galsworthy visits Brighton diamond-cutting factory of disabled soldiers and spends three nights in Birmingham to attend the Conference of Delegates for the Disabled, a regional meeting associated with the second inter-allied conference and exhibition held three months earlier in London.

Late October–early November. Galsworthy continues work on *The Burning Spear*
November. Reveille issue number two published.

1919

23 January. Another Sheaf published simultaneously in Britain and America by Heinemann and by Charles Scribner's Sons, respectively.

1 February. Galsworthy travels to America to begin a lecture tour, which includes an address to the American Academy of Arts and Letters.

February. Reveille issue number three published; shortly thereafter Galsworthy resigns his editorship of the publication due to 'a certain trouble over censorship of articles . . . which criticized the methods of the Ministry of Pensions . . .'

24 April. The Burning Spear published simultaneously in Britain, by Chatto & Windus, and in America, by Charles Scribner's Sons, under the pseudonym A.R.P.–M.

1920

18 March. Tatterdemalion published simultaneously in Britain by Heinemann and in America by Scribner's; includes 'Cafard', 'Flotsam and Jetsam: a reminiscence', 'Heritage' and 'Poirot and Bidan: a recollection'.
21 April. The Skin Game, published by Duckworth & Co. in England, opens at St Martin's Theatre, London.
20 October. Galsworthy travels to America to undertake a second lecture tour.

1921

Handbook for the Limbless published by the Disabled Society; includes foreword by Galsworthy.
Galsworthy establishes International PEN – the organization of Poets, Essayists and Novelists – with Catherine Dawson Scott.

1922

Twenty-one-volume Manaton Edition of Galsworthy's collected works begins to appear in America, published by Charles Scribner's Sons.

1923

6 April. The Burning Spear (American edition), now attributed to Galsworthy, published by Charles Scribner's Sons in the United States.
15 May. The Burning Spear (English edition), attributed to Galsworthy, published by Chatto & Windus in England.
Beginning in September, the first four volumes of the twenty-one-volume Manaton Edition of Galsworthy's collected works, published in England.

1924

Beginning in January, remaining volumes of Manaton Edition of Galsworthy's collected works published in England.

1925

26 March. Caravan published by William Heinemann in the England, in which 'Cafard' appeared.

Select chronology

1929

Galsworthy awarded Order of Merit.

1932

Galsworthy awarded Nobel Prize in Literature.

1933

31 January. Galsworthy dies in Hampstead, London.

1935

Forsytes, Pendyces and Others, Galsworthy's first posthumous collection of essays, notes and letters published in London by William Heinemann.

1937

Glimpses and Reflections, Galsworthy's second posthumous collection of essays, notes and letters published in London by William Heinemann.

Select bibliography

Archival sources

Bancroft Library, University of California, Berkeley

Papers of Julie Helen Heynemann

Collection of Steve Forbes

Papers of John Galsworthy

Dorset House School of Occupational Therapy, Library and Archive, Oxford Brookes University, Oxford

Printed and photographic material relating to the First World War

Hoover Institution Archives, Stanford University

Hoover Archives Political Poster Collection

Houghton Library, Harvard University

Papers of Sir William Rothenstein

Imperial War Museum, London

Department of Documents: Papers of Rudolf Sauter
Department of Printed Books: Women at War Collection
Department of Art (in co-operation with the Manchester Institute for Research and Innovation in Art and Design), Manchester Metropolitan University: 'Posters of Conflict: The Visual Culture of Public Information and Counter-

Select bibliography

information. Online at http://www.vads.ac.uk/collections/IWMPC.html, accessed 8 July 2008.

Library of Congress

George Grantham Bain Collection of News Photographs
Gary Yanker Collection of Political and Propaganda Posters

Lord Roberts Workshops archives held by the Forces Help Society and Lord Roberts Workshops, London

Printed material related to the Lord Roberts Workshops, ca. 1914–18

National Archives of the United Kingdom

Document classes consulted include T 1 (Treasury Board Papers and In-letters) and INF 4 (Ministry of Information and Predecessors: War of 1914 to 1918 Information Services)

National Archives of the United States

Records of the American National Red Cross

Princeton University Library

Archives of Charles Scribner's Sons

Queen Mary's University Hospital Library and Archive, Roehampton

Printed material, manuscripts and photographs relating to the history of Queen Mary's Hospital

Newspapers and periodicals

Aberdeen Journal
Adams County Union–Republican
American Journal of Care for Cripples
Argosy
Boston Evening Transcript
British Journal of Nursing
British Medical Journal
Carry on: A Magazine on the Reconstruction of Disabled Soldiers and Sailors and Soldiers
Church Family Newspaper
Daily Mail
Dublin Express

East Anglican Daily Times
Electrical Industries
Evening Standard and St James's Gazette
Everybody's Magazine
Glasgow News
Globe
Grocers' Journal
Hansard
Huddersfield Examiner
Hull Daily Mail
Irish News
Jewish Chronicle
Liverpool Courier
Liverpool Daily Courier
Living Age
Manitoba Free Press
Middlesex and Buckinghamshire Advertiser
New Castle News
New Statesman
New Witness
Newcastle Chronicle
Newspaper World
Oakland Tribune
Observer
Punch
Recalled to Life: A Journal Devoted to the Care, Re-education, and Return to Civil Life of Disabled Soldiers
Reconstruction
Reveille: Devoted to the Disabled Sailor and Soldier
Scotsman
Sheffield Daily Telegraph
Southampton Times
Spectator
Springfield Republican
Times (London)
Times Literary Supplement
Western Daily Press
Westminster Gazette
World

Contemporary works: books, articles, and official publications

A.R.P.–M. [John Galsworthy]. *The Burning Spear: Being the Experiences of Mr John Lavender in Time of War*. London: Chatto & Windus, 1919

The Blinded Soldiers and Sailors' Gift Book. London: Jarrold & Sons, 1915

The Book of the Homeless (Le Livre des sans-foyer). London: Macmillan, 1916

Conférence interalliée pour l'étude de la rééduction professionnelle et des questions qui intéressent les invalides de la guerre du 8 au 12 mai 1917. Paris: Imprimerie Chaix, 1917

Camus, Jean. *Re-education of the Maimed*, translated by W. F. Castle. London: Balliere Tindall & Cox, 1918

Devine, Edward T. *Disabled Soldiers and Sailors Pensions and Training: Preliminary Economic Studies of the War*. New York: Oxford University Press, 1919

Dunton, William Rush. *Occupation Therapy: A Manual for Nurses*. London: W. B. Saunders, 1915

Fabes, Gilbert Henry. *John Galsworthy, his First Editions: Points and Values*. London: W. & G. Foyle, 1932

Harris, Garrard. *The Redemption of the Disabled: A Study of Programmes of Rehabilitation for the Disabled of War and of Industry*. New York: D. Appleton & Co., 1919

Galsworthy, John. *Justice: A Tragedy in Four Acts*. London: Duckworth & Co., 1910

——*A Sheaf*. William Heinemann, 1916

——*Addresses in America, 1919*. London: William Heinemann, 1919

——*Another Sheaf*. London: William Heinemann, 1919

——*Tatterdemalion*. London: William Heinemann, 1920

——*The Skin Game: A Tragi-comedy*. London: Duckworth & Co., 1920

——*The Burning Spear: Being the Experiences of Mr John Lavender in Time of War*. London: William Heinemann, 1923

——*Captures*. London: William Heinemann, 1923

——*Works of John Galsworthy*. Manaton Edition. London: William Heinemann, 1923–24

——*Caravan: The Assembled Tales of John Galsworthy*. London: William Heinemann, 1925

——*Forsytes, Pendyces and Others*. London: William Heinemann, 1935

——*Selected Works. Glimpses and Reflections*. London: William Heinemann, 1937

——*The Burning Spear. Villa Rubein*. London: Heron Books, 1970

——*The Forsyte Saga*. Oxford: Oxford University Press, 1999

Harris, Garrard, and US Federal Board for Vocational Education. *The Redemption of the Disabled: A Study of Programmes of Rehabilitation for the Disabled of War and of Industry*. New York: D. Appleton & Co., 1919

John Hodge *et al*. *The Inter-allied Conference on the After-care of Disabled Men: Second Annual Meeting, held in London, May 20 to 25, 1918. Reports presented to the Conference*. London: HMSO, 1918

——*The Inter-allied Conference on the After-care of Disabled Men: Second Annual Meeting, held in London, May 20 to 25, 1918. Supplement to Volume of Reports*. London: HMSO, 1918

Howson, George. *Handbook for the Limbless*. London: Disabled Society, 1921

Inter-allied Conference on the After-care of Disabled Men. *Report on the Inter-allied Conference for the Study of Professional Re-education, and other Questions of Interest to Soldiers and Sailors disabled by the War, held at Paris, 8 to 12 May, 1917*. London: HMSO, 1917

Jones, Robert. *Notes on Military Orthopaedics*. London: Cassell & Co., 1917

——(ed.). *Orthopaedic Surgery of Injuries*, 2 vols. London: Oxford Medical Publications, 1921

Kaye-Smith, Sheila. *John Galsworthy*. London: Nisbet, 1916

Keith, Arthur. *Menders of the Maimed: The Anatomical and Physiological Principles Underlying the Treatment of Injuries to Muscles, Nerves, Bones and Joints*. London: Hodder & Stoughton, 1919

King Albert's Book: A Tribute to the Belgian King and People from Representative Men and Women throughout the World. London: *Daily telegraph*, in conjunction with the *Daily Sketch*, the *Glasgow Herald*, and Hodder & Stoughton, 1915

McKenzie, Robert Tait. *Reclaiming the Maimed: A Handbook of Physical Therapy*. New York: Macmillan Co., 1918

McMurtrie, Douglas C. *A Bibliography of the War Cripple*. New York: Red Cross Institute for Crippled and Disabled Men, 1918

——*The Evolution of National Systems of Vocational Reeducation for Disabled Soldiers and Sailors*. Washington, DC: United States Government Printing Office, 1918

——*Reconstructing the Crippled Soldier*. New York: Red Cross Institute for Crippled and Disabled Men, 1918

Macpherson, W. G. *History of the Great War based on Official Documents. Medical Services: General History*. London: HMSO, 1921

Ministry of Pensions. *Instructions and Notes on the Treatment and Training of Disabled Men*. London: HMSO, 1917

Pearson, Arthur. *Victory over Blindness; How it was Won by the Men of St Dunstan's and how Others may Win it*. London: Hodder & Stoughton, 1919

Prince of Wales's Hospital for Limbless Sailors and Soldiers, Wales and Monmouthshire, *Cardiff: The Story of the Hospital*. n.a.: n.a., 1918

Princess Marie-José's Children's Book. London: Cassell & Co., 1916

Princess Mary's Gift Book. London: Hodder & Stoughton, 1914

The Queen's Gift Book in Aid of Queen Mary's Convalescent Auxiliary Hospitals for Soldiers and Sailors who have Lost their Limbs in the War. London: Hodder & Stoughton, 1918

Reports by the Joint War Committee and the Joint War Finance Committee of the British Red Cross Society and the Order of St John of Jerusalem in England on Voluntary Aid rendered to the Sick and Wounded at Home and Abroad and to British Prisoners of War, 1914–1919, with appendices. London: HMSO, 1921

Roberts, Henry D. (ed.). *The Inter-allied Exhibition on the After-care of Disabled Men, Central Hall, Westminster, 20 to 25 May 1918, Catalogue*. London: Avenue Press, 1918

Select bibliography

Told in the Huts: The YMCA Gift Book Contributed by Soldiers and War Workers.
London: Jarrold & Sons, 1916
Wharton, Edith. *The Book of the Homeless.* London: Macmillan & Co., 1916

Secondary works: books and articles

Alper, Helen (ed.). *A History of Queen Mary's University Hospital, Roehampton.* London: Richmond and Twickenham and Roehampton Healthcare NHS Trust, 1996
Anderson, Julie. '"Spare your tears": representing and narrating blind bodies in Britain, 1915–1925.' Mansfield College, Oxford, 2006. www.inter-disciplinary. net/mso/hid/hid5/s3/html
Atkin, Jonathan. *A War of Individuals: Bloomsbury Attitudes to the Great War.* Manchester: Manchester University Press, 2002
Audoin-Rouzeau, Stephane, and Annette Becker. *1914–1918: Understanding the Great War.* London: Profile Books, 2002
Barham, Peter. *Forgotten Lunatics of the Great War.* New Haven, CT: Yale University Press, 2004
Barker, Dudley. *The Man of Principle: A View of John Galsworthy.* New York: London House & Maxwell, 1963
Barry, Jonathan, and Colin Jones (eds). *Medicine and Charity before the Welfare State.* London: Routledge, 1991
Batten, Sonia. 'Forgetting the First World War', *Journal of the Centre for First World War Studies* 2: 2 (July 2005), www.jsww1.bham.ac.uk/fetch.asp?article= issue4_batten.pdf
Bennett, Arnold. *Letters of Arnold Bennett.* London: Oxford University Press, 1966
Bogacz, Ted. '"Tyranny of words": language, poetry and anti-modernism in England in the First World War', *Journal of Modern History* 58 (1986): 643–668
Bond, Brian. *War and Society in Europe, 1870–1970.* Oxford: Oxford University Press, 1986
Bourke, Joanna. *Dismembering the Male: Men's Bodies, Britain and the Great War.* London: Reaktion, 1996
Bracco, Rosa Maria. *Merchants of Hope: British Middlebrow Writers and the First World War, 1919–1939.* Oxford: Berg, 1993
Braybon, Gail. *Evidence, History, and the Great War: Historians and the Impact of 1914–1918.* London: Berghahn Books, 2003
Buchli, Victor (ed.). *The Material Culture Reader.* Oxford: Berg, 2002
Buitenhuis, Peter. *The Great War of Words: British, American, and Canadian Propaganda and Fiction, 1914–1933.* Vancouver: University of British Columbia Press, 1987
Burke, Peter. *Eyewitnessing: The Uses of Images as Historical Evidence.* London: Reaktion, 2001

Butlin, R. A. *Historical Geography: Through the Gates of Space and Time.* London: Edward Arnold, 1993

Cecil, Hugh, and Peter Liddle. *Facing Armageddon: The First World War Experienced.* London: Cooper, 1996

Coats, Robert Hay. *John Galsworthy as a Dramatic Artist.* New York: Scribner's, 1926

Cohen, Deborah. *The War Come Home: Disabled Veterans in Britain and Germany, 1914–1939.* Berkeley, CA: University of California Press, 2001

Cole, Sarah. *Modernism, Male Friendship, and the First World War.* Cambridge: Cambridge University Press, 2003

Collins, Theresa M. *Otto Kahn: Art, Money and Modern Times.* Chapel Hill, NC: University of North Carolina Press, 2002

Cooter, Roger. 'Medicine and the goodness of war'. *Canadian Bulletin of Medical History* 7 (1990): 147–159

——*Surgery and Society in Peace and War: Orthopaedics and the Origin of Modern Medicine, 1880–1940.* London: Macmillan, 1993

Cooter, Roger, Mark Harrison and Steve Sturdy (eds). *War, Medicine and Modernity.* Stroud: Sutton Books, 1998

——*Medicine and Modernity.* Amsterdam: Rodopi, 1999

Croman, Natalie. *John Galsworthy: A Study in Continuity and Contrast.* Cambridge, MA: Harvard University Press, 1933

DeGroot, Gerard J. *Blighty: British Society in the Era of the Great War.* London: Longman, 1996

Dupont, V. *John Galsworthy: The Dramatic Artist.* Paris: Didier, 1943

Dupré, Catherine. *John Galsworthy: A Biography.* London: Collins, 1976

Eksteins, Modris. *Rites of Spring: The Great War and the Birth of the Modern Age.* London: Bantam, 1989

Evans, Martin, and Kenneth Lunn. *War and Memory in the Twentieth Century.* Oxford: Berg, 1997

Forty, Adrian, and Susanne Kuchler. *The Art of Forgetting.* Oxford: Berg, 1999

Fréchet, Alec. *John Galsworthy: A Reassessment*, translated from the French by Denis Mahaffey. London: Macmillan, 1982

Fussell, Paul. *The Great War and Modern Memory.* Oxford: Oxford University Press, 1975

Galsworthy, Ada. *John Galsworthy: An Appreciation together with a Bibliography.* London: Heinemann, 1926

——*Over the Hills and Far Away.* London: Robert Hale, 1937

Gerber, David. *Disabled Veterans in History.* Ann Arbor, MI: University of Michigan Press, 2000

Gillis, Leon. *Fifty Years of Rehabilitation at Queen Mary's Hospital, Roehampton.* London: British Council for Rehabilitation of the Disabled, 1989

Gindin, James Jack. *The English Climate: An Excursion into a Biography of John Galsworthy.* Ann Arbor, MI: University of Michigan Press, 1979

——*John Galsworthy's Life and Art: An Alien's Fortress*. Basingstoke: Macmillan, 1987

Glover, Jon, and Jon Silkin (eds). *The Penguin Book of First World War Prose*. London: Viking, 1989

Holloway, David. *John Galsworthy*. London: Morgan-Grampian, 1968

Hudson, W. H. *Far Away and Long Ago: A History of my Early Life*. London: Dent, 1918

Huyssen, A. *Twilight Memories: Marking Time in a Culture of Amnesia*. London: Routledge, 1995

Hynes, Samuel Lynn. *A War Imagined: The First World War and English Culture*. London: Bodley Head, 1990

——*The Soldiers' Tale: Bearing Witness to Modern War*. London: Pimlico, 1998

Jordanova, Ludmilla. 'Medicine and visual culture'. *Social History of Medicine* 3: 1 (1990): 89–99

Keen, Paul, and Ina Ferris (eds). *Bookish Histories*. London: Palgrave, 2009

Kern, Stephen, *The Culture of Time and Space, 1880–1918: With a New Preface*. London: Weidenfeld & Nicolson, 1983

Kingery, David. *Learning from Things: Method and Theory of Material Culture Studies*. London: Smithsonian Institution Press, 1996

Kortem, Barbara (ed.). *The Penguin Book of First World War Stories*. London: Penguin Books, 2007

Koven, Seth. 'Remembering and dismemberment: crippled children, wounded soldiers and the Great War in Great Britain'. *American Historical Review* 99: 4 (1994): 1167–1202.

Küchler, Susanne. *The Art of Forgetting*. Oxford: Berg, 2001

Leaska, Mitchell A. (ed.). *The Virginia Woolf Reader*. New York: Harcourt Brace Jovanovich, 1984

Levitch, Mark. *Panthéon de la guerre: Reconfiguring a Panorama of the Great War*. Columbia, MO: University of Missouri Press, 2006

Lubar, Steven W., and David Kingery (eds). *History from Things: Essays on Material Culture*. London: Smithsonian Institution Press, 1993

MacMinn, George Rupert. *College Readings in the Modern Short Story*. Boston, MA: Ginn, 1931

Marković, Vida E. *The Reputation of Galsworthy in England, 1897–1950*. Beograd: Filološki fakultet, Beogradskog univerziteta, 1969

Marrot, Harold Vincent. *The Life and Letters of John Galsworthy*. London: Heinemann, 1935

——*A Bibliography of the Works of John Galsworthy*. London: Elkin Mathews & Marrot, 1928; reprinted New York: Franklin, 1968

Masterman, Lucy. *C. F. G. Masterman: A Biography*. London: Nicholson & Watson, 1939

Messinger, Gary S. *British Propaganda and the State in the First World War*. Manchester: Manchester University Press, 1992

Mikhail, E. H. *John Galsworthy the Dramatist: A Bibliography of Criticism*. Troy, NY: Whitston, 1971

Mosse, George L. *Fallen Soldiers: Reshaping the Memory of the World Wars*. Oxford: Oxford University Press, 1990

Nellis, Michael. 'John Galsworthy's *Justice*'. *British Journal of Criminology* 36 (1996): 61–84

Neil Pemberton, 'Enabling the past: new perspectives in the history of disability'. *History Workshop Journal* 61 (autumn 2006): 292–295

Ott, Katherine, David Serlin and Stephen Mihm (eds). *Artificial Parts, Practical Lives: Modern Histories of Prosthetics*. New York: New York University Press, 2002

Pick, Daniel. *War Machine: The Rationalisation of Slaughter in the Modern Age*. New Haven, CT: Yale University Press, 1993

Piper, Andrew. *Dreaming in Books: The Making of the Bibliographic Imagination in the Romantic Age*. Chicago: University of Chicago Press, 2009

Potter, Jane. *Boys in Khaki, Girls in Print: Women's Literary Responses to the Great War, 1914–1918*. Oxford English Monographs. Oxford: Clarendon Press, 2005

Prost, Antoine. *In the Wake of War: les anciens combattants and French Society*. Oxford: Berg, 1992

Quinn, Patrick J., and Steven Trout (eds). *The Literature of the Great War Reconsidered: Beyond Modern Memory*. Basingstoke: Palgrave, 2001

Reynolds, Mabel Edith Galsworthy. *Memories of John Galsworthy*. London: Robert Hale, 1936

Reznick, Jeffrey S. *Healing the Nation: Soldiers and the Culture of Caregiving in Britain during the Great War*. Manchester: Manchester University Press, 2004

Ross, Stewart Halsey. *Propaganda for War: How the United States was Conditioned to Fight the Great War of 1914–1918*. London: McFarland, 1996

Sanders, Michael, and Philip M. Taylor. *British Propaganda during the First World War, 1914–1918*. London: Macmillan, 1982

Saunders, Nicholas J. *Trench Art: Materialities and Memories of War*. Oxford: Berg, 2003

——*Matters of Conflict: Material Culture, Memory and the First World War*. London: Routledge, 2004

Saunders, Nicholas J. and Paul Cornish (eds). *Contested Objects: Material Memories of the Great War*. Abingdon: Routledge, 2009

Shalit, Leon. *John Galsworthy: A Survey*, translated by Ethel E. Coe and Therese Harbury. London: Heinemann, 1929

Shukla, Sheo Bhushan. *Social and Moral Ideas in the Plays of Galsworthy*. Salzburg Studies in English Literature. Salzburg: Institut für Anglistik und Amerikanistik, Universität Salzburg, 1979

Simmrell, V. E. 'John Galsworthy: The artist as propagandist'. *Quarterly Journal of Speech Education* 13 (1927): 225–236

Smit, Jan Hendrik. *The Short Stories of John Galsworthy*. Rotterdam: van Sijn, 1947

Squires, J. Duane. *British Propaganda at Home and in the United States from 1914 to 1917*. Cambridge, MA: Harvard University Press, 1935

Sternlicht, Sanford V. *John Galsworthy*. Boston, MA: Twayne Publishers, 1987

Stevens, Earl (ed.). *John Galsworthy: An Annotated Bibliography of Writings about Him*. De Kalb, IL: Northern Illinois University Press, 1980

Stromberg, Roland N. *Redemption by War: The Intellectuals and 1914*. Lawrence, KS: Regents Press of Kansas, 1982

Taylor, A. J. P. *Beaverbrook*. London, Hamish Hamilton, 1972

Turner, David M., and Kevin Stagg (eds). *Social Histories of Disability and Deformity*. London: Routledge, 2006

Waites, Bernard. *A Class Society at War: England 1914–1918*. New York: Berg, 1987

Waller, Philip J. *Writers, Readers, and Reputations: Literary Life in Britain, 1870–1918*. Oxford: Oxford University Press, 2006

Watson, Frederick. *The Life of Sir Robert Jones*. London: Hodder & Stoughton, 1934

Watson, Janet S. K. *Fighting Different Wars: Experience, Memory, and the First World War in Britain*. Cambridge: Cambridge University Press, 2004

West, Anthony (ed.). *The Galsworthy Reader*. New York: Charles Scribner's Sons, 1967

Westwell, Ian. *World War I: Day by Day*. St Paul, MN: MBI Publishing, 1999

Whalen, Robert Weldon. *Bitter Wounds: German Victims of the Great War, 1914–1939*. Ithaca, NY: Cornell University Press, 1984

Winter, Jay. *Sites of Memory, Sites of Mourning: The Great War in European Cultural History*. Cambridge: Cambridge University Press, 1995

——*Remembering War: The Great War between Memory and History in the Twentieth Century*. New Haven, CT: Yale University Press, 2006

Winter, Jay, and Antoine Prost. *The Great War in History: Debates and Controversies, 1914 to the Present*. Cambridge: Cambridge University Press, 2005

Winter, Jay, and Jean-Louis Robert (eds). *Capital Cities at War: Paris, London, Berlin, 1914–1919*. Cambridge: Cambridge University Press, 1999

——*Capital Cities at War: Paris, London, Berlin 1914–1919*. Vol. II, *A Cultural History*. Cambridge: Cambridge University Press, 2007

Wohl, Robert. *The Generation of 1914*. London: Weidenfeld & Nicolson, 1980

Wollaeger, Mark. *Modernism, Media and Propaganda*. Princeton, NJ: Princeton University Press, 2006

Woodall, Samuel James. *The Manor House Hospital: A Personal Record*. London: Routledge & Kegan Paul, 1966

Woodward, John, and David Richards (eds). *Health Care and Popular Medicine in Nineteenth Century England: Essays in the Social History of Medicine*. London: Croom Helm, 1977

Woollacott, Angela. ' "Khaki fever" and its control: gender, class, age and sexual morality on the British home front in the First World War'. *Journal of Contemporary History* 29: 2 (April 1994): 325–347

——'Dressed to kill: clothes, cultural meaning and World War I women munitions workers', in Moira Donald and Linda Hurcombe (eds), *Gender and Material Culture*. Vol. II, *Representations of Gender from Prehistory to the Present*. Basingstoke: Macmillan, 2000

Wright, David. 'The Great War, government propaganda and English "men of letters", 1914–16'. *Literature and History* 7 (1978): 70–85

Theses and dissertations

Knoester, Maarten Willem. 'Faith of a novelist: religion in John Galsworthy's work', Ph.D. dissertation, Leiden University, 2006

Linker, Beth. 'For life and limb: the reconstruction of a nation and its disabled soldiers in World War I America', Ph.D. dissertation, Yale University, 2006

Perry, Heather. 'Recycling the disabled: army, medicine and masculinity in World War Germany, 1914–1922', Ph.D. dissertation, Indiana University, 2002

Sprott, Mary Esther. 'A survey of British wartime propaganda in America issued from Wellington House', M.A. thesis, Stanford University, 1921

Index